Advertising as Culture

Advertising as Culture

Edited by Chris Wharton

intellect Bristol, UK / Chicago, USA

First published in the UK in 2013 by
Intellect, The Mill, Parnall Road, Fishponds, Bristol, BS16 3JG, UK

First published in the USA in 2013 by
Intellect, The University of Chicago Press, 1427 E. 60th Street,
Chicago, IL 60637, USA

A catalogue record for this book is available from the
British Library.

Cover designer: Holly Rose
Copy-editor: MPS Technologies
Production manager: Bethan Ball
Typesetting: Planman Technologies

ISBN 978-1-84150-614-2

Printed and bound by Bell & Bain, Glasgow.

Contents

Acknowledgement

We would like to thank all the people and organisations that have helped in the preparation of this book – in particular Vanessa Maughan for assistance in research and editing.

Introduction – advertising and culture

This book is about advertising and culture. Advertising is a significant aspect of modern societies and plays an important part in economic activity. It is a highly visible component of everyday life and increasingly of contemporary culture. The book considers culture as a broad category of human endeavour and experience. It takes a multidisciplinary approach drawing on media and cultural studies and the study of history and of art history, sociology, politics and political economy for ideas and explanations that can be applied to advertising and culture. Indeed the book's contributors are drawn from each of these areas of academic enquiry. Their contributions represent strands and tensions in the relationship between different aspects of culture, such as fashion, art, popular music, politics and media, and the world of advertising. The book raises the question of how, to what effect and with what intensity, advertising features – as the Advertising Standards Authority, the UK's advertising regulator, recently put it – as a 'common subject' in our cultural lives. The book deals with advertising and culture primarily within a British context, but in an increasingly globalised world many of its themes and issues are relevant to societies where advertising is a growing presence.

Terms and definitions

This book explores the *relationship* between advertising and culture and this introduction outlines the book's scope, content and themes. To begin with, a tentative exploration of the terms central to the enquiry is needed. By its very nature a book titled *Advertising as Culture* has already brought these two things together as a combination of words in language. It has created a *conjunctive* relation between advertising *and* culture, linking and articulating two separate, but now connected, ideas or concepts. We rely on language, not just to deal with concepts but to be able to talk about and share our experiences. Advertising and culture are recognised and experienced in the everyday, sensuous experience of lived reality. We see, hear, read and react to advertising and we live out our lives in and through culture surrounded by its activities and artefacts.

Having established the conjunctive relationship between advertising and culture as represented in language, we need to break them apart, to explore them in their *disjunctive* existences. Therefore to begin our exploration of what we mean by these terms we need to remove the *conjunctive*: that is, take the 'and' out of advertising and culture. This will enable us to engage with them primarily on their own terms.

So what do we mean by advertising? At one level advertising is a specific form of communication that provides information, raises awareness or instigates interest in a particular product or service. As part of marketing the intention is usually, but not always, to increase the use or consumption of the item that the advertisement or advertising campaign is promoting. This is usually in the interest of increasing turnover, sales and profits but wider social benefits may occur. Advertising in this sense is a means towards an end.

Advertising is also an industry with organisational and institutional structure. It is an important part of advanced market economies providing a channel for capital and employment, careers and training in a range of occupations from creative work to finance and research. It also has an ideological role; as Judith Williamson suggested a generation ago, it provides 'structures of meaning' (1978: 12). At its core is the activity of advertising: of creating advertising campaigns. This involves not only individual workers and agencies involved in marketing strategies, promotional and creative work but also organisations that represent the interests of the industry, research organisations, regulatory bodies and a wider media interest.

Advertising output is prodigious. From telephone to television, radio and Internet to billboards and cinema and from handhelds to handbills: it is very much part of the everyday and the everywhere. Advertising has become as Leiss et al. have suggested 'an integral part of modern culture' (2005: 5).

So having briefly explored what we mean by 'advertising', we can now pose the same question of 'culture'. Cultural Studies, according to Jim McGuigan, has made the distinction between, '"Culture" with a capital C' and, 'lower-case culture as the medium of social communication' (2010: 2). In everyday use, 'capital C culture' is often thought of in the way Raymond Williams referred to it as the 'works and practices of intellectual especially artistic activity' (Williams 1983: 90). This might include what is termed 'high' culture, extolled by Victorian thinkers such as Matthew Arnold as 'the best that has been thought and said'. In today's world this can appear crowded out by 'lower case culture', the popular culture that is increasingly a product transmitted and experienced through a rapidly expanding media technology. Raymond Williams offered a working definition of culture that identifies three components: the 'documentary', the 'ideal' and 'way of life'. The 'documentary' refers to texts and artefacts, the material aspects of culture and the 'ideal' can be the standards and norms of culture against which other cultural elements are compared. The 'way of life' refers to the forms of behaviour and 'structures of feeling' that a 'people, a period or a group' have in common. Crucially for Williams each of these is a necessary component to a definition of culture. On this basis we can picture different cultural formulations from global to local communities and from social class to gender to artistic or consumer culture. Inserting different documents that are associated with different cultural traditions and imagining ideal forms and how these are important to different ways of thinking, feeling and behaving can help us give shape to the cultures we inhabit and to ones we are less familiar with.

On this basis we can restore the conjunctive: bring back together – reunite the concepts of advertising *and* culture, perhaps recognising that consumer and media culture are closely related phenomena. For many people advertising, media and consumption are experienced as a common culture (Willis 1990; Williams 1990). A common culture is by its very nature one that is shared but perhaps also as Terry Eagleton, following Williams, suggests: culture is 'common only when it is collectively made' (2000: 119). Culture, then, is always contested: whose culture; what meanings does it have; what kind of work does it do and in whose interest? Rojek puts it more strongly: 'Cultural Studies insists upon conceptualising culture as the intersection of force and resistance' (2007).

Scope and outline

The scope of the chapters that follow are both broad in approach and in subject matter, ranging from fashion through popular music to politics. Two strands are apparent. The first deals generally with the social and cultural role of advertising and the second with specific areas of culture, such as fashion, where advertising features prominently.

The first strand considers how advertising has developed and become an essential economic and social element of a society largely driven by the imperatives of capital. Advertising has a broad set of functions from information to entertainment and from persuasion to myth and mystification. Several chapters are relevant to an exploration of these. In particular 'Advertising – a way of life', 'Spreads like butter', 'Media and advertising' and 'Selling politics' deal specifically with these matters.

The second strand analyses areas of culture where advertising plays a significant part. For instance, advertising draws on the artistic, cultural and technical expertise of workers in areas such as art and design and information technology. It utilises and reappropriates ideas, designs and artefacts produced in these areas and in addition creates its own productions and products that can be analysed using criteria associated with these areas of cultural production. 'Handbags and gladrags' deals with fashion, 'Music and advertising' and 'The cultural economy of death' with popular music. The world of modern art is explored in 'Art and advertising', and that of computing and information technology in 'On-line digi ads'. The wide range of cultural areas dealt with in the book is symptomatic of the depth and breadth of advertising in contemporary society.

The chapter 'Advertising research' and to a lesser extent 'Spreads like butter' consider the different perspectives and forms of research that might be applied to a society in which advertising is a prominent feature and to advertising's links with culture.

Chapter outlines

The first chapter, 'Advertising – a way of life', 'by Tony Purvis, offers an analysis of how culture in Europe and America and increasingly in Asia and China 'continues to be shaped in relation to advertising and advertisements'. Exploring the works of Williams, Barthes,

Freire, Merton and Žižek, this chapter offers a telling critique of contemporary advertising. It opens and concludes with a visit to the sets of *Mad Men*, a television drama about the world of advertising: '*Mad Men*'s irony goes some way in exposing how these PR campaigns sit jarringly next to cultural oppression and social segregation, and where the same uncanny silences that punctuate the script's dialogue and sets shout loudly of discontent and division in the culture itself'.

In Chapter 2, 'Advertising research', John Fenwick and Chris Wharton provide a critical introduction to research theory and practice examining a variety of theoretical perspectives, competing traditions and academic approaches that underpin social research as applied to advertising. The chapter looks at research design, methods and techniques of enquiry. Advertising research is presented as constituted by both industry enquiry into its own products and activities and by critical research conducted from outside the world of advertising. The chapter asks what constitutes research in this field, making a distinction between informal and systematic research and outlines the core components of research: qualitative and quantitative approaches; primary and secondary aspects; sampling; choice of method and analysis of findings; ethics and values. The chapter explores the application of research to advertisements and to people and their cultures.

In Chapter 3, 'Spreads like butter – culture and advertising', Chris Wharton looks at the importance of technology to advertising, the development of different advertising forms and the cultural significance of advertising agencies. Advertising has increased its hold on culture over time, filling more spaces, screens and channels than ever before. The chapter considers homology: how contemporary advertising 'fits' with culture. This is identified in three stages: firstly, in the production and creation of advertising campaigns; secondly, as a highly visible presence in a range of media forms that circulate in social and cultural experience; and thirdly, in advertising's subsequent reception by audiences who bring their own cultural experiences to bear. The chapter is concerned with how advertising enters, fits and flows through contemporary culture and the kind of meanings it might have for people.

The fit between advertising and culture is represented in several chapters through an analysis of the world of fashion, art and popular music. In the first of these, Chapter 4, 'Handbags and gladrags – the rise and rise of accessories in fashion and advertising', Hilary Fawcett looks at the development of fashion-accessory markets in Britain in the post-war period and how advertising adapted to changed economic and cultural circumstances. Women's magazines are shown to be crucial to the promotion of fashion, to markets and a culture increasingly associated with celebrity and the 'consumer's desire for status and identity' in which easy credit and 'impulse buying has been condoned and accepted in an advertising culture which justifies extravagance with "because you're worth it"'. She concludes that the 'hedonism and aspiration that has marked consumer cultures in the past twenty years is now up for question'.

Judith Stevenson in Chapter 5, 'Music and advertising – a happy marriage?' examines the close relationship between advertising and popular music. Acknowledging the complexity and ambiguity apparent in the reception of adverts that use pop music, she explores the symbiotic relationship between music and advertising. The chapter argues that 'for many people music is an essential part of their lives and an important aspect of identity. Generations are defined by popular music'. Research suggests that music is an important factor in the lives of one of the main target groups for advertisers: 16- to 24-year olds. Her themes include music in fashion advertising, connections between Pop Art, pop music and ads with a look at rock band The Who and a case study of the motif of the young crowd in contemporary adverts.

In Chapter 6, 'The cultural economy of death – popular music and advertising', Paula Hearsum explores the triple concoction of advertising, music and death, 'an intoxicating mix which harnesses the intense and dynamic relationship between a listener, a dead musician and the music itself'. The chapter explores the use of posthumous musical releases, the re-packaging of material to coincide with anniversaries of a musician's death and the release of biopics, soundtracks and back catalogues which aim to increase sales by advertising the demise of the musician. From Elvis to Amy Winehouse, the 'industry of death requires all elements of the relationship to work in synchronicity: the advertising industry, the popular music industry, musicians and audiences'.

Chapter 7, 'Art and advertising from the 1880s to the present' by Malcolm Gee, is a further exploration of a symbiotic cultural relationship. As advertising expanded and became established in the modern period it 'appropriated and adapted visual styles and approaches developed in the sphere of fine art … fine art practices themselves have been increasingly influenced by an awareness of the visual characteristics of advertising, and the place that these occupy in modern consciousness'. The chapter explores forms of modernism and how the general principle of abstraction and techniques like photomontage were complementary to the aims of advertising. The chapter ends with an examination of contemporary practice and concludes that 'whereas in the 1890s, advertising, via the poster, aspired to the prestige of art, art today is both attracted and threatened by the power of advertising'.

Online computer-based digital advertising is a relatively new experience. David Reid in Chapter 8, 'On-line digi-ads', explores the genesis of computing and online advertising, recognising how this has, in its multiple forms, taken hold not just of the newly developing online culture but more widely in the already established world of marketing and consumer relations. This is an important area of enquiry recognising a cultural shift where the globalised world searches amongst commodity forms for entertainment, knowledge and education. The quotidian culture of the everyday learns to appreciate the real anew and the exciting potential of the virtual takes form as new ways to purchase and consume. The chapter provides an overview of digi-online forms.

Advertising and its techniques are not only used by the private sector to promote and sell goods and services to the masses, they are also used by politicians, political parties and governments to promote their products to the public. Politicians seek to convey their personal attributes and personalities; political parties strive to publicise their ideologies, programmes and visions; while governments aim to communicate their messages, policies and services.

In Chapter 9, 'Selling politics – the political economy of political advertising', Andrew Mullen makes the case for a critical political economy approach to the study of political advertising. Developed over a century ago by the state, political advertising has become an important element of the 'propaganda-managed democracies' (Chomsky 1995: vi) that have developed in Britain, the United States and other capitalist, liberal-democratic societies. It has proved effective in shaping political attitudes, beliefs and behaviours following its pioneering use in selling war in the early part of the twentieth century. It is applied to selling ideas such as capitalism and the nation, political parties, politicians and political candidates. The amount spent on political advertising increased significantly as it became an integral aspect of the political system and integrated into public relations and other corporate communication strategies. Ever more effective propaganda means that the space within the public sphere for informed and lively debate is constantly under attack and this is made worse by an education system which fails to properly inform citizens about advertising, the media, politics and sociology.

Monika Metykova in Chapter 10, 'Citizens and consumers – media and advertising', looks at advertising as a source of finance for the media industries. The chapter outlines how advocates of privately run commercial media systems argue that this is the way of guaranteeing independence from political and economic interference. The market may well serve the interests of consumers, but advertising revenue competition means that audience volumes determine media contents. This is likely to privilege consumer interests over those of the citizen. Nevertheless, public service broadcasting has an obligation to civic culture. Regulation is of crucial importance in securing public interest in communication and ASA and Ofcom play a key role in United Kingdom advertising. There has been a general shift away from citizen-oriented regulation with increasing reliance on self-regulation rather than direct statutory regulation. The chapter argues against 'underestimating the connections between the roles that media play in democratic societies, the ways in which they obtain funding for their activities and the regulatory frameworks that governments put in place.'

Themes and issues

A number of key issues, themes and concepts essential to a critical approach to advertising and culture are identified and developed in these chapters. As an increasing presence, advertising's forms and influences are colonising ever increasing areas of experience forming a 'way of life' that although relatively recent is often taken for granted. Homology and symbiosis are attached to this and are important concepts to apply to advertising and culture. These are followed by an analysis of 'power and oppression', 'identity', 'creativity', 'pleasure' and 'desire' associated with advertising. The themes of 'history' and 'technology' are also central to several of the chapters.

The idea of advertising as an element of culture and a strategic aspect of a modern way of life is developed from the work of Williams and outlined and explored in Chapter 1,

'Advertising – a way of life' and Chapter 3, 'Spreads like butter'. In Chapter 3 advertising *homology* is linked to this and the fit between advertising and other forms of culture and the everyday ordinariness of its manifestations is introduced as an essential element of modern culture. The symbiotic relation between music and advertising is explored in Chapter 5 and between art and advertising in Chapter 7. The *power* of commodity capitalism is shown, in 'Advertising – a way of life', to be closely linked to advertising and culture and functions through oppression and by its very nature helps define and maintain inequalities. Chapter 9, 'Selling politics', continues an exploration of the theme of power, as it operates in the overt aspects of political advertising and the machinery of the state but also in its role in securing a more general class-based hegemony. Chapter 10, 'Media and advertising', also deals with that aspect of advertising power secured through media funding and the subsequent privilege afforded to the narrow category of consumer culture over that of civic culture and the wider interests of citizens. This chapter also deals with the issue of advertising regulation which can limit the power of organisations and elites in this respect.

The importance of social *identity* to an analysis of advertising is raised in Chapter 5, 'Music and advertising', where identity and identification with popular music and advertising texts, particularly by young people, is examined. In Chapter 4, 'Handbags and gladrags', the place of fashion and fashion advertising is explored in the construction of femininities. More generally, in 'Spreads like butter' identity is explored as one important element of decoding strategies manifest in advertising readings. 'Advertising – a way of life' offers a broad analysis of the theme where identity is associated with consumption rather than other shared experiences based on the productive aspects of work and labour. The critical tools of culture and audience theory are shown not so much to undermine the industry's preoccupation with brand-related consumer identities, but used by the industry to identify a larger market share. 'Media and advertising' is concerned with consumer and citizen identities. Investigating identities is a theme of Chapter 2, 'Advertising research', where both critical research and advertising industry research are shown to share similar methods of enquiry if not the same ends. The nature of *creativity* as it is channelled through the technical means of advertising production and the organisation of advertising agencies is examined in 'Spreads like butter'. It is further explored in Chapter 7, 'Art and advertising', through reference to artistic styles, techniques, applications and outlets in the area of art and graphic design which have impacted on advertising. *Pleasure* and *desire* are recurring themes in the book where the overstated promise of happiness and the conflation of desire with need are discussed in 'Advertising – a way of life' and linked to Raymond Williams' analysis of advertising as a 'magic system'. This theme recurs in Chapter 6, 'The cultural economy of death', in relation to the popular music industry and in 'Handbags and gladrags' with fashion and fashion advertising. Two further areas remain to be mentioned: *history* and *technology*. To a greater or lesser extent history features in each of the cultural areas that comprise our enquiry. From an outline of social and economic developments associated with modern political advertising to the relationships and crossovers between technical and aesthetic features of modernist and postmodernist art, design and advertising. This latter is explored in 'Art and advertising', and in 'Spreads like butter' some of the technological changes that made modern advertising possible are explored in terms of their formal rhetorical possibilities. Chapter 8, 'On-line digi-ads', deals with a variety of online advertising forms and technologies that place advertising and promotion in the midst of a very contemporary way of life.

Conclusions

Advertising is a very visible part of the modern world we inhabit. Culture builds on existence – it creates a way of life; of knowing, exploring and appreciating the world. This book explores how advertising and culture sit alongside each other and often overlap. Its themes of 'history', 'technology', 'a way of life', 'homology', 'power', 'oppression', 'identity', 'creativity', 'pleasure' and 'desire' are important to a study, understanding and analysis of advertising and culture. What we make of this 'way of life' and this analysis will depend on a number of factors – primarily on our visual and mental image of advertising, culture and society. This and any reconfiguring of that image or the reality that lies behind it will depend not just on that analysis but on our stake in the social and economic order and our place in the world.

To return to the initial premise of this introduction, advertising and culture are not synonymous: a distinction between the two can be made. The culture of a people or a community in its widest sense has, or given the pace of globalisation is soon likely to have, advertising as a significant part of it. In Williams' terms advertising is a documentary element which pervades culture in a highly visible way and as a way of life where thought and behaviour associated with promotion and competition define the industry, its products and social effects. In addition advertising competes with other cultural elements for attention and allegiance. It aspires to the ideal.

But is it possible to imagine culture without advertising or with only a minimal connection? In developed societies increasingly sophisticated advertising constantly requires culture to draw on for ideas, references and creativity as a space outside of its own self-referential and insular limitations. In many ways it needs a life world outside of its own to exist.

Over time, advertising changes and develops: changing function, content and style. It exists, like everything else, within poles of possibilities between advancement and disappearance. Its trajectory appears to increase its spread and intensity across time and space. However, targeted regulation like that in the city of Sao Paulo has curtailed the excesses of outdoor public advertising. Technological innovation especially the Internet and virtual development traverses traditional boundaries, with distinctions between cultures and economies, public and private spheres, domains and spaces becoming indistinct or even turned inside out. Advertising either elbows out non-commodity form, crowding out cultural space or mellows, finding gentler forms and accommodations and a softer mode of address. In the mean time, advertising and culture are here to be studied – together or apart.

References

Eagleton, T. (2000), *The Idea of Culture*, London: Blackwell.

Leiss, W., Kline, S., Jhally, S. and Botterill, J. (2005), *Social Communication in Advertising*, London: Routledge.

McGuigan, J. (2010), *Cultural Analysis*, London: Sage.

Rojek, C. (2007), *Cultural Studies*, Cambridge: Polity.

Williams, R. (1983), *Keywords*, London: Fontana.

—— (1990), *Culture and Society*, London: Hogarth Press. First printed 1958.

Williamson, J. (1978), *Decoding Advertisements: Meaning and Ideology in Advertising*, London: Marion Boyes.

Willis, P. (1990), *Common Culture: Symbolic Work at Play in the Everyday Cultures of the Young*, Milton Keynes: Open University Press.

Chapter 1

Advertising – a way of life

Tony Purvis

Don Draper: This is the greatest advertising opportunity since the invention of cereal. We have six identical companies making six identical products. We can say anything we want. How do you make your cigarettes?

Lee Garner, Jr.: I don't know.

Lee Garner, Sr.: Shame on you. We breed insect repellent tobacco seeds, plant them in the North Carolina sunshine, grow it, cut it, cure it, toast it …

Don Draper: There you go. There you go.

[Writes on chalkboard and underlines: 'IT'S TOASTED.']

Lee Garner, Jr.: But everybody's else's tobacco is toasted.

Don Draper: No. Everybody else's tobacco is poisonous. Lucky Strike's … is toasted.

Roger: Well, gentlemen, I don't think I have to tell you what you just witnessed here.

Lee Garner, Jr.: I think you do.

Don Draper: Advertising is based on one thing: happiness. And do you know what happiness is? Happiness is the smell of a new car. It's freedom from fear. It's a billboard on the side of a road that screams with reassurance that whatever you're doing is OK. You are OK.

Lee Garner, Sr.: It's toasted. [Smiles]

Lee Garner, Sr.: I get it.

(From: *Mad Men* (AMC, Lionsgate Television), Season 1, Episode 1 (July, 2007))

Culture is ordinary: that is where we must start. To grow up in that country was to see the shape of a culture, and its modes of change. I could stand on the mountains and look north to the farms and the cathedral, or south to the smoke and the flare of the blast furnace making a second sunset. To grow up in that family was to see the shaping of minds: the learning of new skills, the shifting of relationships, the emergence of different language and ideas. … Every human society has its own shape, its own purposes, its own meanings. Every human society expresses these, in institutions, and in arts and learning. The making of a society is the finding of common meanings and directions, and its growth is an active debate and amendment under the pressures of experience, contact, and discovery, writing themselves into the land.

(Raymond Williams 'Culture is Ordinary', in Highmore 2002: 92)

Reading culture

*M**ad Men* (2007–)[1] is a television drama whose characters people a culture in which every aspect of that culture is read in symbolic ways. Don Draper, lead character in the series, knows that the PR/advertising firm Sterling Cooper, if it is to produce effective readings of culture via its advertisements, must make the ordinary and mundane seem extraordinary and magical. It does this via a promise of happiness, something Draper himself has yet to find. But Draper knows he needs to make a living. He knows, too, that the 'mad men' with whom he works are part of the same culture, the one in which the freedom and consumer choice promised in the advertisements make sense only against the backdrop of capitalism's production of oppression and dissensus. Whilst most people do live very ordinary lives, the series exposes how the oppression of some groups, most notably those on low incomes, but also women and African-Americans, experience the culture in ways which throw a clearer light on the actual realities of consumer-capitalism's fantasies of freedom and choice. Nonetheless, Draper's own life is ordinary; and he is believable because his ordinariness is shared by those others whose stories are told in *Mad Men*'s narrativisation of the 1960s.

Williams' observation, that culture is ordinary, is one which refers to the same period as *Mad Men*. Indeed, his work during this period is written in an attempt to both celebrate this ordinariness and critique the social divisions (based on social class, income distribution, and access to education and housing) which capitalism wrought. The 1950s and 1960s were decades in capitalist history that saw consumerism and advertising become more dominant than in all the previous decades of the twentieth century (Fox and Lears 1983). But they are also decades when the wealth and glamour imagined in advertising is also matched by enormous poverty and social inequality. If the identity of the consumer is one which seems universal, so too are the effects of a free market which ensures that happiness is not quite so universal. *Mad Men* invites us to re-read the symbolic spaces of culture and to visualise the ordinary and the obvious as the very sites in which happiness and oppression are lived on a daily basis. Williams' view of culture also asks us to think about the symbolic dimensions of our lives in a new way. His reading is one which sees in the activities of everyday life the kernel of community. 'Culture for Williams is not, or should not be, what separates people, but what joins them in community. Culture is not for the discerning few, but for the many. It is characterized by aesthetic and intellectual scarcity only in its alienated, elitist forms' (Brantlinger 1991: 77).

This chapter will examine the ways in which culture, principally in Europe and America, though increasingly Asia and China, continues to be shaped in relation to advertising and advertisements. Central to this discussion is the theory and practice of *reading* culture. Here, the noun is not intended to signify an activity which is reserved for a privileged few who, equipped with a specific education and learning in (high) *Culture*, thereby possess greater insights into everyday life. Nor does it make assumptions about literacy where the term refers to the teaching of reading and writing in schools or literacy classes. Nor, indeed, is reading necessarily concerned with learning specific theories and methods by which to read media texts, as sometimes occurs in undergraduate courses dealing with structuralism, deconstruction, semiotics or film analysis. By suggesting that culture can be read, however, the chapter is also proposing that culture is legible but not in ideologically transparent or politically neutral ways. Rather, reading is here used in the sense Paulo Freire deploys the term in his analysis of oppression, and it denotes reading as a critical activity which is always alert to culture's political and ideological dimensions. *Pedagogy of the Oppressed* (1972) outlines his call for cultural activism grounded in such reading, and it grows out of his experiences working with the poor on literacy programmes in Brazil.

Freire's critique proposes that capitalism's economic inequalities, which are reproduced in the shape of division and oppression, are made credible because of the way they are legitimised and made to appear tolerable. Reality which becomes oppressive, he argues, 'results in the contradistinction of men as oppressors and oppressed. The latter ... must acquire a critical awareness of oppression through praxis of this struggle. One of the gravest obstacles to the achievement of liberation is that oppressive reality absorbs those within it ... Functionally, oppression is domesticating' (Freire 1972: 27–8). Commenting on the naturalisation of domestic culture via popular media and advertising, Roland Barthes's *Mythologies* ([1957] 2000) is one of the first major analyses to consider how oppression becomes legitimised in culture. It is not his claims in the name of structuralist methodology which are significant in *Mythologies* so much as the instances, the settings and routine activities Barthes actually chooses in his reading of culture. Because palpably obvious, and thus often ignored, his own 'starting point' is the 'falsely obvious' and 'a feeling of impatience at the sight of the "naturalness" with which [media] dress up a reality'(11).

Barthes, like Williams, does not bequeath a theoretical method by which students should read texts so much as he brings to the foreground the oppressive, paradoxically pleasurable dimensions of everyday life dressed up by the mass media. Raymond Williams in 'Advertising: The Magic System' (1980; first written in 1961) shows how the 'magic system' of advertising and its glamour can make us overlook the toil and suffering entailed in all production. When history can pass as nature, assisted by the credible ordinariness of advertisements, and when routines and practices are habituated, so oppression can be legitimised without too much displeasure and remain unaltered. The legitimisation process, argues Freire, where oppression is domesticated, is often achieved via pedagogy, as opposed to propaganda (1972: 41–44), and usually through the form and content of education but additionally in the culture's ways of transmitting information (1972: 45–59). Consumer-driven economies use advertising and product branding (Klein 2000) to transmit information in order to manipulate and influence demand (and thus the flow of money), though it is the impact of schooling which first interests Freire. Focusing on the form and transmission of culture, rather than being overly concerned with its final definition, is one of his most important contributions to cultural theory. However, concise summaries of culture and advertising will be useful in this initial mapping.

Way of life: culture and advertising?

Both terms, whilst open to theoretical contention and dispute, can be summarised with relative ease. Richard Hoggart (1957), Williams (1958; 1961), and more recently Terry Eagleton (2000; 2011), working within the trajectory established by Williams, see culture as a whole way of life. Culture is universal; and although specific ways of life are marked by distinct beliefs and values, culture's universality resides in its closeness to the everyday life (Gardener 2000; Highmore 2010; Sheringham 2006). Yet advertising, too, is arguably universal, close to everyday life, laden with values and ideologies, something brought poignantly to the fore in AMC' s *Mad Men*. 'I give you money, you give me ideas', advises series lead character Don Draper (Series 4, Episode 7). Here is how the Institute of Practitioners in Advertising (the UK's lead industry-professional body) similarly describe their identity fifty years on from Don Draper: 'Advertising presents the most persuasive possible selling message to the right prospects for the product or service at the lowest possible cost' (Gordon 2011: 24–25). It is a definition which more exactly appropriates advertising's impersonality in today's culture, and one which moves away from the more innocently conceived notion that defines advertising as notification, warning and information.

The two terms, then, if left to common sense, pass unnoticed. Viewed, however, in the context of oppression, culture as 'way of life' is something for which people are prepared to die (e.g. the 'troubles' in Iraq and in Afghanistan have been constructed in the media as cultural (Lewis 2005; Miller 2004); and historically, it is advertising, deployed as an apparatus of the state, which has recruited large numbers via an interpellation addressed on behalf of a country ('We') which really needs 'You'. (A recent example of how this 'we/you' interpellation, via images and voice-over, is the recruitment video for the Swedish Army: http://www.buzzfeed.com/donnad/realistic-swedish-army-recruitment-ad).

Culture's universality, often because of mass media, is today experienced in local ways before it is realised geographically or transnationally. Advertising, moreover, is not so much a system used in order to inform or provide notice as it is origin and source of information per se, something which, as Michael Moore's *Fahrenheit 9/11* shows, disturbingly legitimises warfare. People wage war in culture; yet advertising is so inescapably linked to the domain of the political economy as to be in a more uncannily magical position of influence and determination than Williams conceived in his important critique of advertising in 1961.

It was during the 1960s and 1970s that definitions of and relations between culture and advertising were being considered in some detail. Although the work of F. R. Leavis (Leavis and Thompson 1942), and Horkheimer and Adorno (1947), had earlier added to the competing theories of culture and advertising, it was the sheer size of the advertising industry from the 1950s that propelled critical attention. It is also during this period that culture is ambivalently conceived as *problem* (and thus as cause of modernity's moral decline), and *solution* (where it is imagined as a way of achieving modernity) (Eagleton 2000). Thomas Merton, Roman Catholic monk and social critic, comments on advertising's power under capitalism and captures something of its contradictory sacred-secular status, comparing it to transubstantiation. In the way that the bread and wine during the mass are transformed, becoming for the faithful 'the body and blood of Christ', so it is with advertising. Merton contends that advertising 'treats all products with the reverence and the seriousness due to sacraments' (Merton [1965] 2009: 232). His comments are insightful and draw attention to form and content together, central also to the work of Marshall McLuhan (1964) and also Freire. Merton writes how the form and content of technological innovation, something which is potentially 'de-humanising and destructive' (Hall 2011: 34), serve to alienate people 'while at the same time summoning them to cooperate in the work of their own alienation. The machinery of alienation is then tightened up, and social control becomes more and more arbitrary' (Merton, op. cit.: 257).

Vance Packard's *The Hidden Persuaders* (1957) makes similar claims, and it becomes seminal in the emerging anti-advertisement discourse which influenced American cultural criticism during the 1960s. Some of Packard's account is retraced in Ivan Preston's *The Great American Blow-Up: Puffery in Advertising* (1975) which examines how the exaggerated and deceptive content of some advertisements is received in American law and the litigation culture which ensues. More recently, Rosemary Hennessy's *Profit and Pleasure* (2000) adds to the corpus of work which critiques media, culture and advertising. She examines particularly the strategies of visibility and visualisation at work in advertising and consumer culture and which, in Hennessy's analysis, operate as forms of oppression. She comments how we read, see and perceive is 'historically produced cultural knowledge' (95) and that how we read and see should not be severed from the 'social relationships of labor and power commodity capitalism is premised on'.

Across much of this criticism, Hennessy rightly comments that Williams' own reading of culture remains seminal. Culture is common and its materiality is 'ordinary', Williams contends. It is, suggests Eagleton, important to us in similar ways to 'personal dignity and security, [and] freedom from pain, suffering and oppression' (2000: 100). Williams and Eagleton stress culture's earthiness and the sense of belonging people have to the land and to each other. 'Culture is something we live for', something associated with 'affection, relationship, memory, kinship, place' (Eagleton 2000: 131). Williams and Eagleton are of course alert to the qualitative and aesthetic judgements which have beset discussion of culture and which has often been heavily inflected by Matthew Arnold's discussion of culture, civilisation and anarchy (Arnold [1869] 1960). Eagleton retraces how 'Culture' has been perceived as an answer and mass culture as a problem. Associated with permissiveness and anarchy, popular-media culture is read in terms of its deficit status, and a return to 'Culture' (more closely aligned with Western-European Civilisation) is the way out of the mess associated with modernity and, today, postmodernity. Historically associated with Leavis, whose specific contribution is frequently misrepresented, the popular culture-as-deficit legacy is alive and well. The hugely popular American drama from the 1980s, *Little House on the Prairie* (1974–83, NBC; and since 2008, rerun by the Christian-based network CTS), exemplifies how the past is recast as more civilised than America's postmodern, fractured present. Two popular dramatisations with a more nuanced logic of past-present informing their narratives, and which directly reference advertising, are to be found in Channel 4's (UK) series *Shameless* (2004–) and AMC's *Mad Men* (2007–), which is explored in more detail later in the chapter. Advertising, moreover, is itself alert to the power of old- and new-world imagery in its campaigns. 'Even the word "new" is charged with extra meaning: however well your old widget performs, a new one MUST be even better! [Advertisements] take great delight in saluting retrofuturism's undeniably appealing sense of style' (see http://weburbanist.com/2009/03/29/retrofuturistic-ads-selling-a-brighter-tomorrow/).

Reading the words and worlds of culture and advertising: Paulo Freire

A way of life is bigger and richer than the culture/civilisation bifurcation above might suggest. If we consider 'political' activism during the last thirty years, then it is clear that much of this has been 'cultural' in focus. During 2011, so-called pro-democracy movements across North Africa have drawn attention to culture, and not the economy, in the fight against oppressive regimes. Since the 1940s, critics such as Adorno, Leavis, Williams and Freire highlight culture's pivotal role in effecting change; and media technologies of the last ten years have amplified how this change is communicated transculturally (Lewis 2005, 2008). Whilst the economy is central in determining the material conditions in which culture is lived, nonetheless, struggle is often waged in the name of cultural identity (ethnicity, gender, religious faith, and national identity). In Freire's logic, culture's complexity is actually its very ordinariness; and the ordinary, because obvious, is often, as Barthes argues, elided or dismissed. Freire's demand that approaches to, and forms of, cultural literacy be organised in democratic, collective ways (1972: 135–40), is all the more significant because of his own commitment to pedagogy and his desire to work with others in speaking out against oppression. He underscores a commitment to forms of critical literacy, where education might promote readings of culture which facilitate cultural transformation. In that sense, he shares much in common with Williams and Eagleton as well as elements of Slavoj Žižek's recent work (2008, 2009, 2011; see also Žižek's endorsement of critical work by Freire, in McLaren 2000, McLaren et al. 2010).

Freire does not propose a particular theory or vocabulary which can then be applied to texts. His notion of 'banking' offers an alternative route of analysis and considers why education constructs learners who accept rather than challenge subjectivity. Under this system, knowledge, Freire argues, underpins existing inequalities in a culture which is less open to democratic reform. People and institutions entrusted with education deposit information, but this services on-going oppression (learners are constructed around deficiency) as opposed to critical reflection. Knowledge, Freire argues, perpetuates structural inequalities and culture remains unchanged. Today's notion of 'agency', 'audience' research', 'media consumer' and related keywords in some 'populist' cultural studies (McGuigan 2011), similarly replicate the discourse of advertising. Agency is restored once a product is purchased. However, such a model similarly replicates the very discourse which legitimises deficiency. Freire challenges this kind of 'schooling' approach, arguing that it ultimately dehumanises educators and educated alike. 'The capacity of banking education to minimize or annul the students' creative power and to stimulate their credulity serves the interests of the oppressors. ... The oppressors use their "humanitarianism" to preserve a profitable situation' (Freire 1972: 47).

The impact of the oppression which Freire describes is more widespread than his own experiences in Brazil. 'Cultural literacy' too often bolsters a singular narrative whose modes of intelligibility ensure the dominant culture is 'common' (as in widespread) but not commonly owned; and consent is achieved via a tactical use of official culture in education. Freire suggests, however, that no one is culturally illiterate or deprived, and nor are citizens dispossessed of a culture. To the extent that literacy and cultural literacy are also concerned with the everyday practice of making sense of social relations, so forms of literacy which remain in the service of 'powerful groups' (similar to Žižek's argument about 'leadership' ([2010] 2011)), are always more suited to preserving the basic inequality of capitalism. Asking questions about how media consumers 'use' television, or how advertisements are encoded in relation to personal identity, fails to interrogate the legitimacy of the very media form and content being transmitted in the first instance. The promise of agency remains deferred and, in the words of McGuigan, 'cultural analysis remains one-dimensional' and capitalism remains 'cool' (2011: 11). Whilst citizens are taught to read and write, continued subjectivity is guaranteed if access to the sources of power and cultural self-determination remain mysteriously inaccessible. 'It is impossible to understand literacy ... by divorcing the reading of the word from the reading of the world, that is, having the experience of changing the world' (Freire 1987: 49). Freire's concept of reading signifies an approach to culture which does not view citizens as 'adaptable or manageable beings' (1972: 47); people are not 'illiterate' in the conventional sense, but are discouraged, sometimes prevented, from developing a 'critical consciousness' of the culture.

Žižek's ([2010] 2011) very recent analysis of capitalism, including advertising, as well as the spaces of capitalism which provide pleasure (he appropriates Jacques Lacan's notions of the symptom and *jouissance*), makes comparable observations to those of Freire. Žižek suggests that there are no inherent problems or pleasures with culture and that, in fact, the problems are ones which require a reading of oppression through an analysis of capitalism's leadership. Recasting the words of Saint Paul, Žižek states that cultural struggle 'is not against actual corrupt individuals, but against those in power in general, against their authority, against the global order and the ideological mystification which sustains it' (2011: xv). The ideological mystification to which Žižek refers is compounded by media and advertising under capitalism, and he provides a close analysis of China's economy. Such mystification is referred to as advertising's *magic* by Williams, and his observations over the later sections of 'Advertising: The Magic System' ([1961] 1980) are prescient. It is not advertising's potential for vulgarity or indecency which bothers Williams or Žižek; and both caution against criticism based on aesthetics and decoding of signs. Williams in particular underlines his concerns about forms of criticism which stress consumption and consumer identity. Emphasis on the latter is ultimately an endorsement of the culture of the market as opposed to a critique of a system whose logic insists on 'consumers', an identity solely constructed for the purposes of the market and not the culture. Rather (and the parallels with Freire and Žižek are to be underlined), it is advertising's *cultural* power over the manipulation and distribution of goods and services which needs to be addressed. 'An out-dated and inefficient kind of information about goods and services has been surpassed by the competitive needs of the corporations, and these increasingly demand not a sector, but a world' (1980: 195).

The problems Williams imagines in his essay uncannily resemble today's global capitalism. Globalisation, and particularly global media and advertising, what Taylor and Harris call the *mediascape* (2008), mean that engagements with, and interventions in contemporary culture occur in relation to mass-media technologies and representations (Taylor 2010: 91–119). Although access to technologies remains unequal, most people do not live outside of the global culture which advertising and PR companies display in advertisements. It is to be recalled that Barthes's analysis of mystification is by way of a critical engagement with the obvious. The mystification to which Žižek alludes is one which is also packaged in the very obvious 'face-to-face' formats of new-digital media and popular culture ([2010] 2011: 342–352). For instance, the media's uncovering of a scandal, as Žižek emphasises, does not bring to an end the 'upbeat message' ([2010] 2011: 408). He shows how advertising's cheerful constructions of the world blur the actual facts so that fiction can easily displace the truth. As a consequence, appraisal of the truth of the facts becomes difficult.

Culture, happiness and personal dignity

The preceding arguments become all the more important if, in reading culture and advertising, oppression can be challenged. The power of media and advertising is not to be underestimated. Merton, foreshadowing more recent criticism, captures something of the influence media images and advertising exercise over thinking and behaviour.

> We need to recover the belief that it is worthwhile and possible to break through the state of massive inertia and delusion created by the repetition of statements and slogans without meaning … The arbitrary, fictitious and absurd mentality – reflected in its advertising and entertainment particularly – must be recognized as an affront to man's personal dignity.
>
> (Merton, op. cit.: 257)

Merton's bringing together of the terms 'culture' and 'advertising' in a discussion about human dignity, also invites a consideration of a more problematic equation: advertising is culture to the extent that advertisements reflect a way of life; yet culture is itself a form of advertising, promoted and represented in the form of identities, language communities, physical spaces, and textual arrangements. Culture does not require advertising or advertisements. Nonetheless, all social relations are shaped in cultures marked prominently, if not inescapably, by advertisements, something explored satirically and sensitively in AMC's *Mad Men*. In the series, Sterling Cooper is driven by practice (how to do good ads), and theory (how to do better ads). The theory and the practice combine in the production of the advertisement itself. The drama shows how companies involved in PR, advertising and allied industries are peopled by workers whose lives are shaped around the very fictions produced in the advertising industry where people earn a living. Outside of the office, characters re-emerge as the very consumers who live with the myth of agency they helped to construct in the firm's division of labour. In the workplace, the division of labour and people in the production line means some workers have greater agency than others; and in the division of consumption, income differentials mean that some workers have far less agency than others. Advertising, however, is ever-present, and its symbolic dimensions are rarely questioned unless the market fails.

Advertising's own textual arrangements, alongside its methods, grammar, and effects continue to be scrutinised in media and cultural studies. However, advertising and PR companies have themselves benefitted from media theory's own engagement with audience research and textual analysis. In the gathering of data, PR firms ensure that the illusion of agency is foregrounded in all campaigns (Gordon 2011: 132–155). Indeed, PR and advertising firms encourage more critical applications of media theory than many media studies courses, showing how the frameworks which have provided media studies with a disciplinary, academic identity can be re-deployed in order to keep the advertising and PR industry ahead of the critical field and also very profitable (Gordon 2011: 27–97). Despite the contribution of media theory to the analysis of culture, advertisements and brands are affected by the interventions of media theory only when the theory can make the brand sell with greater ease. If this were not the case, advertising and advertisements would cease to persuade in the way they do today. Arguably, what is referred to as 'audience studies' helps advertising to operate even more successfully in that it provides the very critique upon which PR firms rely in the construction of the market.

The language and effects of advertisements, whilst they might *seem* intimate, addressed to a 'you' and a 'me' via the discourses of representation, consumption and identity (du Gay et al. 1996; Mackay 1997), are ultimately impersonal and inhuman to the extent that advertising industries care little about personal effects (or affects) so long as products achieve sales. Whilst advertisements provide the illusion of agency, the illusion is effective precisely because the impersonal, commanding power of the economy has been provisionally displaced in order that the 'person' might seem more important than the mass-produced images in which s/he is interpellated. The brand, constructed as the object which will bridge the gap between the subject who lacks and the new way of life promised in the advertisement, will ensure the subject's life will be *sans manqué*. *Mad Men* shows that whichever way audiences finally decode or re-encode the message, in the sphere of the market, meaning is paramount *only* if sales fail. Advertising tells us that we lack objects/brands which can make us and the culture 'whole'. Desire is satisfied on the basis of a belief that the purchase of an object (which we lack) will make us complete. Advertisements, for example, promoting cars, holidays, cosmetic surgery, or a second home, aim to sell products to subjects who are encouraged to believe that, with the product, life will never be the same.

The myths and promises of advertising, the selling of identities, and the construction of corporate, alternative or indeed resistant subcultures through advertising, make sense *inside* the capitalist economy and which advertising promotes. There is no inside/outside culture in capitalism, as *Mad Men* clearly exposes, and arguments about agency and autonomy make sense inside capitalism itself. To examine advertising is to examine culture. However, it is to examine a way of life from the perspective of the images and texts of a system which, whilst it remains fundamentally economic in its determination, is nonetheless imagined in the domains of identity and way of life.

Mad men, mad world?

These two spheres, of identity and way of life, are central to *Mad Men*'s narrative.

> Vinyl upholstery and mirrored walls, but brand new. It's after work, but the women have their hair done and each man's tie is pushed to the top of his collar. Highballs and martinis clink under quiet music and everywhere are the sights and sounds of smoking.
> (Source: Set directions: *Mad Men*, Series One: Episode 1)

In the series, Sterling Cooper's campaigns and advertisements are built around a cultural imaginary external to the office where the 'martinis clink' and where it all seems 'brand new'. This space is conceived as universal (everyone shares the culture), and as goal-driven (people get on with each in the cause of the 'American Dream'). The narrative is textured by the myth of a unifying national history where people are brought together around *common* cultural values. These American values, however, are subsequently passed off as universal. The set directions from Series One, Episode 1, construct this world with such obviousness that in the watching of the drama, the obvious – precisely that which is most ideological – is easily bypassed. Again, the set directions arrange this world with some clarity.

> Images and sounds from late 1950's and early 60's advertising: Doctors selling cigarettes. Athletes selling liquor. Bathing suit models with vacuum cleaners. And most importantly, proud Dads with their perfect wives and children driving their cars to some green suburban utopia. We get a sense of the time and its ideals.
> (Source: Set directions: *Mad Men*, Series One: Episode 1; opening set)

This period, described as one most typifying the 'culture of consumption' (see Fox and Lears 1983), is also one marked by civil rights, anti-war demonstrations, feminism, class politics in the form of trade unionism, and countercultures. Whilst the drama might appear to consign the 'reality' of these historical-political spheres to *Mad Men*'s extra-textual margins, they are never absent and serve always to highlight the individualism which capitalism's advertising industry helps create and exploit during the 1960s. The dyadic focus of the series is firstly on advertising as an industry and the concomitant generation of 'belief in the business' in order to survive; and secondly on the advertisements themselves, whose fictions of happiness require another set of beliefs. The latter beliefs become acts of faith, and are converted into sales returns once consumers buy the product, promoted as the object of desire in the advertisement. At the same time, increased sales make sure Sterling Cooper's profitability and viability are maintained. The advertisements and images make sense in a culture where the mediascape is built on advertising flow. All advertisements attempt to promote sales on the basis of representations (Gordon 2011: 24–27) or 'image speak' (Schutzman 1999: 12). Such images re-configure the culture in the shape of the object of desire (an imaginary future is a one in which the product is owned), simultaneously promising contentment in the present (Bennett 2005a, 2005b). The advertisement is a text of culture yet it is one which promotes the sale of a product *and* a particular way of life.

The promotion of a way of life and a brand is something which companies today have exploited in the name of (so-called) green- and eco-cultures, the Innocent drinks company being a recent example of such ethical narratives (Simmons 2008: 11–29). Žižek, citing a full-page Starbucks advertisement from *USA Today* (4 May 2009, p. A9) argues that the 'buying into a coffee ethic' is an 'exemplary case of "cultural capitalism"' (2009: 53). Within that 'cultural' logic, the metaphor 'adverting is culture' would appear to make complete sense. However, advertising seeks additionally to legitimise both the act of purchase and the object. As a consequence, the consumption of the text and the product appear necessary and thus 'natural'. In *Mad Men*, to use the earlier argument of Barthes's, 'newspapers, art and common sense constantly dress up a reality which, even though it is the one we live in, is undoubtedly determined by history' (op cit: 11). The more successful the representation, the more the object, and the activities surrounding its ownership (browsing, shopping, purchasing and self-identifying), are accorded the status of nature as opposed to history. On the basis of a purchase, consumers (who are also workers in the division of labour) return their income to the cycle of production, buying back a part of the culture from the wages which were earned in the making of the product. The exchange of money, however, operates according to an allied logic, so that 'identity shopping' is bound up with shopping for the object itself, where language and identity are all-important. The soft drinks company Innocent 'has found more and more ways to communicate essentially the same message. It has been able to do this by creating a tone of voice *so engaging* that you will want to read on' (Simmons: 71; emphasis added).

Mad Men exposes how, supposedly happier with our lives once we purchase a car or buy the latest fragrance, we nonetheless go shopping for more and more objects, and always on the basis of advertising's promises. The production and consumption of consumer objects, tied as it is to advertising, simultaneously sustains the advertising industry itself and so the incessant flow of images and meanings is maintained. Desire becomes conflated with need and demand via evermore intense, innovative advertising campaigns. In the case of some soft drinks, it is precisely desire and not the drink (or need) which is being purchased. Žižek explains how Coca-Cola is 'the direct embodiment of … the pure surplus of enjoyment over standard satisfactions, of the mysterious and elusive X we are all after in our compulsive consumption of merchandise' (2001a: 22). This does not mean contemporary consumers are more compulsive or consumerist, more duped or less ethical than the past. Sterling Cooper, not unlike PR companies today, does not ask consumers to evaluate the ethics or aesthetics of the advertisements which the industry spawns. Companies then and now are largely impervious to the results of textual evaluations of advertisements undertaken on degree programmes, unless this is in order to identify a potentially larger market share (Gordon: 37–66). Since the 1960s, semiotics, feminist theory, and audience ethnographies have served as critical tools in the decoding of visual-textual representations and deployed in collections by Mackay (1997), and Hermes (2005). However, the discipline cultural studies, some have argued, has had little impact on the subjection and manipulation of consumers under capitalism (Hennessy 2000; McGuigan 2011; Žižek 2001b), and particularly PR regimes (Dinan and Miller 2008).

Whilst the critical approaches of media and cultural studies certainly serve an important purpose in foregrounding the reading of culture, the obsession with identity-based criticism has not ultimately undermined the industry's own obsession with the myriad images deployed in the construction of the brand and the exploitation of identity. The contradictory logic of capitalism, which Marxist criticism has long argued, (John Rees 1998; Alex Callinicos 2010) is that it generates its own critique. The critical readings of culture by oppressed groups generated a profoundly vocal, politicised critique of the culture during the decade in which *Mad Men* is set. These readings of culture took place despite the prevailing cultural criticism in the academy, and often as a direct challenge to the economy as much as hegemonic cultural representations of identity. Thus, identity-based criticism, whilst it might raise questions about regimes of 'neoliberal governmentality', 'versions of intersectionality' and 'underlying essentialisms' (McRobbie in Gill and Scharff, eds, 2011: xii) does nothing to interrogate the very economic modes which allow such cultural criticism, or indeed identity for that matter, to appear intelligible. Indeed, the contradictory, cultural dissensus reflected in the many counter-mainstream manifestos of the period in which *Mad Men* is set, are ones which seek to question fundamentally the economic bases which sanction oppression and which simultaneously foreground and privilege identity.

Re-presenting culture and advertising

Mad Men exposes these massive contradictions in culture. This is often achieved formally, by means of the drama's setting, its depiction of social spaces, the use of gesture and stillness, and the silence of the high-rise cityscape. Similar to the personal tragedies of lead characters, whose private grief rarely disrupts the public workplace, so the political mainstream attempted to dismiss the economic and cultural contradictions of the period. The double-voiced, *dialogic* dimensions of culture (Holquist 1990), are echoed in the advertising texts themselves. It is not as a result of inherent textual instabilities of advertisements that the culture may be called into question (Taylor and Harris 2008: 1–14). Indeed, the deconstruction of the advertisements comes about not on the basis of an *a priori* desire to subvert its dominant meaning; such ambivalence is already in the text. Rather, there is instead something more obvious, to recall the arguments of Barthes, Freire and Williams, in the very oppressive culture from which the advertisements emerge. The cigarette campaign in Episode One of *Mad Men*, and the promotion of the 'toasted seed' which is transformed into *Lucky Strike*, hides from view the real cost and waste of cigarette manufacture. It does not follow, however, that those involved in the manufacture of cigarettes were necessarily content workers or believed *Mad Men's* narrative about happiness.

Žižek, too, has shown that even so-called ethical consumption (he cites coffee and water), is never as ethical as the advertising might imply. Cigarette advertisements today are arguably far more ethical than most others in that at least they warn that we will die. The belief is that the Third World is being assisted under capitalism's return to an authentic experience associated with the 1960s. Accordingly, 'the price is higher than elsewhere since what you are really buying is the "coffee ethic" which includes care for the environment, [and] social responsibility towards the producers' (Žižek 2009: 54). By purchasing coffee and making a contribution to the 'Ethos Water' programme, consumers are encouraged to believe that 'we are not merely buying and consuming' but are 'simultaneously doing something meaningful, showing our capacity for global awareness' (54). Moreover, whilst advertisements might appear to depict society's ethical choices (via the new moral identification with a brand), this is always in order to sell the product as widely as possible. Such attention to cultural and ethical difference conceals the fixed economic sameness which unites people in the division of labour and the mundane routines of daily life. These advertisements, similar to the ones in *Mad Men*, are spaces upon which some identities are more conspicuously inscribed as *different*. A final extract from set directions illustrates this point:

[MORNING] From the air, we see an elegant modern glass building. Below, the hats on the tops of men's heads swarm like ants through revolving doors. [ELEVATOR] A middle-aged black man mans the controls of the crowded elevator. Three young execs, KEN, DICK, and HARRY, in apparently identical suits take off their hats and crowd to the back of the elevator.
DICK: 'Twenty-three.'
HARRY: 'Oh, but not right away.'
An attractive YOUNG SECRETARY, holding her purse to her chest, steps on the elevator and turns her back to them. The three men look her over and nod to each other approvingly.
(Source: Set directions: *Mad Men*, Series One: Episode 1)

Whilst racism and misogyny today are materialised in different ways, the set directions for *Mad Men* show clearly how oppression occurs in spaces as blatant and obvious as the elevator, the city's streets and the wider communities. Yet the difference which race and gender appear to make visible in this sequence itself comes about because of the cultural sameness of the wider public space whose homogeneity is metonymically signalled in the three young men who are '*apparently* identical' (emphasis added).

Culture *is* ordinary

Western mainstream culture, the series shows, is peopled by groups who live uncannily alongside an excluded and often silent *other*. Despite the agency which consumer capitalism and advertisements promise, this culture operates oppressively. Advertising has to win all consumers and all identities, not simply those made visible in the cultural mainstream, but it cannot do this with parity because of the economic division of labour and the subsequent construction of people, in the words of Freire, as 'objects' and not 'subjects' in their own affairs. This stress on identity is paralleled in the workplace, in civil rights, and in the advertising industry's proliferation of identities. The products and campaigns advertised in the world of *Mad Men* require and imply a division of labour which, under capitalism, will always legitimise some ways of life, or certain identities, more than others. The series shows a business and PR world whose advertisements and products are available 'for all', tied harmoniously and democratically to the American dream. However, *Mad Men*'s irony goes some way in exposing how these PR campaigns sit jarringly next to cultural oppression and social segregation, and where the same uncanny silences that punctuate the script's dialogue and set shout loudly of discontent and division in the culture itself. Here, the real object being produced and consumed is human labour.

This assignation of subjects to lower positions in the division of labour, something which in the world of *Mad Men* is also gendered and racialised, is a division which must also compete with capitalism's contradictory production of subjects as free agents in the imaginary which is cultural consumption. Freire writes that 'every approach to the oppressed by the elites, as a class, is couched in terms of [a] false generosity' (1972: 103). However, if gender and ethnic identities are coded in relation to subjection via the division of labour, the consumer is encoded with a sense of power. Work identity is experienced as subjection whereas consumer identity equates sovereignty. Advertisements do not sell to subjects so much as they interpellate consumers as free, willing agents who supposedly act with autonomy. In *Mad Men*, characters' positions as consumers are not dissimilar to those today, based around the necessary selling of labour in a market place, where advertisements hide from view the other labourers and promote, instead, an image of consumer autonomy. Freire suggests that the selling as opposed to the owning of one's labour means that labour itself is depersonalised (1972: 150). However, his argument is one which does not negate consumption. It would be short-sighted to simply or uncritically dismiss consumption as consumerist or hedonistic or oppressive per se (Littler 2008). Similarly, it is difficult to argue that agency is a redundant concept if alternative-hedonism and anti-globalisation lobbies today, and civil rights and feminist campaigns in the past, have been able to exercise a limited agency in promoting counter-discourses in old and new-media formats.

Perhaps the problem with the agency-focused model of media, as Taylor (2010) lucidly discusses, is that it tends to reify agency so that consumer 'choice' is read first of all as agency (freedom to choose as an equal) and that this subsequently valorises the imagined democracy of perfect competition and the market. As Freire has expounded, capitalism and markets do not possess a morality or conscience (1972: 96–108). Thus, the pursuit of profit still requires a state to maintain certain conditions within which that profit may be legitimised: education, agency, choice, and morality. The state in such circumstances must make itself available to be used by those on the lowest social rungs. Here, advertising works as an appendage of the state, where the ideology of equal cultural citizenship (we can buy this or that object) acts to dampen more critical, dialectical forms of inquiry. In an argument which anticipates shows such as *The X-Factor* (2004–) and *American Idol* (2002–), Freire writes that ideology is at its most effective in the myth 'that anyone who is industrious can be an entrepreneur [and] worse yet, the myth that the street vendor is as much an entrepreneur as the owner of a large factory' (109). Despite these conditions, Freire's optimism, something he shares with Williams, is one which shows how, in the context of oppression, individuals and groups have necessarily toiled collectively in order to question the very causes and conditions of a reality where division is made to seem inevitable.

Mad Men, too, dramatises how culture is founded on mutuality, interrelatedness and cooperation. In the advertising industry, people necessarily work together. Moreover, characters live lives in a culture outside of work and do ordinary things such as taking holidays, socialising, travelling, or simply passing the time. These signifiers of people's daily life amplify theoretical accounts of culture which itemise its mundane, ordinary and repetitive schedules. In Williams' meticulous reading of culture, it is indeed the ordinary where a way of life happens. However, as this chapter has argued, ordinary life chances – what some refer to as 'agency' – are not equal. Nonetheless, Freire's pedagogy is one which believes that people will be 'truly critical … if their action encompasses a critical reflection which increasingly organizes their thinking and thus leads them to move from purely naïve knowledge of reality… to one which enables them to perceive the causes of reality' (101).

References

American Idol (2002–), Freemantle Media North America: Fox.

Arnold, M ([1869] 1960), *Culture and Anarchy*, London: Cambridge University Press.

Barthes, R. ([1957] 2000), *Mythologies*, London: Vintage.

Bennett, D. (2005a), 'Getting the Id to Go Shopping: Psychoanalysis, Advertising, Barbie Dolls, and the Invention of the Consumer Unconscious', *Public Culture* (Duke University Press), vol. 17, no. 1 (February 2005), pp. 1–25.

————— (2005b), 'Desire as Capital', in N. Bracker and S. Herbrechter (eds), *Metaphors of Economy*, New York and Amsterdam: Rodopi, pp. 95–109.

Brantlinger, P. (1991), 'Raymond Williams: "Culture is Ordinary"', *Ariel: A Review of International English Literature*, 22:2, April; pp. 75–81.

Callinicos, A. (2010), *The Bonfire of Illusions: The Twin Crises of the Liberal World*, London: Polity.

Dinan, W. and Miller, D. (2008), *A Century of Spin – How Public Relations Became the Cutting Edge of Corporate Power*, London: Pluto Press.

Du Gay, P., Hall, S., Janes, L., Mackay, H., and Negus, K. (1996), *Doing Cultural Studies: The Story of the Sony Walkman*, London: Sage.

Eagleton, T. (2000), *The Idea of Culture*, Oxford: Blackwell.

————— (2011), *Why Marx Was Right*, New Haven, CT: Yale University Press.

Fahrenheit 9/11 (2004), Dog Eat Dog Films; Moore, M.

Fox, R. W. and Lears, T. J. (eds) (1983), *The Culture of Consumption: Critical Essays in American History, 1880–1980*, New York: Pantheon.

Freire, P. (1972), *Pedagogy of the Oppressed*, London: Penguin Books.

Freire, P. and Macedo, D. (1987), *Literacy: Reading the Word and the World*, South Hadle, MA: Bergin and Garvey.

Gardener, M. (2000), *Critiques of Everyday Life: An Introduction*, London: Routledge.

Gill, R. and Scharff, C. (eds) (2011), *New femininities: postfeminism, neoliberalism and subjectivity*. Basingstoke: Palgrave.

Gordon, A. E. (2011), *Public Relations*, Oxford: Oxford University Press.

Hall, G. (2011), 'Another Kind of Trifling', *The Merton Journal: The Journal of the Thomas Merton Society of Great Britain and Ireland*, Eastertide 2011, 18:1, pp. 33–40.

Hennessy, R. (2000), *Profit and Pleasure: Sexual Identities in Late Capitalism*, New York and London: Routledge.

Hermes, J. (2005), *Re-Reading Popular Culture: Rethinking Gender, Television and Popular Media Audiences*, Malden, MA; Oxford: Wiley-Blackwell.

Highmore, B. (2002), *Ordinary Lives: Studies in the Everyday*, London: Routledge.

————— (2010), *Studies in Ordinary Lives*, London and New York: Routledge.

Hoggart, R. (1957), *The Uses of Literacy: Aspects of Working Class Life*, London: Chatto and Windus.

Holquist, M. (1990), *Dialogism*, London and New York: Routledge.

Horkheimer, M. and Adorno, T. W., ed. G. S. Noerr, trans. E. Jephcott ([1947] 2002), *Dialectic of Enlightenment: Philosophical Fragments*, Stanford: Stanford University.

Klein, N. (2000), *No Logo*, London: Flamingo.

Leavis, F. R. and Thompson, D. (1942), *Culture and Environment: The Training of Critical Awareness*, London: Chatto and Windus.

Lewis, J. (2005), *Language Wars: The Role of Media and Culture in Global Terror and Political Violence*, London: Pluto.

————— (2008), 'The Role of the Media in Boosting Military Spending', *Media War and Conflict Journal*, 1:1), pp. 108–117.

Little House on the Prairie (1974–83), Ed Friendly Productions, NBC.

Littler, J. (2008), *Radical Consumption: Shopping for Change in Contemporary Culture*, Maidenhead: Open University Press.

Mackay, H. (1997), *Consumption and Everyday Life*, London: Sage.

Mad Men (2007–), Matthew Weiner; Scott Hornbacher: AMC.

McGuigan, J. (2011), 'From Cultural Populism to Cool Capitalism', *Art and the Public Sphere*, Intellect, Volume 1:1, pp. 7–18.

McLaren, P. (2000), *Che Guevara, Paulo Freire, and the Pedagogy of Revolution*, Lanham, MD: Rowman and Littlefield.

McLaren, P., Macrine, S., and Hill, D, (eds) (2010), *Revolutionizing Pedagogy: Educating for Social Justice Within and Beyond Global Neo-Liberalism*, London: Palgrave Macmillan.

McLuhan, M. (1964), *Understanding Media: The Extensions of Man*, New York: McGraw Hill.

Merton, T. ([1965] 2009), *Conjectures of a Guilty Bystander*, New York: Doubleday.

Miller, D. (ed.) (2004), *Propaganda and Media Distortion in the War on Iraq*, London: Pluto.

Packard, V. (1957), *The Hidden Persuaders*, New York: Pocket Books.

Preston, I. ([1975] 1996), *The Great American Blow-Up: Puffery in Advertising and Selling*, Wisconsin: University of Wisconsin Press.

Rees, J. (1998), *The Algebra of Revolution*, London and New York: Routledge.

Retrofuturistic advertising: http://weburbanist.com/2009/03/29/retrofuturistic-ads-selling-a-brighter-tomorrow/). Accessed May 2011.

Schutzman, M. (1999), *The Real Thing: Performance, Hysteria, and Advertising*, Hanover and London: Wesleyan University Press.

Shameless (2004–), Paul Abbot: Channel 4 (UK).

Sheringham, M. (2006), *Everyday Life: Theories and Practices from Surrealism to the Present*, Oxford and New York: Oxford University Press.

Simmons, J. (2008), *Innocent: Building A Brand From Nothing But Fruit*, London: Marshall Cavendish.

Swedish Army; recruitment video: http://www.buzzfeed.com/donnad/realistic-swedish-army-recruitment-ad. Accessed May 2011.

Taylor, Paul A. (2010), *Žižek and the Media*, Cambridge: Polity Press.

Taylor, P. and Harris, J. (2008), *Critical Theories of Mass Media: Then and Now*, Maidenhead and New York: Open University Press.

The X-Factor (UK) (2004–), Talkback Thames: ITV.

Williams, R. (1958), *Culture and Society*, London: Chatto and Windus.

—— (1961), *The Long Revolution*, London: Chatto and Windus.

—— (1980), *Problems in Materialism and Culture: Selected Essays*, London: Verso.

—— ([1958] 2002), 'Culture is Ordinary', in Highmore, B., *The Everyday Life Reader*, London and New York: Routledge, pp. 91–100.

Žižek, S. (2001a), *The Fragile Absolute – or, Why is the Christian Legacy Worth Fighting For?*, London: Verso.

—— (2001b), *Did Somebody Say Totalitarianism? Five Interventions in the Misuse of a Notion*, London and New York: Verso.

—— (2008), *Violence: Six Sideways reflections*, London: Profile Books.

—— (2009), *First As Tragedy, Then As Farce*, London and New York: Verso.

—— ([2010] 2011), *Living in the End Times*, London and New York: Verso.

Note

1   See Plate 1: Mad Men – John Slattery ('Roger Sterling', left), Jon Hamm ('Don Draper', centre) and January Jones ('Betty Draper', right) – courtesy of Lionsgate Home Entertainment's *Mad Men: Season One*.

Chapter 2

Advertising research

John Fenwick and Chris Wharton

Introduction

This chapter explores research methods and advertising, providing a critical introduction to research theory and practice in societies where advertising has become a core feature of daily life. The discussion maps a variety of theoretical perspectives, competing traditions and academic approaches underpinning social research, including positivism and interpretivism together with perspectives drawn from postmodernism, gendered research and phenomenology. It examines social research designs, methods and techniques of enquiry as they may be applied to advertising. Perspective and research designs outlined in this chapter might be applied to music, fashion, art and design, politics and other areas as they relate to advertising and are explored in this volume. Advertising research is understood as being constituted by both industry enquiry into its own products and activities and by critical research conducted from outside the world of advertising.

This chapter discusses the question of what constitutes research, making a distinction between informal and systematic research. It outlines the core components of research: qualitative and quantitative approaches; primary and secondary aspects; sampling; choice of method and analysis of findings; ethics and values. The chapter explores the application of research to advertisements and to people and their cultures. It is intended that the chapter will assist those wishing to know more about the practice of advertising research and provide a critical analysis for researchers who seek to appraise existing studies or embark upon their own research projects into the industry and its products.

Understanding research in relation to advertising

In seeking to understand advertising research, we eschew prior decontextualised definitions of 'research' or 'advertising' on the grounds that the meaning of these terms is to be located in their practical *use*. Research after all denotes a range of distinct techniques and *activities*. Nonetheless, in order to provide a context for the discussion to follow, it is useful to begin with a brief consideration of what is commonly understood as 'research'.

It may seem that everyone is or has been involved in research, whether this involves doing the background work for an academic essay, being employed in a public institution like the National Health Service, acting in a research capacity in a media organisation, or, mundanely, in making a consumer choice before buying a mobile phone, car or some other commodity. 'Have you done your research?' is a commonplace everyday term. The *Sage Dictionary of Social Research Methods* lists a variety of terms encountered when studying research or carrying it out. It usefully explains what research design, research problems, and research bargain 'mean' and their significance to research, yet there is no entry for 'research' itself (Jupp 2006). The meaning is taken for granted. The *Collins* dictionary suggests that research is a 'scientific study to discover facts' yet reference to the term 'scientific' introduces a controversial debate relating to the proper methods of enquiry which will be explored further in this chapter. As we will find when alternative theoretical approaches to research methodology are brought into the debate, the meaning of research may start to be less clear as we look at it more closely.

Therefore, at minimum, let us regard formal research as a mode of investigation and enquiry which is planned and systematic rather than ad hoc or taken for granted. It is a reflective and evaluative activity, involving a research question to which it seeks an answer. More specifically, research aims to obtain *organised and systematic* knowledge of the object of enquiry and it is this rigorous quality that distinguishes research from unplanned common sense apprehension of the world.

Of course, research may come to the same conclusions as everyday common sense reasoning. Research may confirm what we think we already know. If so, it is not wasted: it provides support and strength for reaching a conclusion that we may otherwise reach only through intuition or guesswork. An extensive and expensive advertising campaign may thus proceed with more confidence in its supporting data.

Furthermore, an understanding of research methods permits us not only to undertake the informed practice of research, it – crucially – allows us to evaluate the research done by others, whether in academic environments or in the advertising industry by asking questions such as: how many people were interviewed? How were they selected? How justified are the researchers' conclusions? Could the research have been carried out differently?

> Training in research methods provides you with an awareness of what constitutes good and poor research. It therefore provides a platform for developing a critical awareness of the limits and limitations of research that you read.
>
> (Bryman and Bell 2011: xxxv)

Research, then, is about the rigorous and systematic investigation of the world around us. But as soon as we reach this tentative conclusion a major problem arises: there is no obvious, uniform, universal way of seeing the world. Our ways of seeing are mediated by factors including our culture, our personal politics or religion, our age and our stock of intellectual and emotional experience against which we, on a daily basis, assess what there is to see. Competing perspectives on the world vary from place to place – culturally within nations, as well as more obviously between wholly different societies – and over time. We do not see the world as a Renaissance artist did, nor as the ancient Greeks saw it. The elaboration of the mathematics of perspective in European art did not only change what was painted, it changed what was seen and what was 'understood' amongst artists and audiences. Ways of seeing are also shaped by our theoretical views of what the world is – the window through which we view reality – which we can refer to as our paradigm, our way of making sense of what is around us. These paradigms might be those of the liberal, the neo-conservative, the anti-globalisation activist, the fundamentalist Christian or Muslim, the Marxist, Feminist or Anarchist, the humanist and many more: there are innumerable bases from which we can make sense. Apprehending the world is conditioned by theoretical choices, which may present themselves to us as concrete intellectual or emotional alternatives or may simply be taken for granted, hidden away from explicit interrogation. The Western liberal secular tradition which underpins so much academic research, and which also tends to characterise commercial advertising research, constitutes a particular paradigm in itself. It does not denote the absence of a paradigmatic choice.

Similarly the *practice* of research is conditioned by theoretical choices: the detached clinical approach of the scientist who seeks to count and measure the products of research (how many people? how many think this, or that?) or the empathic approach of the researcher who wants to get closer to how people feel and react. We shall in this chapter refer to the former as the positivist, the latter as the interpretivist. Advertising research has a place for both.

Whatever your choice of theoretical approach to research, it *is* a choice. Research practice is about values and ideology as well as about techniques and research tools; theory and method are interconnected. This fundamental theme will now be explored further in setting out some core elements of research methodology.

The core components of research method

Research methods can be categorised broadly as either qualitative or quantitative. Qualitative methods are interested in meaning rather than measurement: the feelings, opinions and subjective perceptions of individuals or groups. Qualitative researchers seek to gain insight into the ways in which people make sense of the world. Crucially, qualitative researchers are not the detached neutral observers of textbook scientific method; they are involved in and engaged with the topic of their research. The qualitative researcher stands at the heart of the research rather than being separated from it. In contrast, quantitative methods are focused upon measurement rather than meaning, seeking to reach statistical conclusions that can be generalised across a wider population. At the very least, the quantitative researcher collects empirical data that describes a population statistically. Ideally however, the data will be of sufficient rigour to enable statistical tests to be performed upon it, for instance cross-tabulating variables such as gender or age with, say, the decision to buy a particular product.

Qualitative and quantitative research both represent broad approaches. Within each tradition there are several distinct methods of investigation. Qualitative researchers may use methods such as observation, participation, focus groups or exploratory interviews, each of which can provide insight into how individuals or groups feel about something or how they perceive the object of study. Researchers may even join the groups they study in order to gain first-hand access to the meanings, feelings and culture of the group, an ethnographic method which derived originally from anthropological studies of other cultures. Quantitative researchers use different methods of investigation, all of which are concerned with numerical measurement. The experimental method of the laboratory scientist resides within the quantitative tradition but is little used in social science beyond some areas of psychology. Quantitative researchers make greater use of the social survey, a method which is able to collect a large volume of data for a wide population, capable of statistical analysis and quantifiable conclusions. Such information is standardised, collecting common data from the research population, and is not concerned with the nuances of individual feelings and perceptions. It aims for robust generalisation.

The distinction between qualitative and quantitative research is fundamental and all methods of research relevant to advertising can be regarded as part of one approach or the other. However, it is not simply a matter of choosing one approach to another on pragmatic or opportunistic grounds: the two approaches represent alternative traditions in social theory and philosophy, two contrasting paradigms of how we apprehend the world. Are we aiming to *explain* the world through generalisations deriving from a received notion of what scientific method entails, in which we seek to perfect our detachment, and banish subjective meaning and our own values as a researcher to the periphery of our concerns? Or, are we aiming to *understand* the world through engagement with the perceptions and feelings of individuals and groups, where subjective meaning and the involvement of the researcher is absolutely central? This is the key choice in research method, from which all else follows.

Whether adopting a qualitative or quantitative approach, there are some essential common areas to consider before embarking upon research. These are principally:

- *Whether to use primary research methods* (that is, collecting original information first-hand, for the first time, for the purposes of the specific research study) *or to use secondary sources* (that is, information which already exists and was collected by others, including previous research in this field or the secondary information routinely generated by commercial organisations and governments). Both have their place. Clearly secondary sources are abundant and usually cheap, but we cannot always know the circumstances of their creation or the confidence we can place in them.
- *How to select the sample for the research.* It is not usually possible to study the whole population in which we are interested. Qualitative and quantitative researchers alike must select the sample with which they are going to carry out primary research (and within secondary research, the 'sample' from a range of possible sources). This constitutes the research population. Qualitative researchers select a sample in order to address their key research questions and to illuminate the concepts in which they are interested, a process of 'theoretical sampling' which fits with the paradigm adopted by the researcher. Quantitative researchers select a sample which is statistically representative of a wider

population: only in this way can the quantitative researcher produce the generalisation in which they are interested. The matter of sampling is complex, not only in the technical sense (for the quantitative researcher) of how to select, say, a random representative sample for a large-scale population survey, but in the more difficult sense (for the qualitative researcher) of the conceptual bases on which selection is being made. This is compounded by the tendency of ethnographic-style research to generate far more information than can ever be used; hence effectively introducing a second sampling stage after the information has been collected. The transparency of sampling decisions in qualitative research is thus an issue for careful consideration.

- *Finding the right method to address your initial research question.* The differences between the two research traditions are fundamental, and it is not only a matter of contrasting methods of investigation. The qualitative and quantitative approaches ask *different kinds of questions.* It is because of this that they employ different methods. A researcher who seeks to establish whether a causal link exists between different variables or, perhaps more realistically, whether different variables are statistically correlated to a greater extent than would be expected by chance, will be bound to employ quantitative methods. Qualitative techniques simply would not provide an answer to questions about correlation or causality. Such a researcher is testing a hypothesis, possibly as part of a wider attempt at testing theory. While strictly speaking any hypothesis can never be proven (and a great deal of caution is required in talking of proof in research) it can manifestly be disproven – only one observation is needed to disconfirm a stated hypothesis. A researcher who seeks instead to understand the meanings people give to their actions, or to find out how they feel, or to comprehend the culture of a group from within, is not testing theory. Such a researcher is *building* theory, starting from the data and generating tentative understandings of the topic at hand. Such a researcher will necessarily be working in the qualitative tradition. Quantitative methods could not provide the required answers. Theory testing is a process of deduction. Theory building is a process of induction. This is a key distinction in research method in any area of social science and is important to wider applications of method in advertising and elsewhere.
- *How to analyse the results.* Upon completing the process of information gathering, by whatever method, there may be a temptation to think that the research task set by your demanding employer, your unreasonable tutor or even your own free enquiring spirit is almost over. However, this is the point at which the hard work begins. Quantitative research requires a process of data analysis through one of the standard available computer packages, usually producing, at the outset, frequency distributions (descriptive one-variable presentations of your data), cross-tabulations (relating one variable to another) and multi-variate analyses (establishing relationships, if any, between numerous variables). With due attention to technical accuracy, writing-up the textual interpretation of such results need not be lengthy or demanding, if data suitable for addressing your research question were entered in the first place. Qualitative research tends to generate rich results which typically require a more lengthy process of analysis

and interpretation. It may be possible to group responses to qualitative questions into categories suitable for manipulation through available analysis packages and in this way essentially to quantify some of the responses to qualitative answers, a process adopted in, for instance, content analysis of advertising. However, qualitative data analysis involves a close attention to detail, to meaning and to robust interpretations which will withstand scrutiny. It takes time. Results are built up through an inductive process which may inform further research. Indeed, it would be entirely feasible to adopt qualitative methods to establish a hypothesis which is subsequently tested by deductive quantitative methods.

Whatever methodological approach is adopted, it is essential to have clarity: what are our research questions? What is our research population? What do we hope to achieve from the study? Do we have access to the necessary sources (primary or secondary)? Provided there is such clarity, then research practice can permit a great diversity of approaches, none of which is better than the others: the issue is whether the methods are fit for purpose and, above all, whether they address our stated initial research questions. Whatever method is adopted, concerns of reliability and validity remain central. The terms are not synonymous. Reliability denotes the extent to which the techniques were accurate, whether (in a standardised survey) the questions were asked in the same way, and whether another researcher carrying out a repeat study would obtain consistent observations: '… reliability is fundamentally concerned with issues of consistency of measures' (Bryman and Bell 2011: 157). Validity denotes the extent to which the research actually investigates what is purports to investigate, the link between the concept or phenomenon at hand and the research tools employed to carry out the research. In quantitative research, validity would be a matter of whether the measure is really measuring what it claims; in qualitative research, validity might refer to the closeness of the link between our concepts – say, 'alienation' – and our claim to find evidence of what it means to the people we are observing. Reliability is a technical issue that, although not always simple to address, is conceptually straightforward. Validity, especially in qualitative research, may be conceptually complex and it requires considerable attention throughout.

Competing theoretical traditions

Research theory and research practice are closely interlinked. Choice of practical methods is underpinned and informed by choice of guiding paradigm. Theoretical choices include the stance we take toward:

- ontology: the nature of being and existence
- epistemology: the nature of belief and of how we can have knowledge about the world
- cognition: the practical process of acquiring knowledge

The quantitative research outlined above is based upon a view of the world as an objective and measurable entity. Its ontological assumption is that the world already exists as an external reality, and is available for empirical investigation. In terms of epistemology, research can generate broad generalisations based on measurement of the world, and can even attempt to formulate universal statements – laws – of human action. This perspective, derived from a conventional interpretation of the scientific method, is consistent with the paradigm of *positivism*. Social science research can, from this perspective, be scientific in its ontology and its epistemology, proceeding to test its theories through deductive processes.

Of course, not everyone accepts this paradigm. First, it will readily be accepted by researchers of all theoretical hues, even those who accept the theoretical premises of positivism, that achieving the demands of scientific enquiry in the messy world of human society is challenging. It is even, some might say, impossible: scientific method might be desirable, but we will never for practical reasons achieve it. Secondly, and a fundamental matter of principle rather than one of practice, positivism can be challenged on the grounds that it is based on a misconception. The world is not an externally existing entity waiting to be measured. Ontologically, it is a bundle of meanings, understandings and social constructions, generated by people. The world is constituted (that is, made real) through its recognition by people. Take away that recognition, and that world does not exist. Epistemologically, we can only understand this through appreciative enquiry in the form of interpretive qualitative research. The tools of the positivist researcher can tell us nothing of this world. Thirdly, the least developed but perhaps most important objection to positivism is that it misunderstands the scientific method on which it claims to be based. It is rooted in a received textbook caricature of science where investigators are detached, where their observations do not affect what is being studied, and where objects of enquiry can be in only one place at a time. In contemporary science, particularly sub-atomic physics, none of these statements is true (Fenwick and McMillan 2010: 198). Science itself does not follow the received notions of positivist social enquiry and thus, in essence, positivist research gets science wrong.

This misunderstanding of scientific method is based within the historical period at which positivist social enquiry was being developed. Auguste Comte (1798–1857) is associated with positivism and with early sociology and an attempt to create a coherent form of understanding of the world rather than speculation about it. This was based on natural science techniques but although humans and the societies they inhabit can be studied as an aspect of nature there are important differences, for instance, between animal and human behaviour. Human beings are conscious and reflexive beings interpreting and learning from their past, recreating and consciously changing themselves and the world they live in.

Qualitative research assumes a distinctive paradigm in understanding the social world. It adopts an interpretivist rather than positivist orientation, building its conclusions through induction based on direct observation and close proximity to people's thoughts, feelings and actions. Its method is built upon the varying perspectives of individuals, and the ways in which we all construct the social world we inhabit. We ascribe meaning and reality to the world around us. Philosophically, interpretive methods are consistent with phenomenology, a perspective which has its origins in the work of Franz Brentano (1838–1917) who aimed to create a psychology based on *intentionality*, a key phenomenological concept denoting relationship to an object. Brentano was interested in the world being 'recognised or discovered': a world with an 'immanent objectivity' (Brentano [1874] 1995). Edmund Husserl (1859–1938), crediting the influence of Brentano, went on to develop phenomenology as a major philosophical perspective (Husserl [1901] 2001). What was Husserl's phenomenology? Husserl was interested in the 'structure of subjective acts' and, like Brentano, with intentionality – the link between the act of seeing and what-is-seen. Later, Alfred Schutz (1899–1959) would bring the phenomenological approach to social science, through his focus on the mundane everyday 'life world', intentionality, the 'natural attitude' of shared meanings, and 'common-sense experience of the intersubjective world in daily life' as the basis of sociological knowledge (Schutz [1932] 1967).

Phenomenology is sometimes – erroneously – thought to discard the possibility of any knowledge of real objects. Husserl, philosophically, was largely indifferent to the question of whether objects exist as mental or physical things (or whether they exist at all). The importance of the phenomenological perspective today lies in its concern with meaning, apprehension of the social world, interpretation and the connection between object and perception. This perspective may be highly relevant for advertising research.

Such different research methodologies reflect underlying differences of theoretical orientation. Consistent with this, different approaches within applied advertising research reflect choices between competing heuristic paradigms. The existence of competing theoretical traditions within research method corresponds to some fundamental and powerful philosophical choices. Postmodern researchers may admit different elements of research practice into their studies, borrowing from different traditions as seems fit for the purpose at hand, adopting an eclectic approach to method which eschews any grand theorising or meta-narrative. Feminist researchers, in addition to providing a critique of research which is used to support male-dominated power relations, may adopt research methods which themselves seek to empower the research subject through telling the story as women see it. This emphasis on providing a voice to the less powerful would tend to propel such research towards qualitative and interpretive methods in the service of those hitherto disempowered, whether through gender or other differentiating factors including ethnicity and class.

Amidst these choices, whether research is used to build theory through inductive processes (commonly associated with qualitative research) or to test theory through deductive processes (commonly associated with quantitative research), it is part of the broad field of 'research method', potentially applicable to the world of advertising research and advertising practice.

Having outlined some key terms in research method, and set out a perspective on research as a critical activity involving both practical and theoretical choices, we now consider the importance of the research context: its political economy and its basis in values.

The political economy of research

Research is a process that is commissioned, funded, carried out and disseminated. Rarely will it involve only the lone researcher in their narrow specialism. It will typically involve many more people, including the commercial organisation or academic institution, managers, field work staff, subordinates, funding bodies, IT staff or others supporting the research process and, in public organisations, perhaps elected representatives. Within this process, there are numerous relationships based on differing interests and different degrees of power. Consultancies and private research companies, or research departments in large organisations, will expect to make a return on investment like any other commercial organisation. Political parties use research organisations and think tanks consistent with differing political positions. The funders of research may have the power of veto over the release of results. Findings in the world of advertising may well be commercially sensitive. In O'Sullivan, Dutton and Rayne's words, there are different organisations and agencies that 'shape, guide and sponsor' research (1998: 321). Beyond the laboratory, research is a political process with its own economy.

Referring to the experience of carrying out contract research for government in the 1980s, McDermott (1987) describes the laborious process of agreeing who would be included in the study, what exactly would be studied, the timescales involved and the pressures to produce results. 'This case study shows that government *does* try to use the research data to legitimate its role, as well as trying to control the framework in which the research takes place. Hopefully the case study has also shown that researchers must recognize the constraints placed on them and recognize the power they themselves have in the negotiations' (McDermott 1987: 142, emphasis in original). The word 'negotiations' is telling here. Research is a negotiated activity, with different actors wielding different degrees of influence. Even where formal agreements have been made, there are numerous gatekeepers who can facilitate or impede the practical progress of any research study.

Within this complex process, different modes of influence are available to the researcher. Within politics and public policy research, Thomas (1985: 100–2) referred to the 'limestone' mode of influence (wherein the researcher mimics the action of water within limestone, unsure what route it will follow or exactly where its eventual impact will be felt), the 'gadfly' role (where the researcher, probably working out with contract or directly commissioned research, is a relatively free spirit in seeking to make an impact wherever they can), and the 'insider' model (where the researcher deliberately resides within networks of power and influence). In the years since this typology was formulated, it is reasonable to conclude that the 'insider' has come to be the dominant mode of influence of research on policy, whether through politically affiliated think tanks or directly commissioned and highly targeted research in the area of public policy research. It is worth considering the application of this explanatory outline to those working in advertising and related research today.

O'Sullivan amongst others refers to 'pragmatic research' which corresponds to research carried out by or on behalf of the advertising industry. Formal advertising industry research is usually referred to as independent or syndicated research which is conducted by a research organisation and the findings are available for a fee to a number of companies or it can take the form of a more customised research conducted on behalf of, and funded by, a specific client. However, much industry research is informal: cultural observations and ideas gathered as part of everyday experience by creatives and other people who work in the industry. The extent to which this is more sophisticated or elaborate than what we identified previously as 'unplanned common sense apprehension of the world' will depend on the individuals and circumstances involved. Industry research is often contrasted with critical research which is conducted by people and organisations operating outside the industry, for instance in universities or organisations such as policy institutes. These are often described as 'not for profit' organisations. Critical research, then, is traditionally viewed as detached: more disinterested than industry research, best positioned to explore wider issues to do with the meaning and centrality of commodities to everyday life or the social and cultural effects of how they are promoted. For instance the think tank Compass recently published research that was concerned with the connections between advertising and consumer debt, and advertising and the commercialisation of childhood (http://www.compassonline.org.uk/). Industry research, on the other hand, is primarily driven by the requirement to create successful advertising campaigns which often involve maximising the sale of commodities. This is not to say that a useful insight into consumer behaviour might not be generated but there is no guarantee that this will find its way into the more general stock of social knowledge or be of value to a critical reflection on what constitutes the good society. Industry research is well placed to evaluate and understand its own products as aspects of a market economy but not to investigate its own role and modus operandi in society.

Finally, the processes of political economy may refer to internal relations within the organisation carrying out research. Leaving aside external networks and the negotiations between actors referred to above, the organisation itself has its own structures, hierarchies and multiple objectives. Research may occupy a low status role within the company, its staff poorly paid and under pressure to perform. Alternatively it may be a key department in which considerable resources are invested. MacRury notes that, within the advertising agency, the research role is 'typically carried through by an account planner', an intermediary figure who links together clients, creative staff and oversees the process (2009: 51). It is worthwhile to consider who carries out this role in different kinds of organisations, and indeed whether the role requires specialist research knowledge or different kinds of skills altogether.

Advertising and values

Beyond the political relationships associated with research and competing influences based upon power and interests, there are several senses in which broader values also form part of the research process. The researchers' own values may draw them to a research area in which they choose to specialise over a long period, for instance researching poverty, or ethical fashion and the practices of Western companies in employing cheap labour, or researching drug use: in these instances, the researcher's values have brought them to their research. In other cases, there may be a commitment to values that is less explicit but important nonetheless, for instance choosing to be employed as a researcher in the public service sector rather than in a private sector consultancy, or working in the research department of a trade union rather than an employer organisation. The researcher here is guided by a notion, perhaps not even consciously recognised, of the values of the organisation and the uses to which research is likely to be put. This implicit assessment of the values of the organisation may not be accurate, but that is not the point: the importance is one of perception, based in personal values. Of course, other researchers may choose the opposite standpoint from that of the examples above.

Irrespective of whether the researcher is a lone scholarly figure, a public or private employee, or a research manager within an organisation, values will assert themselves. Will the researcher accept generous funding, guaranteeing their continuing contract employment, from an unpleasant authoritarian regime? Or from the tobacco industry? Or from a cosmetics or pharmaceutical company testing on animals? Most people will have strong and clear ideas of what is right and wrong in these instances, based on their values and ethical standards.

At first sight, applying questions of values to commercial advertising seems less easy. Indeed some would see advertising as a value-free zone. Yet values are explicitly to be found within advertising in areas of ethical banking and corporate and social responsibility, for instance in the advertising approach of the Co-operative Bank in the UK. In other, seemingly unrelated, areas of advertising, values are important in more subtle ways. Glastonbury essentially serves to advertise social and political causes such as Greenpeace, wherein there seems to be a loose assumed associational connection between liberal campaigns (though, importantly, they should not be too contentious) and, significantly, the young(ish) audience, with perhaps a further assumption of relative affluence and awareness. There are certainly assumptions about the value-base of the audience, accurate or otherwise. This depicts a particular view of the world. The organisations represented at such major public events will have a view of the normative profile of the audience, just as promoters of a major sports event or other public spectacle will have assumptions, probably different ones, about the values of the audience. These assumptions will certainly be of interest to commercial advertisers.

Just as an ethical bank will recognise assumed values amongst its customer 'demographic', this is a process of recognising assumed audience values. But it is also a matter of transmitting and reinforcing values. Sometimes these values can be hard to identify, but we are nonetheless aware of them. The transmission of playful postmodern values, amongst research populations who 'get' it, segmented by age or class, is common in advertising or indeed in TV drama such as the regenerated *Dr Who* series which from 2005 has looked back knowingly at its own past, shared the joke with its audience and then reproduced its fictional reality further. This constructed and reconstructed account of the world becomes part of the object of study, as well as one of the theoretical approaches we use to try to understand it.

Depictions of gender are also part of the realm of values. It would now be unacceptable, for many audiences, to transmit an uncritical non-ironic depiction of traditional domestic gender relations in the home or the workplace. Although this was regarded as acceptable in previous decades, changing values have made it unacceptable, unless detached from literal meaning through knowing detachment, as in the questionable claim of 'lads' mags' that sexism is being handled in some kind of ironic manner. How did advertisers come to this conclusion, how can they 'know' that the world has moved on and that values have changed? One mundane answer is that the large advertising companies, along with the main political parties, run continuing focus group sessions to tell them about the changing ways that people see the world, seeking to track the shifting values of its audience. The much discussed cinema and TV advertisements for Lynx deodorant place an exaggerated emphasis on the power of a product for young males to overcome the critical faculties of a large number of young women who have unaccountably failed to dress themselves fully on the day in question. Of course, it is not serious, and we are complicit with the advertisers in 'getting' it and congratulating ourselves for doing so. However, what precisely differentiates this from a TV advertisement for Hai Karate aftershave in the 1970s – 'be careful how you use it' – which used imagery of a broadly comparable nature, and was also presented with humour and detachment? Even in that decade, its depiction was not serious or literal. Nostalgia is not what it used to be. Nor, it seems, is irony.

A final but important sense in which values, ethics and morality impact upon research lies in the conventions of good practice and ethical standards which research and researchers are expected to follow. Research is after all largely done by the more powerful – including governments, commercial organisations or universities – to the less powerful. The relationship between researcher and researched is not an equal one. In the case of the UK national census participation is compulsory, failure to do so in the 2011 census being punishable by a fine of up to £1000. The research relationship is not normally so draconian. However, in all cases, it is essential to be aware of power differences and to ensure that the research 'bargain' is freely entered into. The concept of 'informed consent' is central to contemporary research practice and few would dispute its ethical desirability. Within qualitative research, covert participant observation where the researcher's role is unknown to the rest of the group for fear of influencing their behaviour has long been a recognised research method. Yet it would today be considered unethical, directly contravening the principle of informed consent. Classic sociological research studies such as 'A Glasgow Gang Observed' (Patrick 1973) would not be carried out today as they would not be approved by any university research ethics committee.

This raises powerful moral questions. In carrying out covert research, can the researcher invoke the argument of the investigative journalist, or the phone hacker, that the end justifies the means? This is, arguably, a potentially convincing argument if the investigation were to uncover a major crime or appalling scandal that would otherwise be left undiscovered. One ethical imperative could be judged to outweigh a lesser ethical objection. Yet it is hard to pursue such an argument in the case of academic research or commercial research related to advertising where the greater good is less immediately apparent.

Any claims by researchers to be value-free are unconvincing. Values are at the heart of research. This is relatively easy to identify in qualitative research, especially in participant 'appreciative' methods where the researchers place themselves within the topic of study. The claims of the positivist researcher to be value-free are also false. Values bring the positivist researcher to the topic and define the object of enquiry. Results are used for specific and perhaps partisan purposes. All researchers have values and ethical standards. At least, we hope they do. Otherwise there can be no moral objection to placing our research expertise at the disposal of monsters and tyrants.

Applied advertising research

Applied research conducted by the advertising industry or by other organisations such as universities or think tanks tends to fall into two categories. The first is focussed on the products of the advertising industry: the advertisements and advertising campaigns it generates and the second on people. In the first approach research tends to draw out the elements advertisements have in common with other social and cultural texts, for instance those of cinema, television and radio programmes, and even novels and paintings. The second approach is interested in people as individuals or as part of populations as audiences, citizens or consumers and the part that advertising plays in their lives. For instance BARB conducts research and provides television viewing figures and data sets for the UK and Postar provides similar research on billboards and outdoor poster sites. Advertising research is also applied to the lives, social backgrounds, culture and attitudes of people working in the industry (Nixon 2003). As we have already suggested advertising research is either quantitative or qualitative in its approach and either or both are used in the study of people and advertising campaigns.

Advertisement and campaign research involves either content analysis or textual analysis. Content analysis is a quantitative method in the positivist and empiricist tradition and it attempts to establish the frequency or volume of certain phenomena in media output. As applied to ads it is intended to measure or quantify predetermined advertising content (Bryman 2004: 181–94). Max Weber in the early part of the last century suggested its use in apprehending social change and could be used to 'measure the quantitative changes of newspaper contents during the last generation'(quoted in Hart 1979: 181–2). Later Berelson defined it as a 'research technique for the objective, systematic and quantitative description of the manifest content of communication' (1952: 18). A recent example of content analysis is *The Guardian* journalist George Monbiot's use of secondary source statistics to suggest double standards on the part of the British newspaper industry that supports UK government targets for cutting carbon emissions but carried numerous advertisements for ecologically unfriendly products associated with air and car travel and the oil industry. For instance one paper advocated that 'people should share car journeys' as 'a simple way to lessen your carbon footprint', but in the same edition carried an advert for Ryanair for £10 flights to France.

This was established by quantifying percentages of adverts to newspaper space over a period of time (*The Guardian,* 14 August 2007). It was also a comparative study establishing how the different newspapers compared over a specified period of time. What it did not establish was the potential or actual effect the advertisements had – how persuasive they were in encouraging this form of behaviour? A more qualitative, textual analysis approach would have been valuable here.

Textual analysis takes numerous forms. It can be based on linguistic approaches which explore the nature and use of spoken or written language or a semiotic analysis of both words and images used in advertisements. It might include a formal, design-based approach to the visual language of the advertising layout. All these forms of textual analysis investigate the meaning and significance the advertisement might have and what this might signify to people. This is the approach taken in the second part of Chapter 3 in this book which offers textual analyses of three advertising campaigns for Persil, L'Oréal and Phones 4U. The textual analysis approach is grounded in the interpretive research tradition. Interpretation of data is present in all research in some form but in interpretive textual analysis it is a highly significant feature and occurs at different stages of the research procedure. In the first instance, advertisements are interpreted by researchers who produce their own 'readings' of adverts. But researchers are also interested in the everyday viewer, reader or listener, who from a range of different backgrounds and in diverse circumstances generate their own readings of advertisements. These too have to be interpreted as part of the research.

The advertising industry is keen to test its products: to discover responses to adverts and to gain knowledge of their likely reception. To this end, research is applied at different moments in the advertising cycle of advertising production, presentation and reception. Data are gathered, interpreted and fed back into the system of advertising production. This is known as the advertising loop. Pre-campaign market research takes the form of enquiry into brands, the suitability of different forms of advertising, the market segment to be targeted and the potential size and nature of, for instance, newspaper or television audiences. Copy testing involves presenting storyboards or early versions of campaigns to a sample of potential consumers and ascertaining their views. A variety of different ways of categorising the feedback that can then be used to adjust the design or presentation of the campaign might include questions of recall, motives for buying, levels of persuasion, involvement and salience. Post-testing research looks at the performance of an advertising campaign once it is has been placed in the public domain. Tracking and longitudinal studies look at the performance and effects of the campaign over a period of time.

Responses to advertisements and campaigns, then, are recorded by industry research prior to, during and after the advertising campaign. These are largely qualitative in approach. Interpretive space is provided by the open-ended questions included in questionnaires and interviews where respondents are encouraged to record in their own words the meanings and significance advertisements have for them. The qualitative approach is also apparent in focus groups and semi or unstructured interviews where discussion is based on values, perceptions and attitudes to campaigns and products. However a questionnaire that includes closed questions requiring a yes or no response and the narrow range of responses generated by a tightly structured interview can be considered a more quantitative form of enquiry. However, questionnaire design is more generally considered a part of quantitative research.

On the other hand, observation as a research method is usually considered as part of the qualitative tradition. It has long been used by social scientists and others to gain an understanding of how people behave and how they interact with others. It is also important in exploring how environments, contexts and social settings have an effect on behaviour. Observation can be the simple activity of the researcher looking and recording from a distance or it can involve participating in the activity or even total involvement in a way of life. One area of interest for advertising studies is that of investigating 'modes of viewing' as an element of people's culture. This research method can be used to further an understanding of how people look at advertisements. Industry research might be interested in increasing the 'visibility' of, for instance, an outdoor billboard or campaign situated in a busy city centre. An example of this is found with out-of-home communication agency Kinetic who carried out an impact study of outdoor advertising viewing in 2009. Here is a description of the procedure from Admap:

> Cameras, tracking the number of eyes on the posters, were mounted on the poster units to measure the reactions of moving people, who were unaware that the research was being conducted. Separate cameras were used to measure footfall and the direction of passers-by. Using technology … the research was able to identify how many people looked at digital compared with static creative executions, and for how long, in a real-life, real-time situation.
>
> (Mawditt 2009)

Although observation as a research method is usually associated with qualitative techniques, such covert observation evidently has quantitative elements – it is based on measurement and is clearly a research programme that can be repeated in the future and the findings compared. It also raises ethical questions. In a surveillance society, does the technology involved in observation render questions of 'informed consent' irrelevant and what kind of control should people have over the data their behavioural patterns create (Spurgeon 2008; Andrejevic 2009)?

A critical research project might adopt a wider approach to this area of enquiry, exploring in a theoretical and systematic manner observation techniques that investigate different ways of seeing and modes of viewing that people use to make sense of and appreciate aspects of their environment – of which only one element is advertising. Looking, gazing and glancing are different ways of viewing and deployed in particular forms in the urban environment of the modern cityscape. People do not look at the world – in both the real and metaphoric sense that this implies – only as potential consumers. They are both in the world and view it from a wide variety of different economic, social and cultural backgrounds, interests and identities. Identity based on consumption is unlikely to tell us all there is to know about people.

Market research and life style studies are unlikely to uncover a common culture based on or aspiring to citizenship, productive labour and community.

Mattelart identified the rise of 'lifestyle studies' and sociocultural trends in advertising studies some decades ago (1991). Advertising research increasingly focuses on subcultures, tribes and belief systems and the mapping of goods onto people's minds in the interest of cultural forecasting. Industry research is concerned with both 'trending' and shaping culture, 'cool hunting' in the interest of increased commodity turnover (Leiss et al. 2005: 428). Critical research is interested in similar themes but for different reasons. Both are at the heart of understanding advertising as culture.

Conclusion

This chapter has offered a guide to and analysis of research method associated with society and advertising. The discussion has covered a range of perspectives, traditions and approaches that underpin social research and that are important to the choice of method. The chapter has outlined the main components of research. Formal research, it was argued, forms a part of organised and systematic knowledge and certain features such as the difference between quantitative and qualitative approaches are fundamental to the choice of method and the wider understanding and discussion of research. Distinctions in advertising research between industry-generated and critical research have an enduring significance. Similarly, research ethics and values are a constant feature of this discourse. Advertising research is widely deployed in an investigation of advertising campaigns and in an understanding of people, populations and audiences in order to glean their responses to advertising and in the process ascertaining needs and creating wants. More broadly in its critical form advertising research features in a wider understanding and critique of economies, societies and cultures of which advertising is increasingly a significant part. Social behaviour, attitudes, values and ideologies are elements of a culture increasingly acknowledged as led by promotion and branding. Advertising research is important to where aspects of culture are increasingly represented in advertising and advertising is viewed as culture. This outline of approaches to research and considerations of research design are relevant to enquiries into advertising and aspects of culture explored elsewhere in this volume.

References

Andrejevic, M. (2009), 'The Work of being Watched', in J. Turow and P. McAllister (eds) *The Advertising and Consumer Culture Reader*, London: Routledge.

Berelson, B. (1952), *Content Analysis in Communication Research*, Glencoe: Free Press.

Brentano, F. ([1874] 1995), *Psychology from an Empirical Standpoint* (translated by Antos C. Rancurello, D. B. Terrell and Linda L. McAlister), London and New York: Routledge.

Bryman, A. (2004), *Social Research Methods*, Oxford: Oxford University Press.

Bryman, A. and Bell, E. (2011), *Business Research Methods*, 3rd edn, Oxford: University Press.

Deacon, D., Pickering, M., Golding, P. and Murdock, G. (1999), *Researching Communications: A Practical Guide to Methods in Media and Cultural Analysis*, London: Arnold.

Fenwick, J. and McMillan, J. (2010), 'Public Policy and Management in Postmodern Times', in J. Fenwick and J. McMillan (eds) *Public Management in the Postmodern Era: Challenges and Prospects*, Cheltenham: Edward Elgar, pp. 192–211.

Gannon, Z. and Lawson, N. (2010), *The Advertising Effect: How do we Get the Balance of Advertising Right*, http://www.compassonline.org.uk/. Accessed 15 November 2011.

Hart, H. (1979), *Social Theories of the Press: Early German and American Perspectives*, Beverley Hills, CA: Sage.

Husserl, E. (2001), *Logical Investigations*, Vols. One and Two, London and New York: Routledge. First published 1900–01.

Jupp, V. (2006), *The Sage Dictionary of Social Research Methods*, London: Sage.

Kelley, A., Lawlor, K and O'Donohoe, S. (2009), 'Encoding Advertisements: The Creative Perspective', in J. Turow and P. McAllister (eds) *The Advertising and Consumer Culture Reader*, London: Routledge.

Leiss, W., Kline, S., Jhally, S. and Botterill, J. (2005), *Social Communication in Advertising*, London: Routledge.

MacRury, I. (2009), *Advertising*, London: Routledge.

——— (2009), 'Advertising Research: Markets, Methods and Knowing Customers', in H. Powell, J. Hardy, S. Hawkin and I. MacRury (eds) *The Advertising Handbook*, 3rd edn, London: Routledge, pp. 46–73.

Mattelart, A. (1991), *Advertising International: The Privatisation of Public Space*, London: Routledge.

Mawditt, N. (2009), *Admap*, September 2009 issue 508, pp. 46–47.

McDermott, K. (1987), 'In and Out of the Game: A Case Study of Contract Research', in G. C. Wenger (eds) *The Research Relationship: Practice and Politics in Social Policy Research*, London: Allen and Unwin, pp. 135–143.

Monbiot, G. (2007), 'The Editorials Urge us to Cut Emissions, but the Ads Tell a Very Different Story', *The Guardian*, 14 August 2007.

Nixon, S. (2003), *Advertising Cultures*, London: Sage.

O'Sullivan, T., Dutton, B. and Rayner, P. (1998), *Studying the Media*, London: Arnold.

Patrick, J. (1973), *A Glasgow Gang Observed*, London: Methuen.

Schutz, A. (1967), *The Phenomenology of the Social World*, Evanston: Northwestern University Press. First published 1932.

Spurgeon, C. (2008), *Advertising and New Media*, London: Routledge.

Thomas, P. (1985), *The Aims and Outcomes of Social Policy Research*, Beckenham: Croom Helm.

Chapter 3

Spreads like butter - culture and advertising

Chris Wharton

Introduction

This chapter is about culture's relation to contemporary advertising. It looks at the importance of technology to advertising, the development of different forms of advertising and the importance of advertising agencies to both culture and advertising. It is about how advertising has increased its hold on culture over time and has, as part of the modern media, come to saturate much of modern experience. Advertising is widely acknowledged as an important element of the present-day world and an essential feature of contemporary society, its economy, ways of thinking, lifestyle and culture. In the days before the Internet, digital and interactive media, Judith Williamson in one of the seminal academic books on advertising referred to print, television, radio and billboard advertising of the 1970s as 'ubiquitous' (Williamson 1978). Advertising fills spaces, screens and channels and more of these are available to advertisers today than when Williamson's book was first published. This chapter considers homology: how contemporary advertising 'fits' with culture. This can be identified in three stages: firstly, in the production and creation of advertising campaigns; secondly, as a highly visible presence in a range of media forms that circulate in social and cultural experience; and thirdly in advertising's subsequent reception by audiences who bring their own cultural experiences to bear. The chapter is concerned with how advertising enters, fits and flows through contemporary culture.

Encoding and decoding

The background method of analysis for this chapter is that of the encoding/decoding model put forward by Stuart Hall in the 1970s and 1980s and developed through the work of the Birmingham Centre for Contemporary Cultural Studies (Hall 1973, Hall 1981). Hall refers to the mass communication process that the model seeks to represent as 'the articulation of linked but distinctive moments – production, circulation, distribution/consumption, reproduction' (Hall 2001: 166). The recognition of these distinctive moments within an overall flow of communication exchange makes the model valuable to a study of advertising and culture. The encoding/decoding model can be extended and the presence of advertising in contemporary culture explored through the encoding-text-decoding media model (e-t-d). If advertisements are encoded by advertisers, creative practitioners, often referred to as cultural intermediaries – ideas, values and information uploaded through words, images and sounds – they have to be decoded by people situated in a variety of economic, social and cultural positions and who bring to the advertisement a range of knowledge, experiences and capabilities.

In the spirit of Hall's 1989 comment that 'if you are going to work with the model, you have to change the model and develop it' the addition of 'texts' between the encoding and decoding aspects of the model gives emphasis to its necessary but unstated element (Cruz and Lewis 1994: 272). In the process, this strengthens the model as a conceptual framework for both theoretical and empirical research. At the simplest level decodings can be categorised into three forms. The preferred reading largely corresponds to the cultural meanings and intentions of the advertising producers. The negotiated reading is one that has been adapted by the decoder to suit local conditions or specific aspects and the oppositional reading is where the decoder refuses to accept the meanings and even the terms of reference of the advertising producer.

In the first part of the chapter the idea of encoding is used to explore the background processes of advertising/cultural production and its grounding in the economy and culture of a period, the choices that are made about the use of specific advertising forms selected from a range of technical, practical and cultural possibilities and the themes and ideas that make up the cultural content of an advertisement. The second part of the chapter deals with the reception of advertising. It is about people and their cultures, the importance of their economic and social backgrounds – the significance, for instance, of class, gender, age, values, belief systems and environments – to decoding advertisements. Culture is an important presence in the encoding, textual and decoding aspects of the process of advertising communication. In the first place as a pool from which ideas and representations are drawn, in the second how advertising and advertisements take their place alongside other cultural forms and in the third how culture is drawn upon to make sense of or reject the cultural meanings the advertisements carry.

Figure 3.1: 'Capitalism isn't working' – TUC Demonstration against the cuts, 26 March 2011. Photograph: Robert Orange.

Encoding – culture and advertising

In order to make sense of how culture is encoded in advertising messages we need to look at advertising history, identifying important moments and changes that have occurred in the development of modern advertising. Advertising history as an area of academic enquiry can be approached like other histories.

The long-established History of Art forms a suitable comparison to advertising history emphasising as it does the cultural significance of the visual. It is concerned with the practice, display and interpretation of painting and other art forms, and shares with advertising history a concern to place texts as the centrepieces of circulation, as visible, historical artefacts. Art history explores the conditions in which paintings are commissioned and produced; the nature and significance of what they represent and the prevailing stylistic and formal circumstances with which they can be compared and contrasted over time. Advertisements, like paintings, can be understood as texts, the products of individuals and of different societies and cultures. In order to make sense of paintings an understanding of what they depict and the ideas they carry requires an understanding of how they fit into the wider world and culture that produced them and to which they refer. This idea of 'fit' between texts and the wider culture is often referred to in advertising studies as 'cultural homology'.[1] Paintings and advertisements are also visible cultural remainders, acting as historical evidence of wider economic and social activities from times past. To take the comparison between art and advertising history further: Raymond Williams could suggest over a generation ago, to the horror of aesthetes and economists alike, that advertising was 'in a sense, the official art of modern capitalist society' (Williams 1980: 184).

A generation ago the name Saatchi and Saatchi epitomised the world of advertising. The global advertising agency connected different social and cultural strands not least those of advertising, art and politics. Notoriously, Saatchi and Saatchi produced the now famous UK general election poster of 1979 proclaiming that 'Labour isn't working' an image and message that still resonates over thirty years later. The campaign helped usher in the Conservative government of Margaret Thatcher and affirmed close connections between politics and advertising. In the 1980s, whilst Thatcher fought mine workers and trade unionists and subsequently destroyed both the mining industry and its communities, Charles Saatchi turned from advertising to art. As collector, speculator, gallery owner and art patron Saatchi was instrumental in creating the Young British Artists (YBA), a group including Tracey Emin, Damien Hirst, Gavin Turk and others, in the tradition of art movements that have long given structure to the History of Art. The work was part of the Sensation exhibition held in 1997 at the Royal Academy. The YBA brand reached its marketing peak in the retrospective held at the Saatchi Gallery in 2003. This was housed ironically in London's County Hall, the former home of the recently abolished Greater London Council (GLC) and seat of resistance to the Tory government of the 1980s. This conceptual combination of YBA art, the GLC, Saatchi and the eighties Tory party under one roof is comparable to one strand of Dada and Surrealist art; the juxtaposition or chance encounter of unconnected elements in strange settings.

The surrealist idea of juxtaposition, which Saatchi and Saatchi drew on in their 1980s Silk Cut advertising campaign, in which the concept of the 'cut' was juxtaposed with the material reality of 'silk' in order to sell cigarettes, became one of the most successful campaigns of its day. The campaign was revived as the 'Not over until the fat lady sings' advertisement, which showed a large female opera singer depicted in a split, purple dress, and became the final UK fag advertisement to appear before tobacco advertising was banned in 2003. Charles Saatchi's campaign shared the juxtaposition idea with that of another cigarette advertising campaign for Benson & Hedges who placed 'gold' in unfamiliar relations, places and situations in order to create a brand identity.

The relation between advertising and politics incorporating art and culture was reaffirmed a few days after the 'iron curtain' separating communist and capitalist Europe began to unravel in 1989. The advertising slogan 'Saatchi and Saatchi first over the wall' appeared on a placard attached to the side of the Berlin Wall facing the eastern half of the city.

Advertising history then, is important to an understanding of the relationship between art, culture and advertising. But where should one start? Where can we claim to discover the first early advertising? When does it become significant to an analysis of culture and advertising and which advertising forms should be included in this account? These are the wider questions of historiography, but only a few reflections on the wheres and whens and a selective reference to significant 'historical moments' can be covered here; those important to our understanding of advertising and culture. There is no single history of advertising – only a series of advertising histories and advertising narratives that commence at different times and in different places.

Historical accounts differ, according to the interests, perspectives and ideologies of different writers. Raymond Williams, writing in the late 1970s, began his account with the line: 'It is customary to begin with the shortest account of the history of advertising by recalling the three thousand year old papyrus from Thebes, offering a reward for a runaway slave'(1980: 170). For Pasi Falk, 'modern advertising' is situated in the second half of the nineteenth century and emphasises the difference between the pre-modern practice of 'informing potential clients and customers of the existence and availability of a certain product' and the early-modern intention to 'stimulate demand' (1997: 65). Williams agrees the intention of the historian should be to trace the development of certain trends that lead to the 'institutionalised system of commercial information and persuasion' (1980: 170). For Leiss et al. (2005: 33), the important markers in the development of advertising are between 'traditional and industrial societies' and from industrial to consumer societies and then the developments that occur within consumer societies. Iain MacRury offers an advertising periodisation which falls under the headings of proto-modern advertising 1600–1780, early-modern advertising 1780–1880, modern advertising 1880–1950 and late-modern advertising 1950–90 (2009: 127). In this last phase we see modern advertising agency functions operating on a global scale and the consolidation and widespread use of media technologies in the interest of advertising, thus creating various advertising forms.

The forms that advertising take are varied and constantly developing. In the twenty-first century retailers and advertisers choose from a wide range of possible advertising forms to promote and market their goods and services. The advertising industry uses specific terminology to differentiate between different advertising forms. 'Above the line' refers to advertising forms such as television, cinema, radio and print that require the purchase of media space and have the potential to create culturally significant and memorable representations. These are the ones that tend to come to mind when we think of advertising. Less culturally significant but nonetheless important in economic terms and as part of the spread of advertising, is 'below the line' advertising, comprising direct mail, retail and point of sales displays (Jefkins & Yadin 2000). These have been joined in recent years by new forms of transmitting advertising. Online advertising is what MacRury and others have termed 'through the line advertising' recognising the importance of the Internet not just as the latest medium to provide advertising but as a potential 'confluence of all media' (Richards quoted in MacRury 2009: 86). The Internet as an evolving system of e-mail systems, websites, networking sites including Facebook and Twitter, and search engines offering business services blurs the distinction between 'above' and 'below' and weaves itself into new cultural homologies. From the Theban papyrus advertising slaves in ancient times to the pop-up ads on today's Internet, advertising takes many forms. Historians and writers on advertising have different interests and choose to select different aspects to discuss. The relationship between advertising and culture, and how the two come together as homology is the important element here.

Outdoor signs and space

Billboards and other forms of outdoor or 'out-of-home' advertising are important elements of contemporary above-the-line advertising. Outdoor advertising prior to illuminated and rotating panels, and the more recent digital boards, was dominated by the printed poster pasted onto available wall spaces. In the early-nineteenth century fly posters tended to use any space available and in 1837 a London act was passed to prohibit this happening without the owner's consent. Other forms of outdoor advertising existed, largely comprising hand-painted texts and images created by sign writers. The advertisements were created by applying a background colour field to the wall or wooden panel and contained within a plain or sometime decorative frame in which words and images would be painted to advertise popular products. This constituted a live street performance of production with painters and sign writers working from a ladder or platform. The work was skilled, often working from a pattern or stencil, on occasions transferring an image onto a wall using charcoal or chalk impressed from a pre-drawn scheme. In some sense the work could be described as a craft, drawing freehand or applying layers of paint requiring balance, measurement, concentration and co-ordination of hand and eye. Perhaps involving as Richard Sennett puts it in his description of the activity of craftsmanship, 'the desire to do a job well for its own sake' (2008: 9).[2]

Sign writing is one of the oldest forms of promoting goods and services and continued well into the age of mechanical reproduction when photography and cinema in the nineteenth and twentieth centuries became important to advertising. Sign writing, like most advertising up to the modern age, was mainly about providing information: what was for sale; where it could be found; and how much it was going for. Preserved amongst the ruins of Pompeii and Herculaneum, Roman towns buried after the eruption of Mount Vesuvius in 79 AD, are the traces of advertising sign writing. The twentieth-century excavator of Pompeii, Maiuri, dismissed these ancient advertisements as mere aspects of commerce that 'deface the simple and severe architectural forms of patrician houses by plastering garish trade signs on the wall' (Maiuri 1960: 188). Perhaps they do from the perspective of the classicist but they also provide historically important material and a cultural record.

Pompeii reveals a complex, ancient world of work and leisure, economic and cultural life, where theatres, bars and shops, temples, bathhouses, homes and gardens line the excavated streets. Workshops where goods were produced front the streets – and the road system as in most Roman settlements extended beyond the forum and out from the town, connecting empire and economic activity and enabling the widespread exchange of goods and information. Here are some examples of Pompeiian advertising. It ranged from the rental of property, 'an elegant bath suite for prestige clients, tabernae, mezzanine lodgings and upper floor apartments on a five year contract' to the promotion of goods and foodstuffs such as the ever popular fish sauce (liquamen and garum) that according to Pliny, Pompeii was noted for (Beard 2008: 110). Electoral slogans were painted onto walls, often in the same style and created by the same hand as advertisements for gladiatorial games, one of the cultural highlights of the town, held in the amphitheatre (Wallace-Hadrill 1994). In one example of a gladiatorial advertisement, the sign writer Aemilius Celer appends his own name as the creator of the advertisement (Beard 2008). The content of these advertisements indicates the significance of goods and activities such as gladiatorial events, the use of bars and the sale of food stuffs to everyday life and how advertising was an important aspect of these activities.

It is not just the range of adverts and the types of goods and services represented that is of interest in the first-century Roman town of Pompeii. Also of significance to an appreciation of the relationship between advertising and culture is the way adverts were made and where they were placed. Often similar techniques were used to create adverts as were used in the decorative arts to paint the more lavish interiors of houses in a variety of different styles. The painting of signs and the creation of images of food and drink found in bars were produced on fresh plaster using the same techniques as the muralists who created the frescoes that decorated the wealthy Roman homes. Similarly it was a mosaic, the arrangement of tesserae, little pieces of stone, formed into decorative patterns and images, that carried the liquamen promotion found at Pompeii and mentioned above. Usually representational mosaics, in addition to geometric style borders, often depicted animals, humans and gods. In the twenty-first century, Interflora, the florist, is still represented by a sign that incorporates the figure of Hermes, the messenger, who in Greek mythology was the god of trade and of crossing and protecting boundaries. Known as Mercury in the Latin world, the figure forms the basis of a logo that still represents the Interflora brand depicted in local flower shops or found winging his way across the Internet announcing online flower shopping. Today Mercury/Hermes carries a stylistic bunch of flowers rather than the caduceus, the symbolic staff of the messenger which would have helped identify the figure in ancient times. What is significant from an understanding of the classical world uncovered in Pompeii and elsewhere is the extent of horizontal homology that is the level of fit between different aspects of culture and economic life where the decorative arts, political signs and the advertising of a range of goods exist side by side, sharing the same spaces and even creative techniques.

When surveying outdoor advertising such as the billboards, panels, adshels (bus shelters with advertisements) and other structures that carry advertisements in the twenty-first-century city or town, the traces of older advertisements, many from the industrial period of the nineteenth and early-twentieth centuries, can often be discerned. In some cases signs have remained constantly visible on buildings, with advertising text and image weathering and fading over the years. Recently these have become known as 'ghost signs'. Some become visible as older facades are removed from walls – or as buildings are demolished new sight lines are created, revealing older signs. Goods still being promoted have often gone out of production and the use value of the promoted products fade, like the visible remains of the advertisements, from living memory. Prices indicated in the old British currency of £.s.d. can only be understood as an example of historical exchange value adding a period feel to the overall design.

Foss Bridge House, constructed in 1878, is a handsome Victorian red-brick and yellow sandstone building, with a decorative façade noted for its arches and pilasters, built alongside the River Foss within the medieval and roman walls that surround the city of York in the north of England. In the twentieth century the building came to house an extensive ironmongers shop. On the side of the building is a painted sign of white letters on a black background announcing 'F.R. Stubbs – tools for all trades'. Enclosed by a white frame, demarcating the advertising space from the colour of the background wall, and like the frames around all advertisements whatever form they take, it gives internal coherence and added prominence to the advertisement and visually closes it off, distinguishing it from other signs and immediate distractions. This sign is now accompanied on the other side of the building by a similar but vertical modern sign that announces a change of function for the building to 'Loch Fyne Seafood' in yellow lettering on a dark background. Although the Stubbs advertisement may have been recently retouched both are authentic signs of their times.

During recent building work in the historical centre of Newcastle upon Tyne close to the remains of the fourteenth-century wall that once encircled the town, a fading, painted

Figure 3.2: 'F.R. Stubbs – tools for all trades', York, 2011. Photograph: the author.

Figure 3.3: 'Loch Fyne Seafood', York, 2011. Photograph: the author.

wall advertisement became noticeable. As in the York advertisement, white lettering on a painted black background was positioned over red-brick, on this occasion on the side of a Victorian pub. A white internal decorative border gives a stylistic sense of the 'old and authentic' and a design coherence and prominence to the Jack Daniel's Tennessee whiskey promotion contained within it. The advertisement looked old but the stencilled image was created as part of a 2008 drinks advertising campaign. The advertisement – like other simulated wall signs that appeared as part of this promotion in Newcastle and elsewhere – had been artificially weathered to give it an aged and worn feel. The advertisement appears as if it has just been uncovered, emerging into new and contemporary sight lines after years of obscurity. Lettering at the bottom of the advertisement announces in modern, young idiom, that 'your friends at Jack Daniel's remind you to drink responsibly' thus revealing within the body of the text, its in-authenticity and paradoxically, despite its friendly stated intentions, drawing attention to its real marketing aim – to sell more alcohol. Numerous copies of these Jack Daniel's promotions in the form of older advertisements, placed in traditional advertising spaces create a postmodern simulacrum, multiple copies of something of dubious provenance, as outlined by Baudrillard and others. In the pursuit of increased sales the campaign attempts to create novelty and cleverness – important elements of culture and advertising – but it merely makes for historical inauthenticity and marketing insincerity.

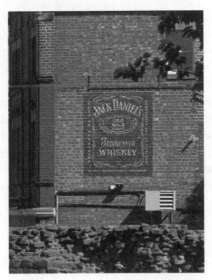

Figure 3.4: Jack Daniel's wall advertisement, Newcastle, 2011. Photograph: the author.

Technology

Advertising is dependent on the media space that different media forms provide, such as space in newspapers, on television and cinema screens and on the Internet. Billboards are often spoken of as being less reliant on supportive media technology: a pure but fading form of advertising relying only on print, paste and paper. Advertising in general is dependent on the technological developments that made those very media forms possible in the first place. In the symbiotic relationship between media and advertising, media needs finance and advertising requires media technology, space and projection. The development of movable type printing in fifteenth-century Europe transformed book production from the labour-intensive hand-produced single books like the illuminated Lindisfarne Gospels (circa 700), to the multiple-copy forty-two-line Bible produced on Gutenberg's press at Mainz in the 1450s. Printing quickly spread throughout Europe. Not confined to religious texts or even just to books, Caxton published a printed version of the Canterbury Tales in 1478, the year after producing a printed poster, known as the Pyes of Salisbury, bearing the request – 'please do not pull down this advertisement'. The development of typographic (movable type) print in the fifteenth century enabled posters to be created more economically and with more detail than xylographic (hand-cut woodblock) techniques allowed. Billboards have developed rapidly in the last couple of decades from a reliance on the technology of the printed word – and the more recent still photography – into digital multi-advertisement screens more comparable in appearance to television or cinema screens and the technology that works them. Newspapers were a further development of movable type printing and newsprint advertising was soon to follow. The development of photography in the early-nineteenth century made possible a range of newspaper representations no longer dependent on hand-drawn images. Metal block printing created more refined and durable imagery than wooden block and the development of photo-chromolithography brought printed colour images to newsprint and to poster advertising.

Developments such as these in the field of communications were important to advertising production and to how advertisements were made and encoded with product information and endowed with ideas drawn from the wider culture. Technological development is fundamental to the creation of, in the words of the Institute of Practitioners in Advertising, the 'most persuasive possible selling message' with all the visual and textual attributes and attachments that came to be associated with late-nineteenth- and twentieth-century advertising.

Agencies

Technological developments were fundamental to the expansion of advertising. One further ingredient however was needed to form modern advertising and cement the relationship with culture. This was the creation of the advertising agency. Advertising agents had been around since the early 1800s performing basic media functions. The first agencies were media space dealers; securing advertising space for clients in the pages of newspapers. The agent bought the newspaper space and then sold it on to an advertiser. Manufacturers and retailers produced their own copy and the agency made money from buying space cheaply and selling it on at a higher rate.

The main function of the first advertising agencies was to deal in commodified space, securing space and by implication time for advertising. Each advertisement has its place within a newspaper column or frame, marked out from other newspaper content, within the television advertising slot or inside the frame of the outdoor billboard. There is also a temporal context: the advertisement exists in time – taking its turn on the hoardings or finding its moment on the screen. These are features common to all adverts – they have duration and spatial presence.

Each advertisement occupies space and time in order to promote the product, service or idea it represents. At the same time it displays an aspect of the wider economy and culture. Each advertisement today advertises the system and ideology of choice that is at the heart of a market economy. Advertising celebrates choice through the spectacle of information, promotion and branding – in classic liberal theory, individuals make their preferences they select the goods they wish to purchase. But these choices are based on inequalities of income, wealth and other aspects of the social. As David Runciman has recently put it, individuals exercising their 'choices and freedoms … are like confetti in the face of the whirlwind power of money' (2011: 11). So advertising has a further function which is to legitimate the existing social system. Although as we shall see later in the advertising decoding process individuals are summoned through shared culture and can come to challenge the dominant meanings ascribed to advertising by rejecting cultural values. Advertising celebrates and disguises but it always acts as a fragment and conduit of culture.

The early-nineteenth-century advertising space brokers and the early-twentieth-century advertising agencies were the outcome of a new form of society based on rapidly developing industrial production in the factories that dominated the towns and cities and organisation of work and class relations. The mass production of goods created mass markets with economies producing commodities and mass consumption on a global scale. Advertising became a necessary aspect of consumption and a significant element of the developing mass media creating new forms and transmissions of information, entertainment and social knowledge. Advertising became not only a necessary part of the economy but a very visible cultural presence.

Agencies – words and images

Advertising agencies developed across the nineteenth and into the twentieth centuries and came to provide a range of other services in addition to space brokerage. Buying and selling-on media space and time required a level of knowledge about the media, its circulation and audiences who were to be transformed into potential customers for the advertised products. The advertising agency role expanded becoming a channel for culture entering advertising.

Much of nineteenth-century advertising was to be found in the newspapers. Advertising guides were produced informing and advising potential advertisers as to the circulation, price and political orientation of the papers. In 1846, Charles Mitchell published the Newspaper Press Directory 'to form a guide to advertisers in their selection of journals as mediums more particularly suitable for their announcements' (Gliserman 1969: 10). Mitchell's directory included advice on advertising taxes, the law and copyrighting. In 1853 the Advertising Tax was abolished as was Stamp Duty on newspapers in 1855. In the late 1860s the Directory was extended to include an index of magazines and periodicals in addition to newspapers.

The 'full service' agency was in place by the 1920s. These supplied the mutually supporting functions of media planning, research and account management, required to mount and direct a successful advertising campaign. They also came to offer the advertiser the necessary means to create an advertisement. Both selling and filling the media space. Copywriting – the production of the textual body of the advertisement – came to be offered as a free service; an inducement and enhancement of the space on offer. This is a crucial cultural moment where the association between artistic and cultural production and the production of advertisements became consolidated and professionalised. The craft and personnel associated with the production of literature such as novels, plays, film scripts, poetry and even journalism make their way into advertising production. Rhythm, alliteration and rhyme important to the creation of literature become sought-after elements of advertising copy. In the late-nineteenth century John Emory Powers became a freelance English language copywriter creating advertisements promoting goods such as Beecham's Pills. The 'Power's style' of advertising copywriting was noted for its simple and direct use of language. In the 1950s, the novelist Fay Weldon's language skills were famously put to use by the UK Egg marketing board to promote egg consumption. Simply prepared but rich in meaning, the strap line 'go to work on an egg' became a familiar slogan of television, poster and newsprint advertising and a staple of popular culture.

In addition, the agencies began to offer the services of illustrators and then photographers, forming the full 'creative' mechanism of personnel and skills for producing an advertisement. The visual language of painting, illustration and then photography and film became part of advertising. For instance, the Surrealist artist René Magritte's relationship with advertising was complex and multi-facetted. He referred to his work in advertising and publicity as 'traveux imbecile' or 'idiotic work'. An example of Magritte's advertising work from 1931 is for Tonny's toffees. He created the image of a black cat and a white dog tearing the wrapper from an oversize toffee to represent the product. Other examples of advertising imagery suggest a more complex relationship between advertising and painting. For instance, Magritte created an advertising image for Belga cigarettes in 1935 in which a woman set against a familiar Magritte blue sky with large white clouds holds a cigarette and directs a penetrating gaze in the direction of the viewer. The female Belga cigarette smoker and the disturbing oil painting The Rape (1934) in which a female head of hair sits on a naked female torso that also stands in for the face share formal and representational similarities. A similar image also appears as the frontispiece to André Breton's pamphlet 'What is Surrealism?' of the same year (Grunenberg and Pih 2011). A motif first deployed in painting and used to represent the group of artists Magritte was part of resurfaces as an advertising image. This is a specific example of a direct cultural homology. Examples such as this remind us of the developing 'fit' between advertising and artistic, literary and cultural production. Artists and writers were quick to put themselves at the service of advertising and advertisers were to borrow people, ideas and motifs from the arts. This then became a two way cultural homology. Advertising feeds off culture and feeds culture with its products – a constant two-way cross over or flow between the world of culture and advertising representation (MacRury 2009: 145–146).

Advertisements are shaped by the art and skill of the wordsmiths and picturesmiths employed in their production. (It is increasingly reliant on research, see Chapter 2 of this volume.) But advertising is also dependent on the enabling technology of the host medium. From the representation of products and creation of promotional methods to the voice, tone and mode of address; the advertisement is shaped by the formal and representational methods of the medium of which it is a part. Formal attributes of an advertisement such as shape, line, movement, colour, perspective, dimensionality and creation of narrative are attributes of the type of media that gives space and time to the advertisement.

Moving advertisements

A good illustration of this is to compare the first British TV advertisement for Gibbs SR toothpaste in 1955 with magazine advertisements for the same product of the 1950s. The 'tingling fresh' magazine advertisement has cool blues and off-white backgrounds that give prominence to the warm red of the SR logo and the accompanying toothbrush. These are part of a formal arrangement: arranged in a similar manner to the display of objects in a still-life genre painting. The magazine advertisement of the 1950s shows an open packet with a toothpaste tube emerging and a centrally placed toothbrush receiving toothpaste from a further tube, suspended like the toothbrush, mid-air. The packet, brush and tube – all converge on the lower left corner of an upright ice-blue block emphasising the 'tingling-fresh' message of the strap line and set against the rectangular shape of the magazine page.

In the TV advertisement based on the same idea the camera pans slowly from left to right across a still scene onto a block of ice, the shape of which is now read against the frame of the television screen (Gibbs SR 1955). The warm/cool connotation of colour in the magazine advertisement is reduced to the black-and-white denotations of early television advertising. Sound is introduced to the advertising effect with the murmur of gently trickling water set against a rippling musical accompaniment behind a voice-over that announces that 'It's tingling fresh'. Toothpaste is deposited on the brush as the tube – drawing away from left to right – creates a slow, hesitant flow of motion. The time of the still-life arrangement has been extended: further scenes that make up this very first British television advertisement show a

Figure 3.5: Gibbs television advertisement, 1955. Source: Advertising Archives.

pseudo-scientific bar chart depicting the creeping advance of gum infection and tooth decay and the rapid movement of a hand vigorously brushing teeth with Gibbs SR toothpaste indicating the solution to the problem. The product and its attributes are represented in different ways in the magazine and television advertisement and imply distinct relationships between the advertisement, product and the viewer. Flow and movement as formal and signifying elements of television and cinema advertising become distinguishing features of much contemporary advertising as the technology became incorporated into a range of screen-based advertising, including the animated digital billboards of recent years.

Creatives and creativity

The creative production of words and images within the new full-service advertising agencies of the twentieth century could be seen to have a close relationship with artistic and literary practice (MacRury 2009: 143) as other aspects of the advertising agency's activities such as research and accounting can be aligned with scientific and economic methodologies. Romanticism – the early-nineteenth-century movement of artists, poets and thinkers that reacted against industrialisation provides the backdrop of thinking for creativity, where 'the ideal form of work was art' (McGuigan 2010: 115). Cultural production, as the agencies developed towards the close of the twentieth century, was still seen no less by the practitioners as part of the 'charismatic ideology of creation' against which Bourdieu offered his more sociological theories of cultural production involving habitus, capital and field (Bourdieu [1996] 1992). The creatives of the advertising industry – the men and women who provide the skills and ideas that make the adverts – were seen as being part of a general social group known as the creative class (Florida 2002: 69). More often they are engaged in what has been termed 'large scale production' that is creating advertising for mass markets. But they are also involved in what Hesmondhalgh has called 'restricted production' which involves a more aesthetic approach that is more comparable to artistic production and which attracts both societal and advertising industry acclaim (Hesmondhalgh 2006: 214). This commerce versus creativity distinction is a familiar one in advertising and cultural production (Nixon 2003: 76).

Members of the creative class have also been described as 'cultural intermediaries'. For Hesmondhalgh following Bourdieu the term 'cultural intermediary' suggests a role as 'critic or social commentator rather than producer of symbolic meaning' (Powell and Prasad 2010). The emphasis here is on the role creatives play in presenting and shaping certain cultural forms and consequent values: cultural intermediaries 'shape both the use values and exchange values, and seek to manage how these values are connected to peoples lives' (Negus 2002: 504). Nixon discusses the formal knowledge of creatives working in the advertising industry based on market research, sale knowledge and the like. This is contrasted with their informal knowledge and observations of consumer culture drawn from everyday experience and includes their own cultural identifications

(Nixon 2003: 35). The creative class in advertising can be viewed as both producers and shapers – 'taste shapers' – of culture (Featherstone 1991; Nixon 2003; Powell and Prasad 2010). This is what Kelly, Lawlor and O' Donohoe refer to as the cultural intermediaries' ability to 'know what was out there' (2009: 139).

To summarise, advertising encoding is the area which precedes the presentation and delivery of the message. The advertising director, creative or designer, working individually or as part of a team is central to this process of advertising production. It creates what Hall refers to as a 'signifying process' and this has been addressed in both theoretical and empirical work (Shapiro 1981; Schudson 1993; du Gay 1997; Soar 2000). It is the process, conditions and relations of production, which contribute to, or in part determine, the nature of the message. Advertising encoding is always a social process carried out in concrete situations and results in the production of messages which should not be perceived as being 'natural' (Fiske 1991; Hall 2001) in the sense that messages merely *reflect* some aspect of nature or culture, which is mirrored, for example, as advertising image or copy which surfaces in the pages and on the screens of the media as an un-ideological and unmediated truth about the world. Advertising encoding emphasises the constructed nature of the media message at least in part as a product of the position of the manufacturer of media messages in social relations, constructed from specific relations of production and then organised into particular ideological configurations. This approach gives emphasis to the constructed nature of advertising texts. Advertising production includes such practices as individual and group conceptual work, producing copy, layouts and sketches, organising service functions, the technical production of film and printing, considering and organising outlets within practical, technological, ideological and cultural parameters (Soar 2000). The process of encoding is the construction, selection, shaping, squeezing and packaging of information and culture into highly structured formats: advertising texts.

The encoding of an advertisement includes formal and informal knowledge and creative skills and abilities of the advertising creative working within the milieu of the advertising agency. The agency is itself situated within a context of research, marketing and sales promotion, and in the wider changing cultural patterning of the contemporary world. As an earlier commentator Judith Williamson suggested, all advertising obviously 'has a function, which is to sell things to us. But it has another function, which I believe in many ways replaces that traditionally fulfilled by art or religion. It creates structures of meaning'(Williamson 1978: 11). As Sut Jhally has put it more recently: 'what are the consistent stories that advertising spins as a whole about what is important in the world, about how to behave, about what is good and bad. Indeed, it is to ask what values advertising consistently pushes' (2000: 30). These stories, meanings and values are not received uncritically as Kate Soper has recently suggested a space is needed 'to challenge the advertiser's monopoly on the depiction of prosperity and the good life' (2011: 30).

In the remaining sections of this chapter, three quite different examples of advertising campaigns from the twenty-first century will help explore how culture is encoded in the

Figure 3.6: L'Oréal, Cheryl Cole, 2009. Source: Advertising Archives.

advertising text and how the culture of the advertising viewer comes to make sense of the advertisement. It also suggests how different types of decoding might come about.

Culture and decoding

In this section, three recent examples of advertising are used to explore how cultural references encoded into advertising texts fit with prevailing cultural factors and how the advertising viewer may draw on their own cultural experiences in order to make sense of and decode advertisements. The three advertising campaigns are the 2004 Persil billboard campaign featuring the Great Britain Cycling Team, a L'Oréal television advertisement fronted by celebrity Cheryl Cole in 2009 and the 'winking Christ' newsprint advertisement for Phones 4U from 2011.

Persil

In 2004 the Team Persil campaign was a prominent advertising feature in many cities in Britain. Its impact was achieved through the size and position of billboards and adshels, the frequency of the campaign, clarity of design, and above all the colossal size of human form representing cycling both as a sport, and as a mode of transport. Unilever detergent company Persil was a sponsor of the Great Britain Cycling Team in 2004 and each advertisement featured a single member of the team wearing the Team Persil cycling strip and helmet and sporting the team logo on their shirt. The team logo comprised the familiar 'Persil' lettering and appeared in the bottom right of each advert. The advertising campaign was prominent across 2004 as the media reported on the Tour de France and the build up to the Athens Olympics in which the Great Britain team competed.

In the city of Newcastle upon Tyne, UK, these advertisements appeared on advertising company J C Deceaux's billboards around car parking areas and on back-lit bus stop adshels. Two advertisements, one featuring a standing cyclist displaying the Union flag and the other the monumental form (portrait, shoulders, torso and upper legs) of a Team Persil cyclist in competition pose were prominent and are discussed here (see Plate 3). These images are good examples of how a campaign takes its place within a prevailing culture and can be understood against a decoding framework of preferred, negotiated and oppositional readings. The readings are in part the product of the urban environment where people find themselves positioned as commuters and travellers. Urban identities are created from many aspects of life, but here the mode of transportation in the city is of importance.

The most visually stunning advertisement in the campaign appeared on a forty-eight sheet poster site (one of the larger-sized billboards) on the edge of a busy city centre car park. A formal description of the poster emphasises the left-hand side of the frame dominated by the image of the cyclist and the right-hand side of the frame by the upper case text: 'removes blood sweat and tears' (see Plate 3). The semiotic potency of the text, with its echoes of Churchill's determined 1940 speech on assuming the British Premiership, is borrowed from the popular axiom emphasising the visible physicality of hard graft and alleviated by the reassuring power of certain detergents to remove these signs. Under this pale blue text, the 'Persil' logo with the accompanying legend 'choice of the GB cycling team' appears in red. The left side of the poster is dominated by the helmet, front portrait shoulders, arms torso and upper legs of the Team Persil cyclist whose form fills the full depth of the framed advertisement. The cropped image is given a powerful presence, the strength of the image of the cyclist upon whose shape light falls giving emphasis to the face, forearms and legs and thus form to the physical exertion involved in competitive cycling. The edge of the helmet and the extended arm creates a strong vertical line that demarcates the image from the text creating delineated space that gives prominence to both. The upper parts of the cycle handlebars create an upward diagonal line that extends across the vertical giving prominence to the text. The image, close to the picture surface, beyond which is a white, flat, even plane that denies any contextual representational function creates a stark, challenging representation. The combination of cropping, lighting and monumentality gives the impression of movement and immediacy in the absence of perspectival features. In combination the colossal image of the cyclist in juxtaposition to the popular phrase 'removes blood sweat and tears' signifies solid, teeth-gritting determination.

Consequently this and other examples of the advertising campaign created a forceful image of cycling as a sport and a positive and challenging icon of cycling more generally. This occurred within the modern city space – one that is increasingly car dominated. The monumentality of the figure visually dominated transit areas of the city such as roads, walkways and car parks. Although these areas are shared with other modes of public and private transport and by pedestrians the speed, volume and presence of the car physically dominates these areas. Recent motoring trends favour higher, wider, larger, less fuel efficient, more powerful private cars associated with driving over rough terrain. In addition to the physical domination of public space by the car as mode of transport is the increasing colonisation of intellectual life by the idea of the car, where notions of ownership, individualism and behaviour are articulated to an ideology of the car.

This observation is in contrast to the enormity of the advertising billboard and size of the figure of the cyclist who appears several times larger than life and towered over the billboards' location on the edge of a popular city car park. This dialectic of reality and representation in which the reversal of dimensions, where the image of the cyclist and cycle is larger than motorist and motorcar registers at the visual awareness level and provides the basis of a reading of the advertisement. This reversal then becomes a feature of decodings that took place within this location.

The preferred reading of this and the other advertisements that made up the campaign involved ideas and representations common in the media and popular culture in which sports coverage and sports-related items formed a significant element of both. Sports personalities, individual and team endeavour, achievements and failures run alongside media coverage of national sides as a significant representational and ideological element attached to national identity, nationalism and the nation state. In this instance this was specified in relation to cycling as a form of transport, the Great Britain Cycling Team, its sponsors and the Persil product.

The validity of the preferred reading that features nationalism and national identity might have been applied to the Persil/union flag advertisement (Plate 3). Using a bold spatial layout, appropriate to the size, shape and lateral layout of a landscape billboard, the left-hand field of the advertising space is given to representation (cyclist and union flag) and the right-hand field to text (redder whiter bluer, Persil). Reading the advertisement from the left, the representative element comprises a young, female cyclist displaying a Union flag and drawing it towards the centre of the advertising field creating an upward curve through the movement of the arm that draws the viewer's eye into the centre of the advertising field and towards the beginning of the slogan. Apart from the flesh tones of the arm and the face framed by a cycle helmet, red and blue over background white form the cycle shirt and union flag, the red band, broad, vertical yet gently curving accentuates the gesture that emphasise the presence of the national symbol. The cyclist's arm and hand gestures towards the right-hand field of the advertisement and the text 'redder whiter bluer' that refers simultaneously to previous Persil campaigns 'Persil washes whiter and it shows', to the detergents product performance and to other qualities articulated by the presence and specific representation of the national symbol. The 'redder whiter bluer' slogan is presented in blue text and the 'Persil' logo in red text, both over the white background that provides the white element of the flag and cyclist's shirt, thus offering a unifying visual background to the two halves of the advertisement: one comprising imagery, the other text. This device brings together the textual, graphological advertising elements to function in an iconic manner, both repeating and emphasising references.

If an element of the preferred reading of this Persil campaign was one of sports-nationalism attached to events such as the Olympic games and other sporting events where cyclists representing Britain were competing, then those significations might also be in play where other aspects of nationalism – political and ideological – are part of the general cultural, decoding atmosphere. The European football championship held in Portugal in June and July 2004 was the occasion for widespread English support for the national team. This was accompanied by an unprecedented flying of the flag of St George from buildings and most noticeably from private cars, vans, taxis and other road vehicles. The meaning of this display of the English national symbol is widely supposed to signify more than support for the national football team. The political and ideological significations are widely contested, from narrow notions of English identity often associated with football hooliganism and forms of xenophobic nationalism; rejection of multiculturalism; acceptance of multiple identities within English culture; an English nationalism and identity defined against other identities in Great Britain or the United Kingdom and the actual and projected political devolutions within the UK to national and regional centres. In the same period the European elections were held on 10 June in which right wing parties campaigned under the standard of the Union flag. The Union flag symbol was central to the campaigns of UKIP, aiming to withdraw the United Kingdom from the European Union, and the British National Party, that took its often racist and xenophobic ideology deep into local communities (Glancey 2004; Bragg 2004). Negotiated and oppositional readings different to preferred sports-nationalist readings may have included ethnic, class or other social aspects that are important elements to formulating readings. These would have been associated with a person's perception and attitude to sport and national teams.

Decodings of this advertisement campaign also occurred in specific urban environments and spatialities comprising living space and movement or transit space. The latter comprises roads, walkways, pedestrianised zones, cycle tracks and car parks. Different decodings will come into being and vary according to historical formulations but will do so within specific localities and spatialities: urban identities are related to the mode of transport used. The relationship of the potential decoder to the preferred reading of the advertisement is in the real sense a relationship between an aspect of urban identity that is pedestrian, motorist, cyclist and the advertisement. Car drivers, passengers, public transport users, pedestrians, cyclists will stand in different relationships to the advertisement and will be party to the formulation of different readings. How might decodings associated with the pedestrian or the public-transport user differ to those travelling in or parking a car? Considerations might include the nature of traffic movement through the city, other travellers, obstructions and dangers. Oppositional readings might stand in resistance to an ideology of sport/individualism/nationalism formulated at the purely political ideological level or conflict with the positive image of cycling and cyclists portrayed in the advertisement. A negotiated reading might accept the preferred reading of sport/individualism/nationalism but be aware of the incongruities in the larger-than-life depiction of a cyclist surrounded by life size and life destroying cars within an overwhelmingly hostile car-orientated urban environment.

L'Oréal

The second advertisement in this section is a television advertisement for L'Oréal New Elvive Full Restore 5 – first aired in September 2009 (L'Oréal 2009). The advertisement sells a product that claims to improve the appearance of hair. The advertisement featured the celebrity presence of Cheryl Cole, described by Wikipedia as 'an English singer, songwriter, dancer, fashion designer, author, and television personality'. Cheryl's busy media presence and status in popular culture has been further secured by being an *X-Factor* judge and 'football wife'. Her working-class background in the north east of England, to which her Geordie accent, although softened through media and celebrity discourse, attests, is an important part of the advertising strategy. These signifiers are important elements, creating links between celebrity presentation, the advertised product and consumer culture.

In the 2009 L'Oréal advertisement, Cole is first seen reclining on a couch in a large, light, spacious, opulent room (Figure 3.6). Red furnishings contrast with a white interior and the striking red of Cole's dress dominates the space as French doors open to frame Cheryl's re-entry into the interior later in the narrative. Red and white dominate and colour is the first element of memorable significant advertising form. A Union Jack rug placed on the floor adds a contrast of blue as does the Union Jack cushion clutched by Cole as she begins the gentle, dance like movement that culminates in the characteristic hair swirl of L'Oréal advertising. This movement is complemented by a sense of rapid flow – the second component of this advertisement's significant form – that follows the celebrity's speedy progress, forward through the depicted interior space, towards the camera and viewer.

The advertisement assembles a series of visual, verbal and textual signifiers of youthful femininity and glamour, celebrity success, talent unleashed, and an English north-eastern working-class figure/culture representing Britain. The significant colour combination of red, white and blue, the national signifiers, were specific to the Cole advert. Similar L'Oréal advertisements for the same product aimed at other national audiences were broadcast in the same year. Different colours dominated the advertisements with blue and grey for Brazil and grey and red for France and other European markets. Similarly, the L'Oréal celebrity and its associations are represented differently in other contemporary New Elvive adverts: by soap opera and the film actress Ana Serradilla in the former and middle-class English and French-speaking Canadian Evangeline Lilly in the latter. Furthermore, L'Oréal's Cheryl Cole has a different script.

From 1973, McCann-Erickson's L'Oréal advertising famously included the 'because I'm worth it' line spoken by actresses and models such as Cybil Shepherd and Jennifer Aniston. The strapline, it was claimed, was intended to be a feminist style affirmation of female strength and individuality. As the campaign progressed through time, it contributed to the company's sales success but at the same time attracting criticism – often seen as an uncomfortable display of celebrity narcissism, the objectification of women and what David Harvey has termed 'the neo-liberal ethic of intense possessive individualism' (Harvey 2008: 32). 'Because I'm worth it', delivered in heavily accented American English became an ambiguous and contested inclusion in popular culture often drawing popular aesthetic and cultural derision.

Throughout the eighties and nineties the advertisements continued to feature a series of female actresses or models who demonstrated the benefits of the L'Oréal product with exaggerated 'hair' movements, overly stylised poses and a general fetishisation of the body and of physical appearance (see Plate 4). A L'Oréal television campaign of the noughties featured Andie MacDowell; a long camera shot of a pair of female legs, a swirl of hair, and spoken references to 'insurance' and the benefits of the product. The closing line of the advertisement changed from the 'because I'm worth it' of the seventies to 'because you're worth it', spoken directly by the actress to the audience. In both cases the exophoric nature of the mode of address is such that the valorisation of actress within text 'I'm worth it' and valorisation of receiver of the text 'you're worth it' become fused. The 'value' of the represented L'Oréal scene, of glamour, body fetishism and surface appearance and the affluent media world of fashion and celebrity is transferred to the position of the viewer of the text. This transference, always open to decoding and interpretation, operates in the sense of Scannell's general understanding of the media message as a 'for-anyone structure' becoming a 'for-anyone-as-someone structure' through creating a sense that the advert, product and its associations are individualised for the receiver of the advertisement (Scannell 2000: 5–24). They become individualised not just by appealing to individual needs but cultural identifications.

'Because you're worth it' of the mid-decade became in the British 2009 advertisement uttered by Cole 'because we're worth it'. Its inclusive mode of address 'we' rather than previously 'you' or 'I' is preceded by the line 'Come on girls, let's say it' delivered without parody or pastiche and is preceded by a momentary pause – a self-referencing but reinstating affirmation of the product and all its attendant signifiers. Reference to Cole's band Girls Aloud is important here and the distinctive Geordie accent, both working class and signifying Britishness, gives voice to the advert. The unity of signifiers – the overall advertising sign articulates the product and celebrity culture to youthful glamour, social class, national and regional culture. Its worth lies in its decoding.

Phones 4 U

A clear example of an oppositional set of readings occurred in 2011 when the *Metro*, a free daily British newspaper, carried an advertisement featuring a cartoon depiction of Christ in a Phones 4 U advertisement. The advertisement first appeared at Easter when Christians traditionally commemorate the death and resurrection of Jesus Christ. The slogan 'Miraculous deals on Samsung Galaxy Android phones' appeared above an image of a Samsung phone and below a cartoon image of a grinning Christ simultaneously winking and giving a thumbs up sign. An 'amplification effect' beyond the initial reach of the advertising campaign can often be achieved by sparking wider media coverage about any controversy surrounding a campaign. However, for the purpose of this enquiry assume that London-based advertising agency Adam and Eve expected a preferred reading of the advertisement that was 'light hearted and humorous'. The Advertising Standards Authority certainly assumed that this was the advertiser's intention but judged that the advertisements were 'disrespectful to the Christian faith and were likely to cause serious offence' and should not appear again. What is clear here in cultural terms is that the advertising agency anticipated a level of shared culture that would in the first instance render the advertisement intelligible. Secondly, that cultural familiarity with the Easter story that finds its meaning as a core article of religious faith is superseded by a playful attitude and ironic detachment from the traditional meaning of signs. The advertisements' references are as much to the thumbs-up, winking figure of 'Buddy Christ' from the 1999 film *Dogma* as to traditional Christian iconography. ASA received ninety-eight complaints challenging the nature of the image, the use of the word 'miraculous' and the publication of the advertisement during Easter. These are the basis of oppositional readings in play during the period of the advertisements publication based on traditional cultural readings and/or adherence to a religious belief system. A preferred reading is likely to be based on an appreciation of a stock of cultural signs largely detached from any referent outside the flow of media images and a negotiated reading on the acceptance of the playful and light-hearted appropriation of traditional signs, which are tangentially and challengingly linked to original meanings. Age and cultural sensibility are likely to be important social and cultural factors in the taking up of decoding positions.

Conclusion

The final section of this chapter has explored advertising campaigns that are specifically culturally situated and take their references from a wide range of cultural factors applicable to their presentation and cultural salience. Social and cultural identities including those associated with class, region, nation and religious belief were identified as significant to decoding these campaigns as were themes such as celebrity and sport. Not only do they stake out the cultural ground requiring that cultural references are appreciated and inviting preferred readings that enable the advertisement to secure their cultural and promotional effect, they are also a point of potential cultural struggle where the advertising viewer brings their own individual and group experiences and values potentially taking form as negotiated or oppositional decoding of the campaign.

As a whole this chapter has attempted to chart three aspects of the relation between advertising and culture. Firstly, that of the production and creation of advertising campaigns which draw on aspects of culture and how these are channelled through advertising agencies. Secondly, that the products of this relationship are displayed through a variety of technologies and advertising forms and become a highly visible presence in a range of media forms. Thirdly, these were shown to circulate in social and cultural experience and draw on audiences' own experiences. They may reaffirm the cultural world they are drawn from or as selected and reshaped representations be the trigger for challenges to the very nature of those representations or even the world they are drawn from.

References

Beard, M. (2008), *Pompeii: The Life of a Roman Town*, London: Profile.

Bourdieu, P. (1996/1992), *The Rules of Art: Genesis and Structure of the Literary Field* (translated by Susan Emanuel), Cambridge: Polity Press.

Bragg, B. (2004), 'Slaying the Racist Dragon' in *Red Pepper*. August 2004.

Cruz, J. and Lewis, J. (1994), 'Reflections upon the Encoding/Decoding Model. An Interview with Stuart Hall', in *Viewing, Reading, Listening: Audiences and Cultural Reception*, Boulder, CO: Westview Press.

Du Gay, P. (1997), *Production of Culture/Cultures of Production*, London: Sage/Open University.

Falk, P. (1997), 'The Benetton – Toscani Effect', in M. Niva and P. Falk (eds) *Buy This Book*, London: Sage.

Featherstone, M. (1991), *Consumer Culture and Postmodernism*, London: Routledge.

Fiske, J. (1991), 'Postmodernism and Television', in J. Curran and M. Gurevitch (eds) *Mass Media and Society*, London: Methuen.

Florida, R. (2002), *The Rise of the Creative Class. And how it's Transforming Work, Leisure and Everyday Life*, New York: Basic Books.

Ghost signs (2011), http://www.ghostsigns.co.uk/archive. Accessed 11 May 2011.

Gibbs, S.R. (1955), Toothpaste television advertisement, http://www.youtube.com/watch?v=pKuEwsEiSp8. Accessed 28 October 2011.

Glancey, J. (2004), 'By George!', *The Guardian*, 20 June 2004.

Gliserman, S. (1969), *Victorian Periodicals Newsletter*, No. 4, April 1969.

Grunenberg, C. and Pih, D. (2011), *Magritte A to Z*, London: Tate Publishing.

Hall, S. (1973), 'Encoding and Decoding in the Television Discourse', Stencilled Occasional Paper, Birmingham: Centre for Contemporary Cultural Studies.

—— (1981), 'Cultural Studies: Two Paradigms', in T. Bennett (ed.) *Culture, Ideology and Social Process*, Buckingham: Open University Press.

——— [1973] (2001), 'Encoding/Decoding', in M. G. Durham and D. M. Kellner (eds) *Media and Cultural Studies Keyworks,* Oxford: Blackwell.

Harvey, D. (2008), 'Right to the City', *New Left Review* 53, pp. 23–40.

Hesmondhalgh, D. (2006), 'Bourdieu, the Media and Cultural Production', in *Media, Culture & Society* 28(2), pp. 211–231.

Jefkins, F. and Yadin, D. (2000), *Advertising,* Harlow: Pearson.

Jhally, S. (2000), 'Advertising at the Edge of the Apocalypse', in R. Anderson and L. Strate (eds) *Critical Studies in Media Commercialism*, Oxford: Oxford University Press.

Kelly, A., Lawlor, K. and O'Donohoe, S. (2009), 'Encoding Advertisements: The Creative Perspective', in Joseph Turow and Matthew P. MCallister (eds) *The Advertising and Consumer Culture Reader,* Abingdon: Routledge.

Leiss, W., Kline, S. and Jhally, S. (2005), *Social Communication in Advertising,* London: Routledge.

L'Oréal (2009), Television advertisement, http://www.youtube.com/watch?v=y3EEIcPkcO4. Accessed 28 October 2011.

MacRury, I. (2009), *Advertising*, London: Routledge.

Maiuri, A. (1960), *Pompeii,* Novara: Istituto Geografico de Agostini.

McGuigan, J. (2010), *Cultural Analysis,* London: Sage.

Negus, K. (2002), 'The Work of Cultural intermediaries and the Enduring Distance Between Production and Consumption', *Cultural Studies* 16 (4), pp. 501–515.

Nixon, S. (2003), *Advertising Cultures,* London: Sage.

Powell, H. and Prasad, S. (2010), '"As seen on TV". The Celebrity Expert: How Taste is Shaped by Lifestyle Media', *Cultural Politics* Volume 6, Issue 1, pp. 111–124.

Runciman, R. (2011), 'Socialism in One County', *London Review of Books* Vol. 33 No. 15, 28 July 2011, pp. 11–13.

Scannell, P. (2000), 'For-anyone-as-someone structures', *Media, Culture and Society* 1 (22), pp. 5–24.

Schudson, M. (1993), *Advertising the Uneasy Persuasion*, London: Routledge.

Sennett, R (2008), *The Craftsman*, London: Penguin.

Shapiro, K. (1981), *The Construction of Television Commercials: Four Cases of Interorganizational Problem Solving*, Stanford: Stanford University.

Soar, M. (2000), 'Encoding Advertisements: Ideology and Meaning in Advertising Production', *Mass Communication and Society* 4, pp. 415–437.

Soper, K. (2011), 'Relax: Alternative Hedonism and a New Politics of Pleasure', *Red Pepper* August 2011.

Wallace-Hadrill, A. (1994), *Houses and Society in Pompeii and Herculaneum*, Princeton, NJ: Princeton University Press.

Williams, R. (1980), 'Advertising: The Magic System', in *Problems in Materialism and Culture,* London: Verso.

——— (1981), 'Analysis of Culture' in T. Bennett, G. Martin, C. Mercer and J. Woollacott (eds) *Culture, Ideology and Social Process,* Buckingham: Open University Press.

Williamson, J. (1978) *Decoding Advertisements, Ideology and Meaning in Advertising*, London: Boyars.

Note

1   The term 'homology' is used here to indicate the fit between an advertisement and the wider culture. This is based on a consideration of content, ideas, theme or style that is found in the wider culture but is attached to or is articulated by an advertising campaign. Homology in cultural studies also indicates the attachment of subcultural groups to objects through a process of appropriation.
2   See Plate 2: John Orlando Parry, 'A London Street Scene' 1835 – courtesy of Alfred Dunhill Museum and Archive.

Chapter 4

Handbags and gladrags - the rise and rise of accessories in fashion and advertising

Hilary Fawcett

This chapter looks at the role of advertising in the development of women's fashion accessory markets in a period marked by massive social, cultural and economic change. Women have played an increasingly important part in consumer cultures since the Second World War. Their growing financial autonomy has contributed to the rapid expansion of areas such as the fashion and beauty industries with their attendant media of women's magazines. Advertising has played a critical role in the expansion of fashion cultures and in the development of what has been described as 'structures of feeling' in relation to female subjectivity and identity. In examining the ways in which British markets in fashion accessories have advanced since the 1950s, we can identify the cultural significance of changing tropes of advertising in relation to construction of femininities and wider issues of class and identity.

There has been a massive expansion in the women's fashion accessory market in the recent past, and as a result of this, advertisements for handbags and shoes have become an increasingly dominant element in fashion magazines, and the fashion media as a whole. Established brands have widened their influence in the global market and numerous new brands have joined this ever expanding and lucrative retailing area. Why is there such an emphasis on accessories, and how has advertising contributed to the success of these products? In order to explore these issues we will first examine the development of fashion accessory markets in Britain in the post-war period, and the ways in which advertising adapted to rapidly changing economic and cultural conditions.

Post-war culture

Frank Mort in discussing Burton the Tailor's 'gentlemanly type' in the immediate pre-war period refers to the significance of fashion and style in the context of the British class system. He describes 'clothes as an expression of status, manners as visible markers of distinction; these rituals were still grounded in a vertical model of class relations' (1997: 22). This continued to be true to a greater or lesser degree after the Second World War and throughout the 1950s, despite the expansion of ready-to-wear fashion markets. Britain in the 1950s was still recovering from the Second World War and whilst the economy was slowly improving and new markets developing, the social order was still more clearly defined than would be the case in subsequent decades. High fashion was the defining system in terms of directional styles in women's fashion. It was Paris, and to a lesser extent Rome, which were central to international fashion trends. If you bought a dress from Balenciaga's Paris salon, it would be remarkable in its design and wonderful workmanship. It was distinctive; you were buying something unique which conveyed not only the status of a Paris original but also the kudos of the extremely prestigious and inimitable Balenciaga label. Across haute couture, highly skilled seamstresses were employed every season to make fashion objects of the highest quality. Advertising for these exclusive clothes was minimal. The designer's success was based on reputation, on catwalk shows and in fashion editorials in magazines such as *Vogue* and *Harper's Bazaar*. If you were wealthy enough to buy a Balenciaga, you were part of an elite international group who visited the couture houses to see and purchase. There were no diffusion lines; the status of the consumer was inviolate. Accessories to accompany these outfits would be bought from exclusive shops and boutiques, like those of Charles Jourdan and Ferragamo. As with high fashion itself these brands did not need extensive advertising budgets, they were promoted in fashion editorials and in elegant and chic window displays in stylish shopping areas such as Bond Street in London and the Rive Gauche in Paris.

Although still a period of gradual change, the 1950s did mark the beginning of broadening fashion markets and a wider access to more stylish mass-produced clothes and fashion accessories than had previously been the case. Economic, social and cultural shifts meant that there was growth in ready-to-wear markets. High fashion might still ultimately call the shots in terms of skirt lengths and overall seasonal directions, but new areas such as the nascent teenage market, meant that at high street level fresh fashion identities were slowly developing. British shoe design, manufacture and retailing in the 1950s expanded within this model. Women's weekly magazines such as *Woman* and *Woman's Own* were cheap to buy and catered for a largely working class and lower-middle-class demographic. These magazines advertised shoes and handbags, alongside other fashion items. According to David Kynaston advertising in these cheaper magazines expanded rapidly and between 1951 and 1958 *Woman* magazine's advertising revenue had quintupled (2009: 664). Modestly priced shoes by British retailers such as Barratts, Dolcis, Manfield, Freeman Hardy Willis and Clarks were promoted, not just in popular magazines but also in newspapers and on billboards. However, just as the difference between a Balenciaga gown and a Marks and Spencer dress was enormous in terms of quality and style, so was the disparity between a pair of Manfield shoes and those made by an exclusive manufacturer such as Charles Jourdan or Ferragamo.

Across all strata of the women's shoe market, stiletto heels were the great style story of the 1950s, and there were advertisements for them across the fashion media. The concept of the stiletto heel might seem glamorous, but the majority of British shoe advertising was still very tame and descriptive. Advertisements at all levels were largely monochromatic, often taking the form of drawings or sketches, with the price located boldly at the bottom of the page. The majority of handbags sold on the high street, were mass produced by British shoe manufacturers such as Manfield or Dolcis, and were made of simulated leather; plastic in other words. One of the great fashion rules of the period was that accessories should match: white shoes, white bag. The major financial outlay was for the clothes, the accessories were usually a much cheaper afterthought. To buy a real leather handbag was seen by most mass consumers as an investment, one that you might make for your trousseau or receive as a very special anniversary present.

In glossy, expensive magazines such as *Vogue* and *Harper's Bazaar*, there were advertisements for accessories, but these represented only a very small percentage of the advertising profile. Accessories were there to compliment the fashion outfit, rather than be items which had equal status to it. Matching shoes and bag were the prerequisites for 'smartness', but in high-end marketing, they are frequently made almost invisible in their tastefulness and subtlety. In accounts of the lives of fashionable young women in 1950s Britain, like that of Emma Tennant (1999), there are detailed descriptions of dresses and other types of clothing, but accessories are hardly mentioned.

Sixties society

It was in the 1960s that the fashion industry in Britain underwent an enormous change and increasing affluence made for the development of significant new markets. As the British economy expanded, unemployment began to fall dramatically. Young people were better educated and a wider demographic had access to further and higher education. Those teenagers, who left school at sixteen, were often able to choose from a range of jobs, a high percentage of which were relatively well paid. Many young people had disposable incomes to spend on clothes and leisure, and markets developed in response to this. Not only did fashion retailing expand and change but in women's fashion new magazines such as *Honey* and *Petticoat* emerged, creating spaces for more imaginative advertising and youth-orientated fashion editorial. Sean Nixon refers to Bourdieu, when describing the advertising profession in the post-war period and its development in the context of the democratisation of schooling. 'Jobs were marked by the openness of modes of entry and career structures were amenable to creative redefinition' (2003: 57). By the mid-sixties art school graduates were playing a significant part in British advertising. They brought with them new perspectives from a liberal visual education as well as an immersion in popular culture. British fashion had benefited from developments in design education which had begun in the 1950s as a result of government reforms; clothes design was the major category that had benefited from the professionalisation of training through new Art College courses, but shoe design also began to be taught in some institutions. By the mid-sixties the British shoe market looked very different from ten years before. New retailers on the High Street including Ravel and Rauol, and they were producing shoes which were highly fashionable, youth orientated and often novel in their quirkiness. Mary Quant and later Barbara Hulanicki at Biba also produced shoes to accompany their clothes ranges, which was a groundbreaking trend in the stylistic integration of accessories and fashionable clothing. Their advertising campaigns were heavily branded and iconic, but the shoes they sold were moderately priced despite this. So at this point in time when the High Street had begun to take over from haute couture in terms of fashion direction, it was possible to buy the most stylish and innovative clothes and accessories for a very modest amount. In the changing rooms at Biba, film stars mixed with secretaries and schoolgirls, all with a common desire to be at the height of fashion.

T. Elliott and Sons was a British company which was very successful in the shoe market in the second half of the 1960s. An old, established firm, they had adapted to the new youth market and by the mid-1960s were at the vanguard of not only shoe design, but also innovative advertising. A large part of their success was predicated on a series of impressive advertising campaigns which connected to the Zeitgeist. These campaigns ran in both high-end magazines and on billboards. The competition for the young market was increasing and Elliott responded imaginatively to the challenge of creating something distinctive and stylish. They employed the graphic designer Paul Christodoulou, who had designed the cover for The Beatles' *Revolver* LP. Christodoulou's style was influenced by Aubrey Beardsley recently rediscovered by a generation with an enthusiasm for Art Nouveau. This was very much a part of a collision of the canonical in fine art and the decorative arts and consumer design in the 1960s. *Alice in Wonderland* by Lewis Carroll was a cultish text in the mid-sixties, with its surreal imagery, and playful use of language (Whiteley 1987: 113). Alice also represented an aspect of the infantilised female imageries of the period. Twiggy, with her young adolescent image, was part of the omnipresent child-woman found across the fashion media.

The Elliott 'Alice' campaign began in 1966 and to add to its distinctiveness, the advertising poster could be bought for 5 shillings and thus you could pin your own version on the wall (Harris et al. 1986: 67). There was a famous BBC television adaptation of *Alice in Wonderland* in 1966, directed by Jonathan Miller, and this was essentially aimed at an adult audience. The British Pop Artist Peter Blake also used Alice as a subject of his painting. The surreal element of the Alice narrative connected with the recreational drug culture of the time, which was so influential in music and in designed objects such as album covers, posters and even fabric designs. In these Alice-influenced Elliott advertising images the shoes and boots become part of a wider cultural narrative which crosses art, literature and consumption. It assumes a common cultural understanding by its audience, but requiring a much more complex and sophisticated understanding than was the case in earlier popular product advertising campaigns.

It was in the later 1960s however that Elliott developed an advertising campaign which had a seminal significance in British shoe marketing and represented part of a new sensibility in fashion photography and fashion advertising. The romanticism of the 'Alice' campaign was left behind for a more knowing and, some might say, cynical approach to the medium. The new campaign was influenced by the iconic nudes of the photographer Bill Brandt and was orchestrated through bill board advertising as well as placements in high-end glossies. The Guy Bourdin style images showed young girls sitting on beaches, wearing only Elliott shoes or boots. The fetishistic and sexual significance of women's shoes here is overt. These images are complex and knowingly connect with a culturally sophisticated young market.

Nature is the backdrop for highly stylised photographic images in which an extremely youthful and beautiful model is shown defined only by her footwear. This is a period in which women became increasing objectified and eroticised in fashion and the media. The allusions to art photography helped to neutralise some of the more disruptive aspects of the iconography. However, the disruptive nature of these images that were emblazoned on billboards across the London Underground were not neutralised strongly enough to prevent founders of London's Women's Liberation Workshop to place campaign stickers saying, 'What are you selling?' across them.

These advertisements were designed to appeal to a sexually enfranchised younger generation. This was the period in which *Hair* was on the London stage (1968) and Ken Russell and other film directors were increasingly including nudity in their productions. The fun and slightly camp allusions to kinky boots found in media in the early 1960s were succeeded by advertising which was more openly engaged with sexuality and in which increasingly prominent photographers from both fashion and fine art backgrounds, were creating powerfully sophisticated and at times disturbing images, with which to promote fashion and fashion accessories. The concept of the absent product begins to emerge in this advertising genre, a genre in which art and advertising connect in ways which were to appeal to an increasingly visually literate consumer market.

It is in the later Elliott boot advertisements and the Guy Bourdin photographic work done for Charles Jourdan shoes, that you see the beginning of the development of the advertising style which continues to characterise fashion photography and high-end accessory promotion (de Bure 2008). Guy Bourdin was arguably the first fashion photographer to shift emphasis from product to image. He had come from a fine art background and was influenced by the paintings of Magritte and other Surrealists. 'Helmut Newton and Guy Bourdin epitomised the trend towards conventions of brutal realism and eroticism. They pushed the limits of fashion photography to produce images that shocked by questioning the foundations of fashion, and making intertextual references to other cultural debates' (Craik 1998: 67). Current fashion advertising has been significantly influenced by Bourdin and campaigns, such as that photographed by Juergen Teller for Marc Jacobs, are hardly distinguishable in style from those groundbreaking campaigns of the late 1960s and early 1970s. It is in the global expansion of these markets that things are radically different and in the past twenty years we have seen the ever-increasing significance of accessories in the fashion economy, as high-fashion clothing has begun to diminish in its market centrality.

Changing advertising cultures

The 1960s marked a critical moment in the growing sophistication of fashion cultures. It was a high point in creativity and change and the subsequent consumer landscape owes much to the developments forged in that decade. Economic problems in the 1970s contributed to a lull in the expansion of fashion markets and it was not until the economic upturn of the

1980s, the so-called Designer Decade that we see new directions and impetus in the production of fashion, fashion magazines and fashion advertising. Punk and post-punk initially affected the aesthetics of the period, but the corporatisation of fashion and the development of new global markets quickly made for an increasingly generic fashion landscape, which by the 1990s was hooked in a predictable recycling of the past. More recently new trends have emerged in the design and marketing of accessories, which have enhanced their significance and status in the context of contemporary fashion cultures and provided an expanding product area for glossy, high end advertising to flourish.

In an article by Zoe Wood in *The Guardian* newspaper in 2011 titled 'It is better to bank on a bag', she reported that 'Hermès is now bigger than Societe Generale', and described how Hermès, renowned for its fashion handbags and a firm with a 174 year history of producing craftsman made fashion items, is valued more highly than France's second biggest bank (3 September 2011). The Birkin bag starts at a price of £5400 and can cost as much as £100,000. They have been leaping off the shelves, not only in Paris, London and New York but in regional cities across the world, as sales outlets have expanded. Hermès is only one brand amongst an ever expanding range of shoe and handbag manufacturers, cashing in on what seems a relentless appetite to extravagantly accessorise. The British accessory firm Mulberry had seen its profits quadruple in 2011, as global markets lapped up their brand, which despite appearances is not an old established firm at all, but one which began in the heritage-aware 1980s. We are in a period of serious economic recession, but the manufacturers of fashion accessories are still making massive profits in a way which confounds expectation. The advertising industry is critical to the success of this phenomenon and it is through an increasing presence of advertising in the printed and digital global media that this massively profitable aspect of fashion retailing continues to flourish.

One might assume that the consumers of these high-end luxury items would be the wives of footballers, Russian oligarchs or that they are celebrities intent on being caught in the lens of the paparazzi. But no, here we are teetering on the edge of economic disaster, and those buying vastly expensive fashion accessories are not part of an exclusive elite, but according to market research, represent a broad demographic. The ship is sinking but better to go down in Louboutins, than Marks and Spencer loafers. For a decade or more luxury brands have been promoted across a wider range of fashion media than ever before. Shoes and handbags are the central and most lucrative elements in the current fashion economy. The availability of easy credit through the noughties and into the present period has meant that buying expensive items on 'plastic' has become an acceptable phenomenon. Impulse buying has been condoned and accepted in an advertising culture which justifies extravagance with the epithet 'Because you are worth it'.

Celebrities such as Coleen Rooney and Cheryl Cole, whose ordinariness, transformed into hyper fashionability, is the main part of their appeal, make the buying of expensive accessories seem more acceptable for those on modest incomes. The days when it was royalty, the mega rich or Hollywood icons who were the standard bearers for exclusive fashion brands are gone. It is now 'the girl next door', who graces the glossies in Jimmy

Choos, carrying her Prada handbag: the girl from the council estate in Newcastle, or the tougher end of Liverpool, is herself now a commodity, a brand promoting other brands. National credit is drying up, but personal debt is being extended by aspirational consumers, still emulating a glamour which is constructed not within the star system, nor on the catwalk, but within the complex web of the fashion and advertising media. Mica Nava speaks of one of the functions of consuming fashion as consolation, 'Consumerism is far more than just economic activity: It is also about dreams and consolation, communication and confrontation, image and identity' (1992: 167). It is possible that consolation plays a larger part in the fevered economic times we live in than in periods of less stress, the buying of Jimmy Choos is to fly in the face of imminent disaster, a reckless but consoling gesture in a very uncertain world. The consumer's desire for status and identity are still key factors in driving the markets, but there is an increasingly febrile desperation about it all as the fashion industry expands ever outwards.

Magazines are central to the promotion of fashion items, and the printed and digital media have rolled out endless new titles in the past twenty years. Some have crashed, but some like the magazine *Grazia* have become new staples in the contemporary fashion media. *Grazia* was first published in Britain in 2007, and cleverly marketed as a cheaper fortnightly glossy, as opposed to the monthly and more expensive *Vogue, Elle, Marie Claire, Red, Harper's Bazaar*, etc. *Grazia* promotes high-end celebrity fashion to a broad readership of young women, and advertises expensive luxury items alongside the high street versions. There is no doubt that the magazine has in some ways contributed to a normalising of the buying of extravagant accessories to its broad readership. Fashion magazines play a central role in the conditioning of taste and identity for young women and magazines like *Grazia* and *Glamour*, another relatively recent addition to the genre, have an identity predicated on the endorsement of celebrity fashion.

> The fashion magazines and fashion press operate within the economy of looking. They also produce distinct cultural values which feed directly into the formation of taste groups for the broader consumer culture. The editors provide the advertisers with an appropriate visual environment within which they can sell their own copy. So the visual pleasures of the fashion pages are actually used indirectly to sell perfume, make-up, shoes, bags, in fact all those goods whose market size allows them to pay for expensive advertising space.
>
> (McRobbie 1998: 197)

The increasing emphasis on accessories in fashion editorial and advertising in the last twenty years is explicable for a number of reasons. Rebecca Arnold states that 'there was a tangible increase in fashion in the early 1990s, prompted by the economic recession that saw numerous fashion designers go out of business and seemed to herald the imminent demise of couture' (2001: 93). It was the development of the perfume and accessories markets that saved many couture houses from going under at this point and has continued to sustain them. Economic factors aside, fashionable clothing has become increasingly generic in style.

Designers have run out of options as one sixties revival runs into another. The High Street immediately assimilates every nuance in directional fashion and sells cheaper and often indistinguishable versions of the original. The time when distinction comprised high quality fabrics, cut and workmanship as in those 1950s gowns by Balenciaga has gone. It is now hard to distinguish the real Stella McCartney from the Primark version. It is easier however to recognise the classic Prada bag, or Blahnik shoes. You can see the logo, the expensive materials used and the meticulous attention to detail. The red soles on Louboutin shoes are a trademark fiercely defended by the firm's legal team. Exclusivity is protected by patented trademarks. To describe someone as wearing Blahniks, Choos or Louboutins, is for them to be immediately defined as successful, glamorous and sexy. The shoes have it; they have become the markers of status and style.

Manolo Blahniks were the first shoes to be an iconic 'must have' in the post-1980s world of high-end accessories and an advertisement from 1992 shows the development of a 'house style' (Figure 4.1). Jimmy Choo and now Louboutin have joined Blahnik as the most referenced luxury brand shoes, filling the pages of chick lit and the shots in chick flicks, and featuring most famously perhaps in the American television series *Sex and the City*. The now-defunct *Sex and the City* was a post-feminist idyll of Jimmy Choos, sex toys and skinny latte. The increasing sexualisation of women in marketing and the media, from Ann Summers to MTV, has affected the significance of shoes in the construction of the feminine ideal. Over the past twenty years or more this identification of glamorous shoes with contemporary femininity has been reflected in increasing numbers of products using shoes as an indicator of what is culturally defined as 'girliness', but in reality means heightened glamour and seductiveness. Birthday cards, cushions, birthday cakes, handbags, etc., have been emblazoned with high-heeled, sexy shoes. Shoes are highly fetishised and long established as sexual objects. We are living in a period of cultural hyper-sexualisation. The iconic cover of the massively successful novel about the fashion industry *The Devil Wears Prada*, shows a bright red stiletto-heeled shoe, the heel of which branches out into the devils trident (Weisberger 2003). The connection between shoes, power, glamour and sex is one which is relentlessly referenced in popular culture.

From the late 1990s, the concept of glamour has been ever more central in women's fashion markets. The body has been on show, and high shoes accentuate calves and thighs contributing to the Jessica Rabbit silhouette, favoured by the media. We have seen the relentless progress of ever more elevated heels and excessively stylised and exotic shoe styles. The kind of shoes worn by celebrities on red carpet occasions, are being worn by women all day and every day. Traditional notions of 'good taste', attached to restraint and a 'less is more' aesthetic, have been largely abandoned by the fashion industry in the promotion of five-inch heels in myriad colours and styles. Women from a wide range of economic backgrounds are buying extremely expensive designer accessories. Just as the fashion shoes become ever more perilous in terms of height and styling, so does the economic situation and yet there is no sign of a slump on this front as sales hold fast.

Shoes and bags have increasingly become the main fashion event, whether on the Web or in the printed media. Looking across fashion magazines, most notably *Vogue*, *Tatler* and *Harper's*, it is clear to see that accessory advertising has taken over from perfume and even clothes advertising as the major area of focus. In British *Vogue*, September 2011, we find forty-seven advertisements for shoes and handbags. Some advertisements, like those for Prada and Armani, combine clothes and accessories. Long-established couture houses have diversified into accessory retailing in the past ten years or more. Most of the advertisements are sumptuous, highly stylised, relentlessly promoting glossy urban chic. With so many brands jostling for attention and many of the products bearing strong similarities to each other, it was never more necessary to create a strong brand image. The minimal text in the double spread Loewe advertisement announces that the firm has been in business since 1846. Increasingly in this competitive arena, long-established firms are stressing their pedigree, to distinguish them as quality brands in an increasingly overcrowded market. The Loewe image is one of a naked woman, lying on a bed holding two strategically placed handbags. The image is beautifully photographed and lit, using a palette of fashionable and subtle blues and greens with splashes of orange in the handbags and the woman's makeup and hair decoration. It has an exotic feel, which references erotic nineteenth-century Japanese prints: opulent and sensual, with an unconventional-looking model indicating that the product does not conform to dominant street glamour.

Prada is another brand which is promoting a less conventional identity on its double-page spread of 'Björk type' young models wearing subtly coloured sequined frocks, with bonnets to match; looking innocent and childlike. The boots and bags although conventional to a degree have colour and design details which are more playful than the majority of the products on display in the magazine. The current Gucci advertisement is much more accessible than those of Prada and Loewe. A large red glossy handbag is placed at the forefront of what looks like a night club lounge, where highly glamorous hostesses seem to be awaiting their evening's trade. It could be an ironic take on Berlusconi's Italy. It is emphatically sexy, as is the advertisement for Versace boots. Italian fashion branding can be subtle, but can often be characterised by a strongly erotic style.

The Tom Ford advertisement in the same issue of *Vogue*, is 1980s New York glamour. Its strong American identity is clearly delineated in a *Bonfire of the Vanities* tableau, all glossy red nails, lipstick and purple glossy bag – an image that stares the recession in the face. One of the most interesting adverts in this selection, is that for Marc Jacobs in which Juergen Teller has photographed Helena Bonham Carter, in a style highly reminiscent of Bourdin. It is a double spread with two separate images, each photographed at an oblique angle, which say as much about the quirky persona of Bonham Carter as the outfit and shoes which are being promoted. Indeed the fashion items themselves are partially hidden. This advertisement stands out as being self-consciously artful, aimed at a consumer who understands the referential framework. Interestingly of all the advertising images Manolo Blahnik's is the most simple. It comprises a coloured drawing of a shoe, but unlike those sketches used to illustrate shoes in 1950s advertising, it is an emphatic and expressive image, indicating the status and inimitability of the brand. For shoes, read Blahnik.

Advertising significantly outweighs editorial in the content of *Vogue*, and the majority of current glossies. It is often difficult to differentiate advertisements from text, in that the photographic style and direction collapses one into the other. There is an article in the September 2011, British edition of *Vogue* which describes the persistent influence of the 1960s on fashion. Indeed the influence of this decade has been present in fashion cultures for many years, and even more than ever in the past decade. Flicking through contemporary magazines and looking at advertising images, there are many that could just as easily have been positioned in a late 1960s fashion magazine. It is as if the fashion media is caught forever at that critical point of expansion and energy. It is a nostalgic preoccupation, which blocks out the dystopian freneticism and desperation for novelty which marks contemporary fashion cultures. It is as if the industry identifies the 1960s as the 'gold standard' in fashion, a point of optimism, certainty and innovation, which continues to engage consumers in looking back, rather than at what may lie ahead.

The increasing financial pressures in the printed media have resulted in the inclusion of ever larger amounts of advertising to shore up production costs. In *Vogue* magazine, from the late 1960s to the mid-1990s, advertising played a relatively small role in the content of the magazine, with accessory advertising being only a very minor part. Perfume and cosmetics, linked to major fashion houses, were a dominant advertising element in the glossies from the late 1980s. In *Vogue*, January 1987, we find only two advertisements for accessories amongst advertisements for clothes, cars, perfume and cosmetics. In *Vogue*, January 1992, the majority of the advertisements were for perfumes, with no advertisements for shoes or bags at all. However, accessories are an even more lucrative market than perfume, and that is something which fashion houses have come to recognise and this explains in part, the significant increase in their prominence in the fashion media.

It is not just magazines, websites and blogs which promote high-end accessories, newspapers desperate for income from advertising also promote exclusive brands. In the September edition of *Lux*, *The Times* newspaper's very metropolitan and high-end fashion magazine, we find their hot list of things to buy includes Céline's 'iconic' Trapeze bag for £2300, and this is very much an average price for a high-end designer bag. The advertisement for the elegant Jimmy Choo boots on the back page has no price tag. Advertising of seemingly exclusive products is price on application, like buying a Picasso or a Van Cleef & Arpels diamond necklace. These items are sold in the global market, in Mumbai and Tokyo, in Dubai and Moscow as well as New York and London. The world economy is in crisis, who knows what lies ahead. The hedonism and aspiration which has characterised the global fashion market in the past fifteen years, is now up for question. Indeed it may be that high fashion and expensive fashion accessories will return to being the preserve of the wealthy elite, just as they were in the 1950s. As with so many things it is difficult to predict the results of what seems to be a significant shift in the global economic order.

For women, fashion provides pleasure, but also significant economic and personal pressures, which are attached to the increasing expansion and impact of fashion cultures and their centrality in the contemporary media. Where at first postmodern culture seemed to offer spaces for difference for women in relation to fashion and fashioning, the reality in the more recent past has been a closing down of difference and an increasing generalisation in terms of female representation and identity. Sex sells, and the representation of female identity has been increasingly reductive in a media suffused by images of youth and glamour. We face an uncertain future economically and socially. Fashion can be fun, but it is also a complex and at times problematic part of the shaping of femininity. I would argue that the advertising media and fashion itself have responsibilities to consumers and society. Shoes and bags may once have seemed a peripheral market on the edges of the fashion industry, but accessories have evolved into an extremely lucrative market which stands at an axis of class, identity and gender. It is a useful model for an exploration of contemporary advertising cultures and their role, both economic and cultural, in the fashioning of femininity.

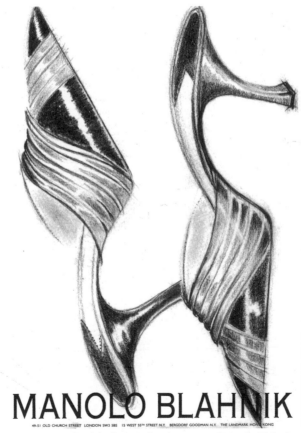

MANOLO BLAHNIK

49-51 OLD CHURCH STREET LONDON SW3 5BS   15 WEST 55TH STREET N.Y.   BERGDORF GOODMAN N.Y.   THE LANDMARK HONG KONG

Figure 4.1: Manolo Blahnik: reproduced courtesy of Manolo Blahnik.

References

Arnold, R. (2001), *Fashion, Desire and Anxiety: Image and Morality in the Twentieth Century*, London: I B Tauris.

Craik, J. (1998), *The Face of Fashion: Cultural Studies in Fashion*, London: Routledge.

De Bure, G. (2008), *Guy Bourdin*, London: Thames and Hudson.

Harris, J., Hyde, S. and Smith, G. (1986), *1966 and All That: Design and the Consumer in Britain 1960–69*, London: Trefoil Design Library.

Kynaston, D. (2009), *Family Britain: 1951–57*, London: Bloomsbury.

McRobbie, A. (1998), *British Fashion Design: Rag Trade or Image Industry*, London: Routledge.

Mort, F. (1997), 'Paths to Mass Consumption' in M. Nava, A. Blake, I. MacRury, and B. Richards (eds) *Buy this Book: Studies in Advertising and Consumption*, London: Routledge.

Nava, M. (1992), *Changing Cultures, Feminism, Youth and Consumerism*, London: Sage.

Nixon, S. (2003), *Advertising Cultures: Gender, Commerce, Creativity*, London: Sage.

Tennant, E. (1999), *Girlitude: A Portrait of the 1950s and 60s*, London: Jonathan Cape.

Weisberger, L. (2003), *The Devil Wears Prada*, London: Harper Collins.

Whiteley, N. (1987), *Pop Design: Modernism to Mod-Pop, Theory and Design, 1952–1972*, London: Design Council.

Chapter 5

Music and advertising – a happy marriage?

Judith Stevenson

The first episode of the new series of the long-running televised talent show *The X-Factor* was screened on the British commercial channel ITV1 on Saturday, 20 August 2011. The programme started at 20.00 and finished at 21.15. Of these seventy-five minutes, at least sixteen were devoted to advertisement breaks. Of the total thirty-two advertisements shown, eight used original popular songs from a range of popular musical genres and decades. Only two out of the thirty-two had no music at all. The remaining nineteen had some form of incidental music. In addition to these sixteen minutes there were a further ten advertisements by the communication company TalkTalk (not the band Talk Talk or their song) who sponsor the show. In these advertisements members of the public act to pieces of music including 'Acceptable in the Eighties' by Calvin Harris, 'Unchained Melody' by the Righteous Brothers and '99 Red Balloons' by Nena.

It could be argued that *The X-Factor* as a musical entertainment show in a prime advertising slot is likely to attract music-orientated advertisements. However, non-music shows across all commercial TV channels have shown a similar pattern; there are an unprecedented amount of adverts, a large majority of which engage with music in some form or another.

The aim of this chapter is to examine the deepening relationship between advertising and music providing an overview and analysis of the ways in which contemporary advertising engages with popular music. The chapter engages with one of the overarching themes of this book; how advertising and culture sit alongside each other and often overlap. However, it is argued that ultimately music and advertising must be seen as two separate entities that have distinctive and disjunctive existences and meanings. This chapter examines themes and issues pertaining to the relationship between music and advertising, acknowledging the complexity and ambiguity apparent in the reception of advertisements that use music. These themes include the motif of the crowd in contemporary advertisements, Pop Art, advertising and The Who rock group; an overview of the cultural appropriation of music in fashion advertising; and a wider analysis of the symbiotic relationship between music and advertising.

The main focus is with advertisements that use original songs that were produced for other purposes rather than produced specifically for advertising. The term 'pop music' is used in this chapter to refer to pop, rock, indie, R&B and other broad genres of popular music as opposed to classical or instrumental styles. Although the majority of examples utilised in the text are from the twenty-first century, many from 2011, older examples will also be used to track and trace the history of the link between advertising and music.

A cultural engagement

Just as changes in technology have altered the face of advertising in the past three decades, changes in the technology and economics of the music industry have altered the way that music is produced. It has also changed the way music is consumed. If you wanted to hear a specific song outside a live performance in the second half of the twentieth century, you would have had to buy the record or wait for the chance to hear it on radio or on one of the limited music programmes on television. There were concerns about the copying of music with the introduction of tape-recording technology, but with legal warnings on the inner sleeves of LPs, musicians and record companies received the vast share of the profits from their work. In the twenty-first century things are entirely different. Information about specific music tracks can be gleaned from a vast array of music and band websites. Tracks can be downloaded within minutes from sites such as Spotify, 7Digital, Amazon, iMesh and iTunes. Although this is often a service that is paid for, it has become increasingly easy to download and access music without the musicians and music companies receiving payment for this exchange. In terms of marketing and business, the changes that have occurred in the past decade have affected the once-omnipotent record companies in a variety of adverse ways. One of the ways that the music industry has coped with this crisis is in its increasing engagement with advertising and marketing.

The most noticeable way music is used in advertising is when an original, often familiar song is appropriated to advertise a product in a television, cinema or viral advert. One of the earliest examples of this was the New Seekers who wanted to teach the world to sing by encouraging increased consumption of Coca-Cola (1971); the saccharine lyrics of the song matched the sweetness of the drink. Stand-out examples in the eighties include the use of a range of classic soul, Motown and blues tracks for Levi's jeans. Every track on Moby's album *Play* (1999) was licensed to different advertisements in the nineties and noughties. Current examples of association between music and advertising include 'Days' by The Kinks for Golf Cabriolet, 'Wipeout' by The Surfaris to advertise MoneySupermarket, 'Glad All Over' by The Dave Clark Five for McDonald's, 'God Only Knows' by the Beach Boys for Volkswagen and Primal Scream's 'Moving On Up' for Kelloggs Corn Flakes. On occasion the same song will be used in more than one commercial; Goldfrapp's 'Ooh La La' can currently be heard in a Vauxhall Corsa advertisement and in a L'Oréal commercial for Spike Fanatic Sculpting Gel. This is the most common connection between popular music and advertising.

In addition, but less frequently, singers and musicians are sometimes employed to advertise specific products. Examples of this mode include pop stars such as Justin Timberlake performing for McDonald's, Michael Jackson and Beyonce for Pepsi and Madonna for Louis Vuitton and Dolce & Gabbana. There are also less obvious and at times totally confounding examples of this association; Lemmy from Motorhead playing classical violin in a commercial for KitKat and slowing down 'Ace of Spades' for Kronenbourg lager, the smoothing out of John Lydon (Sex Pistols, PiL) for Country Life butter, the godfather of punk Iggy Pop contorting with a puppet for Swift Insurance and the Mancunian punk poet, John Cooper Clarke appearing in Sugar Puffs commercials.

Janis Joplin sang about Mercedes Benz and Porsche (1971), Coca-Cola featured in The Kinks' 'Lola' (1970), Listerine and SR toothpaste in 'Germ Free Adolescence' by X-Ray Spex (1978), fronted by the late Poly Styrene and Snuff committing the Shake 'n' Vac advertisement to vinyl (1990): products and brand names have on many occasions cropped up in song lyrics. One of the most popular tracks of 2011, 'Forget You' by CeeLo Green references Atari, X-Box and Ferrari. This follows a long line of tradition in some R'n'B, rap and hip hop that embraces conspicuous consumption, brand names and in which products are referenced in the lyrics to songs, examples include 'My Adidas' by RUN DMC, 'Gin and Juice' (Seagram's and Tanqueray gin) by Snoop Dogg and 'Pass the Courvoisier' by Busta Rhymes.

A further example of the connection between music and advertising is apparent in the sponsoring of venues (O2, Carling), festivals; T in the Park (Tennents), Reading and Leeds (Carling), Wireless Festival (Barclaycard) and music awards; Mercury Music Prize is sponsored by Barclaycard and the Brit Awards by Mastercard.

It might be the case that there is a broader association between music and commercialisation that is apparent in fashion and fashion advertising. Fashion and music came together in the hijacking, re-contextualisation and rebranding of music genres and logos. Northern Soul was an underground aspect of sixties and seventies soul music which thrived on its exclusivity and participant's knowledge of obscure soul tracks. Today the *Northern Soul Keep the Faith* logo is found emblazoned on school satchels.

The terms 'rockstar' and 'rock 'n' roll' and band logos such as Motorhead, AC/DC and the Ramones can now be seen on clothing for children and babies. What was seen in previous decades as underground, rebellious and anti-authoritarian is now viewed as acceptable: a part of mainstream culture and marketing. This is not a new phenomenon; underground fashion, music and culture have often been appropriated by the mainstream, especially since the 1960s, what is missing is the original context. Rock music has essentially been concerned with expressing the concepts of sex, drugs and rock 'n' roll. What was once deemed the cause of moral panics has now been robbed of its original intended meanings. Certain companies can be accused of attempting to co-opt the edginess associated with certain bands and music as a means of achieving a cultural cache.

Companies can also co-opt the cultural cache associated with certain brands that have a long history and association with music. A prime example of this is the purchase of the Converse brand by Nike in 2003 and by default, the cultural and counter-cultural connotations that the Converse brand embodied. This included a range of iconic imagery; a foot dressed in (assumed) Converse hightops in the opening shot of the video for Nirvana's 'Smells Like Teen Spirit' (1991), photographs of The Strokes on their debut LP (2001), images of Thurston Moore and Steve Shelley from Sonic Youth and photographs of the Ramones, The Clash, Nirvana, Green Day and their fans wearing Converse. Converse did not advertise before it was acquired by Nike. It was obvious that something had changed when Will Smith received a pair of 'Converse All Stars Vintage 2004' sneakers in a fantastic piece of product placement in the film, *I, Robot* (2004). In recent years Advertising by Nike for Converse has taken full advantage of the brand's rich musical and cultural connections.

The crowd – a new visual motif?

Styles, themes and motifs in advertising constantly change. Advertising as in all media aims to reflect and mirror cultural trends, fashions and concerns. An emerging motif in contemporary advertising is that of the group or crowd of young people. The 2007 Carling advertisement, 'Belong', begins with an image of a quiet idyllic countryside setting, followed by a close up of two starlings before the camera captures an enormous flock of starlings as they meander and curve, forming biomorphic shapes across the sky. The final frame shows the familiar shape and colour of the Carling Logo, but with 'Carling' replaced by 'Belong'. The soundtrack of this advertisement is by a band called Hard-Fi, repeating the line 'going out tonight' and is titled 'Living for the Weekend'. Carling suggest that they wanted to show 'togetherness and inclusive sociability and to associate Carling with the joy of participating in social activity' (Davidson 2007). Since the appearance of this advertisement, a recurring motif within contemporary advertising has been the representation of a group or crowd. T-Mobile's flash-mob advertisements of the past few years brought a different approach to music and advertising. Other advertisements from companies such as Brothers Cider to Right Guard anti-perspirant show revellers at gigs, festivals or clubs; all beautiful and happy; a new kind of stereotype. Similar poses recur; a crowd of young people jumping in the air in synchronised harmony, a young woman, arm in the air, look of utter contentment on her perfect face, as she moves her head away from the view of the camera, lost in musical reverie. These examples are interesting for many different reasons. The connection between music and advertising in the eighties, through the nineties and into the new millennium was about personalising music – the Sony Walkman, personal stereos, iPods etc., suggested music listening as a private, personal, pleasure. Recent ads using the crowd motif seem to suggest a different perspective on engaging with music in the twenty-first century. Incidentally this is also reflected in advertisements of the past few years relating to gaming products. These advertisements depict groups of people; friends, families, social groups playing Wii, Guitar Hero, etc. This goes against the stereotype of a lone individual engaging with technology. Is this a positive message or just a new way, a new motif to sell things? Could this reflect wider changes within British society and politics – a movement away from the individualistic, to a more collective, communal identity? It is interesting to note that this power of the collective, specifically young people has become apparent in British society in the past year, specifically in the student protests against the increase in tuition fees. Perhaps there is a sense of this in the recent organisation of rioting and looting in London, Manchester and Birmingham in Summer 2011. Much of this was arranged through collective social media such as Twitter and Facebook.

A symbiotic relationship?

The reason that most of us take part in musical activity, be it composing, performing, or listening, is that music is capable of arousing in us deep and significant emotions. These emotions can range from the 'pure' aesthetic delight in a sound construction, through emotions like joy or sorrow which music sometimes evokes or enhances, to the simple relief from monotony, boredom or depression which everyday musical experiences can provide.

(Slobada 1985: 1)

There are a number of reasons why companies are paying large sums of money to use popular songs in their commercials. Music plays an important role in setting the tone for a commercial and can be used for entertainment, to target an audience, and/ or to create an emotional or nostalgic connection with the viewer.

(Belch and Belch 2007: 288)

Music can be the stimulus that ties a particular musical arrangement, jingle or song to a certain product or company … As soon as the tune begins, consumers know what product is being advertised because they have been conditioned to tie the product to the music. Brand awareness, brand equity and brand loyalty are easier to develop when consumers are familiar with the music. This happens when consumers transfer an emotional affinity for the song to the product.

(Clow and Baack 2007: 181)

These statements demonstrate why companies use music in their advertisements. It is not really surprising that advertising has engaged with music in such a variety of ways. For many people music is an essential part of their lives and an important aspect of identity. Generations are defined by popular music. Knowledge of specific genres of music can play an essential role in being accepted as part of a subculture. Clinical trials have found that listening to music can produce the 'happy hormone' serotonin, and aid in the treatment of depression. Studies by Saxton (2005) demonstrate how music is a quintessential factor in the lives of one of the main target groups for advertisers, the 16-to 24-years market. This research demonstrated that music plays a much more significant role in the lives of this age group than sport, cinema or going to the pub. This is why companies turn to and involve music in their enterprises.

The relationship between advertising and music is not only to the benefit of the advertiser or business, it can also, at times, be beneficial to artists, musicians and record companies. It can raise the profile of an artist. Musicians can get their music heard by a wider audience which can lead to increased music sales or even just raising awareness of a specific band or song. A viewer/listener of an advertisement may not consider purchasing the product that is being advertised but may instead buy or revisit the music that is being used in the advertisement. Informal research conducted by the author whilst working in record stores in the eighties and nineties, indicates that advertising significantly affects the stature and status of a band or a song. A frequent question from members of the music-buying public was 'do you have the song from that advertisement?' A significant increase in sales of an artist's work was often evidence of a song being used to advertise a specific product. For instance, Ben E. King's song 'Stand by Me' was released in 1961 and the highest position 'Stand by Me' reached in the British pop charts that year was number twenty-seven. The track was re-released in 1987 coinciding with an advertisement for Levi's jeans. It went to number one in the British charts. 'I Heard it through the Grapevine' by Marvin Gaye revisited the number one spot in 1986, seventeen years after its initial release in 1969, having been the music that accompanied the famous Levi's launderette ad.

However, this symbiotic relationship is not necessarily a win-win situation. As Stephanie O'Donohoe points out in her study of young adults, intertextuality and advertising: 'There was no automatic link between recognising and liking the music and liking the ad which used it' (O'Donohoe 1997). Bands and musicians can lose respect and even fans by allowing their music to be used in a commercial manner. O'Donohoe also mentions in her study negative opinions (pop stars accused of selling out) aimed at musicians who were featured in advertisements (O'Donohoe 1997).

At times musicians and bands may not have total control over the music that they make. The ownership of rights to music is not always straightforward. Music can be used in advertisements against the wishes of those who created the music. Music copyright is complicated and complex, the creators of a piece of music do not always own that music; as Bethany Klein in her book *As Heard on TV: Popular Music in Advertising* points out, authorship of music is not the same as ownership (2009). Klein uses as an example of this the use of The Beatles track 'Revolution' for a Nike advertisement. The song had associations with sixties counterculture and rebellion and seemed to many Beatles fans antithetical to the corporate giant that is Nike. In fact the music was not owned by The Beatles at all but by Michael Jackson who had bought the copyright of some of The Beatles' back catalogue. There have at times been long, protracted court cases over the use of licensing tracks to advertisements, examples of this include Jello Biafra against the rest of the Dead Kennedys to stop the use of 'Holiday in Cambodia' being used in a Levi's commercial and a legal battle between Tom Waits and Levi's over the use of his song 'Heart Attack and Vine'.

In the twenty-first century, one has to wonder if the use of original songs in advertising is working anymore and whether advertising is saturated with popular music. It seems to be the norm now for bands and musicians from a broad range of musical genres to allow their music to be used in advertising.

With more companies than ever using music in their ads, there is concern that the practice has gotten out of hand. Some critics note that watching TV commercials these days is almost like turning the radio dial as more songs from every kind of era and every kind of artist can be heard.

(Belch and Belch 2007: 288)

Pop Art, pop music and advertising

One of the earliest manifestations of the collaboration between music and advertising is the 1967 album by The Who, *The Who Sell Out*. The cover of the album shows the four band members appearing in spoof advertisements for leading brands of the time. Roger Daltrey sits in a bath full of Heinz Baked Beans, Pete Townshend applies a gigantic Odorono deodorant stick to his armpit, Keith Moon covers an enormous blemish on his cheek with a large tube of Medac acne cream and John Entwistle appears in a pastiche of many muscle building advertisements that were prevalent in the 1960s. The songs on *The Who Sell Out* are interspersed with pastiche jingles and advertisements similar to those heard on pirate radio. This embracing of advertising goes far beyond the usual music and advertising relationship, Dave Marsh in his biography of The Who recounts:

At one stage, Chris Stamp (The Who's manager) was approaching potential advertisers to sell space on the album, but he gave up on this plan (it was Pete's idea) when only Coke seemed interested. The Who had done a commercial for the beverage company as part of a campaign in which it hired dozens of pop singers and groups (from Aretha Franklin and Ray Charles to the Beach Boys and the Troggs).

(Marsh 1983: 278)

In some ways this absolute engagement between The Who, music and advertising is not surprising. It could be argued that in many ways, *The Who Sell Out* represents an early example of postmodernism by combining the usually separate identities of music, advertising and art. Utilising pastiche, parody and consumerism were features of sixties and later postmodern culture. Pete Townshend had attended art school and was familiar with theoretical debates surrounding art and culture and along with the rest of the band was very much part of and aware of sixties counterculture and art. Keith Moon wore a T-shirt with a reproduction of a painting called *Blaze* (1962) by the British Pop Art painter Bridget Riley. Iconographical elements associated with Mod fashion (targets, flags) were borrowed from the American artist Jasper Johns' Flag and Target paintings from the fifties and sixties. According to Marsh, Townshend loved Pop Art, covering the walls of his flat with images from a Pop Art book that he had stolen from the Ealing Art School library. Marsh mentions Kit Lambert, The Who's manager, recalling that 'late at night he and Townshend would discuss the concept of The Who as it ought to be, and Kit began to describe The Who as the first Pop Art band' (Marsh 1983: 168).

A major aspect of Pop Art was the embracing of and engaging with popular culture and the ephemera of consumer culture of which advertising was an essential part. The subject matter of Pop Art was the antithesis of the abstraction and purity of modernism that had by the mid-twentieth century become the dominant mode of modern art. Film stars, teen magazines, fashion, consumer products, new technology, comic strips, glamour models and pop stars were consistent motifs in Pop Art. As well as engaging with popular culture for its subject matter, Pop Art used techniques from popular culture, advertising and mass production. The tiny dots that constituted Roy Lichtenstein's paintings were appropriated from newspaper and comic production techniques. Andy Warhol used mass production techniques in his screen prints of Campbell's Soup cans and Coca-Cola bottles, called his studio, the Factory and said 'I want to be a machine'. The American Pop Artist James Rosenquist started work as a commercial artist and billboard painter. Pop Art had perhaps more in common with advertising than it did with the painting, sculpture and fine art practice of previous decades. In 1957, Richard Hamilton said that 'Pop Art should be; Popular (designed for a mass audience), Transient (short-term solution), Expendable (easily forgotten), Low-cost, Mass-produced, Young (aimed at youth), Witty, Sexy, Gimmicky, Glamorous, Big Business' (Hamilton 1982: 28). This created a stronger association with the aims and objectives of advertising than with fine art. The Who's embrace of advertising in *The Who Sell Out* album proved to be an understanding of and an engagement with the broader cultural zeitgeist of the sixties.

Who sold out?

Since the sixties, music by The Who has been used to advertise a range of television programmes (*CSI*, *American Superbowl*) and to advertise a variety of products ('Happy Jack' for the H2 Hummer, 'Join Together' for Nissan Maxima, 'My Generation' for Pepsi and 'Pinball Wizard' for Saab). Townshend, like many musicians who have let their music be used to advertise products, has been accused of 'selling out'. Defending himself against this accusation, Townshend responded:

> Defend myself against whom? The rock 'n' roll thought police? I sell out every time I drag my weary old ass out on the road to play classic rock to beer-drinking saps who should know better. This may be art, but I own the copyright. I come from a musical family. I know music is special. But I also know it is how my family lives. I am quite unsentimental about it, unlike some of our fans.

> (Townshend 2006)

Similarily John Lydon from the Sex Pistols and PiL was widely criticised for appearing in advertisements for Country Life butter, many feeling that the man who embodied the punk ethos should not be engaging with the corporate machine of advertising. However in an interview with *NME*, Lydon states that these ads funded a PiL reunion tour and production of new music:

> I'm permanently out of pocket, but I've got news for you, from the first day I started PiL I was out of pocket. For me it's an ongoing process. For 18 years I haven't been able to fund this, so when the butter advert came along I was more than ecstatic.
>
> (Lydon 2010).

The view that music belongs to the artists who create it is proclaimed by musicians and fans alike. Music forums led by the public such as drownedinsound.com/community appear quite antagonistic to anyone who challenges this point of view. There is a belief that the musicians who created the music 'own' that music and as Lydon and Townshend point out, it is theirs to do with whatever they choose.

Flipside

Critics of commercial culture oppose the deepening of the relationship between music and advertising, arguing that music has value and significance beyond that of commercial gain. There has always been a vehement anti-corporate aspect of music evidenced in the alternative music scene represented by bands like Fugazi, record labels such as Dischord and SST records and music festivals such as All Tomorrow's Parties and the Bowlie Weekender. In addition some of the most famous and successful musicians in the world such as Neil Young and Bruce Springsteen refuse to allow their music to be used in advertising of any sort.

In many ways it is understandable that there is opposition to the use of certain songs being used in advertising. People bring specific meaning to pieces of music and can attach their own personal feelings and emotional connections to them. It makes sense that if you have associated a piece of music with loved ones, a marriage, a memory or a significant life experience you may not specifically want a car, van, yoghurt, breakfast cereal or other product to be associated with this mix. One song will mean many different things to different viewers and listeners. There is not just one reading of a piece of music, it is polysemic, like most art forms it is open to various different, subjective and cultural interpretations. Perhaps this is what jars. Advertisements are less open to this kind of interpretation. Advertisements primarily distribute messages about products and services – there is less ambiguity and ambivalence. The rich experience of listening to and interpretation of music is perhaps narrowed by association with an advertisement.

It seems prudent and astute to acknowledge the complexities of the relationship between advertising, consumerism and marketing and not to see it as a benign connection. Publications such as *No Logo* (Klein 2000) *Culture Jam* (Lasn 1999), essays such as *Advertising at the End of the Apocalypse* (Jhally 2000) and Adbusters online and their magazine point towards the dangers to society, economics and culture that an over-commercialised culture (of which advertising plays an essential part) will inevitably bring. Bethany Klein also warns against the hypercommericialism of culture and uncritical acceptance of the relationship between pop music and advertising:

> That critics, music fans, and musicians express discomfort with and disapproval of the increasingly comfortable relationships between artists and corporations indicates a genuine cultural dilemma. Perhaps an even more pressing dilemma is the quieting of such discourse over time, suggesting a powerless resignation to the contemporary media environment and its associated objectionable trends and practices. Both popular music and advertising exist as cultural-commercial hybrids, making claims of art as well as charges of commercialism subject to deliberation. Dismissing the art versus commerce divide as constructed and the 'sell-out' debates as antiquated conceals the importance of acknowledging and investigating these tensions within and between the popular music and advertising worlds. When fans and critics perceive a line to be crossed, it is not necessary to redraw or reject the line, but to assess who is in control and to what end.
>
> (Klein 2009: 138)

Conclusion

There is no denying the power of advertising. It is everywhere, ubiquitous and omnipresent. Advertising, as this book suggests, engages with all aspects of media and culture in Western, capitalist societies. Culture is complex and ever changing and advertising plays a significant part in this. This chapter has shown that music has increasingly become a major part of the advertising mix. From sponsorship deals, festivals and venues to pop stars appearing in advertisements and their music being used to promote a vast and diverse array of products: it is unlikely that this union is going to end. The interaction between music and advertising is in many ways beneficial to both. However they are separate and distinct cultural forms. Advertising and music are not synonomous: advertising is advertising and music is music. A distinction can and many would argue, must be made. Long may music live its own life with all of its meaningful personal and social associations, separate from marketing and advertising.

References

Belch, G. E. and Belch, M. A. (2007), *Advertising and Promotion: An Integrated Marketing Communications Perspective*, New York: McGraw-Hill.

Clow, K. E. and Baack, D. (2007), *Integrated Advertising, Promotion and Marketing Communications*, New Jersey: Pearson Prentice Hall.

Davidson, D. (2007), 'Carling Belong Ad Escapes Ban despite Volley of Complaints', www.brandrepublic.com. Accessed 2 May 2007.

Hamilton, R. (1982), *Richard Hamilton: Collected Words 1953–1982*, London: Thames & Hudson.

Jhally, S. (2000), 'Advertising at the Edge of the Apocalypse' in R. Anderson and L. Strate (eds) *Critical Studies in Media Commercialism*, London: Oxford University Press.

Klein, B. (2009), *As Heard on TV: Popular Music in Advertising*, Surrey, England and Vermont, USA: Ashgate Publishing Ltd.

Klein, N. (2000), *No Logo*, London: Flamingo.

Knopper, S. (2009), *Appetite for Self-Destruction: The Spectacular Crash of the Record Industry in the Digital Age*, London: Simon & Schuster.

Lasn, K. (1999), *Culture Jam: How to Reverse America's Suicidal Consumer Binge – And Why We Must*, New York: Harper Collins.

Lydon, J. (2010), '*Country Life Butter Adverts are Funding PiL Reunion*', www.nme.com/news/public-image-ltd/5. Accessed 13 July 2010.

Marsh, D. (1983), *Before I Get Old: The Story of The Who*, London: Plexus.

O'Donohoe, S. (1997), 'Leaky Boundaries: Intertextuality and Young Adult Experiences of Advertising', in M. Nava (ed.) *Buy This Book: Studies in Advertising and Consumption*, London: Routledge.

Saxton, G. (2005), 'Collections of Cool', *Young Consumers: Insight and Ideas for Responsible Marketers*, Vol. 6 Issue 2, pp. 18–27.

Slobada, J. A. (1985), *The Musical Mind: The Cognitive Psychology of Music*, Oxford: Oxford University Press.

Townshend, P. (2006) *Performing Songwriter* Magazine, Issue 98, December 2006.

Chapter 6

The cultural economy of death - advertising and popular music

Paula Hearsum

A memorable advertising campaign can stop you in your (musical) tracks. Not only because a notable value of music itself is that it can strengthen the message of an advertising campaign (Dunbar 1990) but in this instance, the triple concoction of advertising, music and death is an intoxicating mix which harnesses the intense and dynamic relationship between a listener, a dead musician and the music itself. It is most powerfully felt when it is utilised to monetise the death of a musician. Like other cultural forms, popular music is open to polysemic decoding, which may shift dramatically when a musician has died depending on the manner in which that death occurred. When culturally mediated through an advertising campaign, Williams' 'magic system' (1961) can be used to shine light on our current 'particular kind of economy' within which for a much troubled music industry, a musician's death is offered as a 'good career move'. Therefore this chapter offers to elucidate the key mechanisms drawn upon after a musician's death, which drive posthumous sales through the examination of advertising campaigns, past and present. In doing so it touches on questions of pleasure, desire and identity associated with advertising and the experience of popular music.

Death and popular music

Popular music has always had an interconnected relationship with death. Whether making pacts with the devil in its lyrical subject matter or with the statistical spike that is the profession's early call to meet their maker (27 Forever Club). Behind the songs and the musicians is an industry, which not only recognises that this is the case but also actively plays on that knowledge to make it work financially to their benefit. The unplanned surge in sales of old material after a musician has died, the harnessing of posthumous releases, re-packaging of old/remixed material to coincide with anniversaries of deaths or the carefully orchestrated and strategic release of biopics and re-releasing of related soundtracks and back catalogues aim to increase unit sales which directly benefit from the advertising of a musician's death. This may be through a strategically conceived campaign or indirectly through media news coverage of that death whereby the material is 'advertised' simply by being mentioned so often through the mediation of their career.

Taken as a whole it is indicative of a well-oiled machine at play. The industry of 'death' requires all elements of the relationship to work in synchronicity in the cycle: the advertising industry, the popular music industry, musicians and audiences. The music must effectively evoke associations of time and place. Conceivably even with an audience who may not have even been alive the first time a piece of music was released. The music industry must be savvy enough to incorporate the 'death' factor into a campaign facilitating consumers to literally 'buy into' the consumption of posthumous material as part of their musical mourning process which, Stromberg (1990) argues in the case of posthumous Elvis Presley sales, is an ideological symbolism of consumerism that the act of doing will change the way they feel, but Duffett (2008) argues often leaves little academic space for fans who consume the music.

Beyond the grave, careers have been restored through the art of advertising and their music given a new lease of life. When it is three dead musical figures that, beyond the grave, compete for the number one spot in *Forbes* annual 'Top Earning Dead Celebrities' list (Kurt Cobain, Elvis Presley and Michael Jackson) there is much to glean from understanding the commercial value of death and how it is repackaged to the living. This chapter, exploring the commercial value of popular musicians' deaths and how they are repackaged to the living, provides examples and case-studies of particular campaigns, highlights recurring devices and also considers what this might suggest about our appetite for the 'consumption' of death which Humphries (1995) wryly calls 'necropop', for profitable ends:

> Record companies aren't slow to resurrect those who have gone before. The opportunities for posthumous marketing are just so tempting. Patsy Cline and Jim Reeves were two of country music's biggest stars, both of whom died in plane crashes in 1964, but that didn't stop the double whammy of a 1981 duet. Thanks to the wonders of modern technology, Have You Ever Been Lonely? brought them both back from the back of beyond. One record, two stars – and both dead … in rock 'n' roll, the opera ain't over, even if the fat lady's dead and buried.
>
> (Humphries 1995)

Whilst academics across disciplines have written about the subject of death and popular music through its use as a recurring theme particularly within genres like hip hop (Kubrin 2005) or even its commercialisation through 'death' or 'dark tourism' (Cohen 1997; Leaver and Schmidt 2009) surprisingly little has unpacked the knowing use of death and consequent anniversaries, to capitalise upon and create new markets. Aural nostalgia is a powerful basis on which to create an advertising campaign. The discipline of advertising has come of age in exploring its own school of thought in combination with Memory Studies, Cognitive Psychology and Popular Music theory: 'The advertising problem under consideration is the improvement of consumers' memory performance to increase advertising effectiveness' (Keller 1987: 316). Tom (1990) built on the work of those interested in consumer behaviour as a result of exposure to memories enticed through advertising exposure and examined the encoding factors at play and their impact in terms of recall, whereby the music itself functioned as a retrieval cue, as opposed to older studies which had looked at non-musical contextual cues. What I suggest is useful here, is to take this a step further to examine how our competing desires around death, in both interest and fear, are drawn upon in the advertising of artists and what that might tell us about our very specific cultural, social and historical views on death, dying and the manner of death. In understanding what interests us about 'buying' death we can learn about our attitudes to life.

The financial framework within which a dead celebrity becomes a commodity is one that can be helpfully understood through Fiske's 'cultural economy' (1992). Fiske suggested, through his revision of Bourdieu's cultural capital that fandom could be viewed semiotically, enunciatively and textually. His framework is useful here to understand the role in which music fans play an active part in the cultural industry surrounding music sales after a musician has died. When a musician dies, whether that fact becomes known through news stories, obituaries or word–of–mouth, a potential musical consumer may make their personal connection to the artist and their music (semiotically). When they hear of a 'new' release, there is a building of that interest through media coverage. This may be in the form of reviews, which discuss the new layer of meaning associated to it, and play on the 'death card' (enunciatively). Finally, as we will see in the case of Johnny Cash later on, they can be involved with helping to create a new cultural product (textually). These cultural economies work because of a particular 'special relationship' we have to music, which is heightened after a musician's death:

There's something pretty peculiar about the whole experience of listening to pop music … It hits at a much more profound emotional level than, say, cinema. It's a very intense relationship. When the person who makes that music dies, it's analogous to losing a relative. Because you're genuinely upset, you start searching for hidden meanings, your mind jitters about all over the place.

(James 2002)

Parallel to the *Forbes* list, *Time* suggested in their 'Most visited grave sites' table that coming in at numbers 4, 5 and 6 are Elvis Presley, Jim Morrison and Bob Marley (Frank Sinatra and Johnny Cash are also in the top 10). Half of the most visited graves are of popular musicians. There is a desire to be close to dead musicians through their physical bodies as well as their bodies of work. Does that suggest that those who accumulate the advertised music of dead musicians are mere inactive users of 'therapeutic crutches' as Jenson argued (1992: 23), there merely to jump to the whip of advertising ploys? The most substantial collection of thought in this area, collated by Jones and Jensen, was their edited work on posthumous fame (2005). In the introduction Jensen posits that this commercialisation of death through the mechanisms of celebrity processes is typically viewed negatively but it could equally be argued that 'when fans mourn dead celebrities, they are symbolically negotiating authenticity, ownership, memory, and identity, all within the institutional processes of mass mediation' (Jones & Jensen 2005: xvi). This is no more true than in the purchase of the music itself.

Whilst posthumous releases have entered the popular music marketplace, noticeably since 1959 after Buddy Holly's death, there has been a relatively recent and marked shift in the nature of that consumption. The trade magazine *Music Week* commented on that shift in demand occurring from 2002:

Call it a shortage of modern-day chart talent, a nice piece of advertising or a sentimental weakness among consumers, but 2002 brought with it posthumous sales on an unprecedented scale.

(*Music Week* 2002: 19)

What they were noting was Aaliyah's 'More Than A Woman', which hit the top of the charts after the 22-year-old died in a plane crash and her work had since won two posthumous awards. How could you not 'read' the video and its music for 'Rock the Boat' (2001) in a different way once you knew she'd died immediately after its shoot? Whilst her ending is not that of the 'Live Fast Die Young' gang once typified by film stars such as James Dean, what is played upon here is that it was a tragic loss because she was not living recklessly. It exposes a pecking order in using the cause of death. An accident brings out sympathy. Incidentally, the choice of Aaliyah's funeral taking place four years to the day of Princess Diana's built on a known outpouring of grief in particular for the dead young women. Our cultural capacity for public mourning and the mediation of grief (Kear and Steinberg 1999) has taken an exponential curve in particular since Elvis's death in 1977.

However, when a musician takes their own life, intentionally or through wreckless behaviour (Kurt Cobain, Nick Drake, Ian Curtis), in terms of the posthumous musical success of the three examples, suicide for popular musicians has not been a negative advertising attribute. In a sadly prophetic note, Michael Hutchence told Q magazine, four years before he committed suicide:

Rock 'n' roll is the perfect scenario for people who need a lot of attention, who were ignored as kids. It's the most indulged, ridiculous situation. It used to be that as a rock star everyone was happy if you killed yourself.

(Hutchence 1993)

Once the musician is dead and the music marketed, we need to ask ourselves are there any losers? Is everyone a winner: the estate and its beneficiaries, the record label and its employees and of course the audience … or have we all lost out? Following the death of an artist, when the longevity of their career is cut short, the market appetite is ripe to listen to unreleased material:

As one advertising executive put it, 'using a dead celebrity is usually cheaper than hiring today's biggest stars'. There is a 'finite' quality to the products that may come along after their death, a quality likely closely linked to the sense of 'lost promise' often associated with the death of young artists whose best work, it is believed, was ahead of them.

(Jones and Jensen 2005: 13–14)

This was visible within a fortnight of the death of Amy Winehouse in July 2011 when newspapers began reporting on the possibility of her unfinished studio work (Topping 2011; Singh 2011). The record industry's monetary gain was no more sharply felt and attacked when Sony music increased the price of Whitney Houston's, *The Ultimate Collection* (1997) on iTunes the day after her death. Their apology and reverting of price did not fully quash rumours that the accidental increase had 'exploited fans' grief' (Michaels 2012). The mounting fervour of excitement to listen to posthumously released material of recording artists parallels that of other dead cultural figures. Death is a great advertising hook. For popular music there are ten distinct ways in which the work can be packaged as a result:

1. Post-production polishing

If 'the day the music died' was 3 February 1959 when Buddy Holly died in an aeroplane crash along with Ritchie Valens and the Big Bopper, then the day it was resurrected was 20 July 1959. This was the date a demo of Holly's 'Peggy Sue Got Married', which had been partially written as a follow on to 'Peggy Sue' (1957) was polished off with backing vocals and guitar and released. A productive decade of posthumous releases for the Holly estate followed and the creation of a new and lucrative revenue stream for dead musicians ensued.

Just as Heath Ledger's performances went into post-production for his posthumous role starring in *The Dark Knight* (2008), we can see its replication in putting the final touches to musical unfinished symphonies. What is then created in the use of a death to market a commodity is a space in which *Cluedo* can be played out by using the (musical) clues in order to attempt to fathom how the death has occurred. For instance, Nirvana's *MTV Unplugged in New York* album (1994) was released seven months after Kurt Cobain's death, leaving critics divided as to whether it gave an understanding into Cobain's suicide or an ethical debate of the MTV Unplugged manipulative format. The five million sales that year and the following Grammy suggest that it was perfectly poised to make the most of the hungry market that wanted an aural, as well as a later visual insight (the DVD was released in 2007), into the mind of a tortured artist. As Coletti suggests: 'Everyone knew this was special. Everyone knew we just saw another side of a very important band. But obviously [everything] gets magnified in the context of what happened later' (2004).

When the deaths are from what are classed as 'natural causes', such as Joey Ramone's death from lymphatic cancer, or Joe Strummer's heart attack, any material they had been working on is often released within the year (Ramone's *Don't Worry about Me* or Strummer's work with the Mescaleros, *Streetcore*). Joey Ramone's second solo album, *Don't Worry About Me* was recorded during the last months of his illness and has been described by critics as a 'fitting epitaph'. What is interesting is that Ramone had already recorded the material knowing he was dying and was seemingly aware of its future release – even if the advertising for it would only begin in earnest after his death. But what of the moral issues of posthumous music when it is released against the wishes of the artists? The case of Jeff Buckley's work is an interesting one as the NME.com music journalist Luke Lewis points out:

> But even when the music is beautiful, the ethics are still dodgy. Shortly before completing 'Grace', Jeff Buckley explicitly stated that he never wanted the opulent-yet-spiteful ballad

'Forget Her' released – but there it is, on all copies of the album released since 2004. Future generations will have no concept of that record without it. Is that right?

(Lewis 2010)

This is even truer of an unclear death, as Buckley, whose autopsy declared death by accidental drowning, typifies. Despite claims that he was not depressed, the speculation that followed included building on the 'capital' of his musician-father Tim Buckley's death through an overdose. The term 'capital' is used in a loaded and knowing way because the impact has a direct correlation to how meaning is made from music in its decoding: 'Great promise, handsome looks and a tragic demise have proved a seductive combination ever since Byron; Buckley's talent and the allure of the music he might have created, mean he is better known now than he ever was while alive' (Anon 2008). Buckley who only released one album, *Grace*, during his lifetime, has had more material and notoriety through recordings of posthumous material which had been repackaged and re-advertised.

2. The virtual artefact

Another parallel with the posthumous work of Ledger is that of work being articulated after death by another artist. Not quite a cover version but more on a par with the work of an understudy. Like Ledger's character, Tony, in *The Imaginarium of Doctor Parnassus* (2009) being picked up by colleagues (Johnny Depp, Colin Farell and Jude Law) there have been musical analogies. Billy Bragg and Wilco's album, *Mermaid Avenue* (1998) created music to accompany some otherwise unrecorded lyrics of Woody Guthrie's and the Manic Street Preachers album *Journal for Plague Lovers* (2009) utilised the 'missing-presumed-dead' colleague, Richey Edwards's remaining lyrics, six months before Edwards was officially declared as 'presumed dead'. The timing of the release was impeccably made to capitalise on a very loyal fan base aware of the upcoming date.

3. Repackaging releases/reissues

Another distinct advertising trench is the shrewd capitalisation using anniversaries of earlier releases. Nirvana's *Bleach* (1989) enjoyed a renaissance on its twenty year anniversary. The re-issue included previously unreleased material and was enjoyed by a nostalgic first time audience as well as a new generation. 'Nostalgic branding' utilises a trump card of memory to both a real and imagined community. Cobain's widow, Courtney Love, has been much attacked for opening up her dead rock star husband's back catalogue using symbolic agency for monetary gain. Her manager, Peter Asher, argued that the new audience might disagree because the continuation of life after death through musical consumption does not have to be seen negatively: 'In my view, if 10 kids hear the song on TV and ask Hey, who was that?' then we have maintained *Nirvana*'

(Lowry and Fine 2006: 80). The flip side of the debate would be an exploitation of time and place through the advertising strategy. Those who were possibly a mere twinkle in a parental eye during the album's inception are the new generation of angst teenagers that Nirvana appealed to the first time round and can take a new reading of the material for the noughties generation.

4. Remastered

An interesting point around authorship comes into play with the advertising of reissues when authenticity as an important musical credential is tampered with. When Elliott Smith's first album, *Roman Candle*, was 'remastered' (as opposed to 'remixed') by the archivist, Larry Crane, he did so to 'improve on' the musical remains interred to the library in order to increase its musical authenticity, a point much utilised in surrounding press coverage supporting its release:

> The intention that I had was to make the album more listenable. I felt that a lot of the guitar 'squeaks' were jarring and very loud, and that many of the hard consonants and 'S' sounds were jarring and scratchy sounding. I felt by reducing these noises that the music would become more inviting and the sound would serve the songs better.
>
> (Crane quoted in Slater 2010)

There is an element of this strategy that is reliant on the psychology of record collecting. With prolific artists, it can be the equivalent of an expensive stamp collecting hobby where there is no hope of completion. However, with a dead musician, their output has an obtainable limitation. Shuker (2004), drawing on Montano's work (2001), suggests that this 'obsession' reveals a 'practice driven by nostalgia' (Montano 2001: 1–2). This relates back to an acquiring of social capital or as Baudrillard and Featherstone suggested, a passion for fashion for collecting. It is also an activity currently changing shape as contemporary collections now include digital versionings (Cunningham et al. 2004). Monetising what was traditionally known as back catalogues has come into the fore in the digital age. Not just in downloading terms, but accessibility to seek out un-marketed material and make the most of what Anderson coined the 'long tail' (Anderson 2006). Rediscovering an interesting soundtrack within a film, being 'recommended' music with online purchasing ('those customers buying this album, also liked this …') or even using Shazam when an old song is played in a café … some music is self-marketed, some is travelling a new trajectory but certainly new possibilities are certainly altering our music information retrieval systems. This coupled to the way in which listening to the music of dead artists has extramusical meaning and allows an accrual of cultural knowledge. Something that also ties back into Fiske's work:

> The accumulation of both popular and official cultural capital is signalled materially by collections of objects – artworks, books, records, memorabilia, ephemera. Fans, like

buffs, are often avid collectors, and the cultural collection is a point where cultural and economic capital come together.

(Fiske 1992: 43)

5. Remixing

This neatly leads on to the advertising of music in a new context to bring music to a contemporary generation which Tankel (1990) suggested involved 'recoding' leading to an aesthetic transformation of the song and its meaning. Elvis Vs JXL's dance remix of the former's 1969 song 'A Little Less Conversation' was used by Nike to advertise the World Cup in 2002. A timing which happily coincided with a re-packaging of Elvis's 30 number one hits. What was a little known B-side became also a lever which propelled Elvis to overtake The Beatles for the most number one hits in the UK … albeit under the proviso that the producer change his name from Junkie XL to JXL to ironically, given the King's cause of death, avoid any association with drugs. And so the Elvis market continued to flourish:

> Elvis's name, image, and music into profits didn't stop with his death in 1977 and that the posthumous continuation (acceleration?) of these practices has contributed in a number of ways to maintaining Elvis's prominence across the cultural terrain. RCA, for instance continues to release profitable 'new albums' of Elvis material (some of it previously unreleased, most of it simply remastered and repackaged) and shows no signs of stopping this practice anytime soon.
>
> (Rodman 1996: 11)

6. Happy coincidence/re-entry

Staying with Mr Presley, happy campaigns can also build on coincidence. It is all in the timing and Elvis's posthumous work was also quick off the starting block. His single 'Way Down' was currently 'on release' in 1977 and shot back up the charts the week following his death. Posthumous appeal has been something much discussed since Elvis's death in particular (Rodman 1996; Marcus 1999; Doss 2004) and more recently as Amy Winehouse's music poured back into the charts both in the UK and USA in the weeks following her death (Music Week 2011).

7. Birthday

There is nothing like a dead musician's birthday to remind a record company to celebrate by advertising some material. News cycles have long been on the case to mark a dead celebrity's birthday so it was never a surprise that on what would have been Elvis's seventieth birthday eighteen of his chartbusters were released (2005). By and large it is birthdays coming round as ten year anniversaries that act as an advertising hook, however, once you have an audience, any anniversary will do. On 26 February 2010, what would have been Johnny Cash's seventy-eighth birthday, Lost Highway Records released his second posthumous record, titled *American VI: Ain't No Grave*.

8. Anniversary of deaths

Why just celebrate a birthday when a death brings a second annual promotional tool? Elliot Smith's *From a Basement on the Hill* (2004) also straddles the category of being reworked as it was incomplete at the time of his suicide. His shocking method (he stabbed himself twice in the heart) also tapped into a morbidity of interest around becoming an investigator into any build up to a death:

> It is a natural impulse to pore over the last album an artist makes before committing suicide, looking for explanations, but it is hardly a healthy pastime. At best, it reeks of morbid curiosity; at worst it fuels one of rock culture's least appealing traits, the urge to romanticise a sad and pointless waste of life.

(Petridis 2004)

9. Cover versions

Joy Division's 'Love Will Tear Us Apart' was released just before Ian Curtis's suicide and in May 1980, a month after his death, reached number one. Whilst their version has already had four releases and is seen as the 'authentic' version, any cover, of which the number is notching ever closer to 200 versions, builds on the history and tragic demise of its original singer and the intended meaning. That is not to dismiss the power that the cover can have on the original version, as Cooper suggests these 'tributes' offer a way to 'enable musicians to transcend death as performing sources ... there is real money to be made in sustaining the postmortem careers of recording superstars. Music as memory becomes music as materialism' (2005: 244).

10. The deathbed album

Whilst a kissing cousin of the post-production polish category, the deathbed album (or single) is not always released close to a death and benefits from a fan's excitement on the unexpected finding of a hidden treasure. For instance, Johnny Cash's posthumous album *American V: A Hundred Highways* (2006) was released almost three years after he died.

Decoding the music made by someone in the knowledge that they were going to die is an advertising opportunity not missed by music critics:

> 'These songs are Johnny's final statement,' producer Rick Rubin said the last time round. What, then, does that make this collection? Can it be more than studio-floor sweepings, stitched together to keep the Cash industry ticking? ...
>
> ... Here, though, it's all ashes. An ominous guitar picks out a lowering landscape, a desolate banjo circles, a drumbeat suggests mortal chains being dragged. And here is Cash's voice, back from beyond, full of stern shadows, telling us this: 'There ain't no grave can hold my body down.'
>
> It's almost as if the whole American Recordings project has been leading up to this advertising opportunity.
>
> (Love 2006)

Whilst the video for his cover of 'Hurt' (2003) was often described as a visual epitaph the 'Cash flow' (an irresistible pun) continued 'textually' too – The Johnny Cash Project for instance, is a project of collective art, which asks fans to contribute their own frames to a video for his most recent posthumous release 'Ain't No Grave' (2010). All a little paradoxical considering that in his autobiography Cash said of Columbia records that in terms of advertising him, he was treated as 'invisible'.

Conclusion

Whilst the highlighted categories are the most common ones to utlise a death to promote music, record companies continue to find new outlets with new technical possibilities. Michael Jackson, who sold in excess of 750 million records whilst he was alive, has since sold 8.3 million albums and 12.4 million digital downloads, which made him the best-selling artist of 2009. Harsh considering that his final years were overshadowed by rumours of financial ruin and plain shocking that Sony is suggested to be releasing ten albums up to 2017 having extended his contract via his family. Sony launched two online research hubs in the UK to examine music advertising in 2010. Their senior director of digital development Federico Bolza articulates the special qualities of popular music:

> [M]usic really matters to people and that, in advertising terms, music companies are fortunate enough to be handling a product that is emotionally powerful and that resonates so naturally and so forcefully to so many. No one worries about a dip in the household detergent market and its effect on the consumer goods industry but pretty much everyone cares about music and has an opinion on the music industry.
>
> (Bolza 2008)

What we can see is that utilising the cause of a death can also reap financial rewards in terms of sales. The demographic group interested in the work of Tupac Shakur and the Notorious

Plate 1: Mad Men - John Slattery ('Roger Sterling,' left), Jon Hamm ('Don Draper,' centre) and January Jones ('Betty Draper,' right). Courtesy of Lionsgate Home Entertainment's *Mad Men: Season One.*

Plate 2: John Orlando Parry, 'A London Street Scene', 1835. Courtesy of Alfred Dunhill Museum and Archive.

Plate 3: Persil, 'redder whiter bluer', Newcastle upon Tyne, 2004. Sketch by Vanessa Maughan. Photographs: the author.

Plate 4: L'Oreal, Cherly Cole, 2009. Source: Advertising Archives.

Plate 5: Jules Chéret, *Saxoléine Pétrole de Sûreté*, 1891. Lithograph. © Victoria and Albert Museum, London.

Plate 6: Lucian Bernhard, *Stiller*, 1907–8. Lithograph. © DACS 2012/Victoria and Albert Museum, London.

Plate 7: Cassandre, *Nord Express*, 1927. Lithograph. © MOURON. CASSANDRE.
Lic 2012-20-05-02 www.cassandre-france.com.

Plate 8: Edward McKnight Kauffer, *Power, the Nerve Centre of London's Underground*, 1930. Lithograph. © Simon Rendall.

Plate 9: Richard Prince, *Untitled (Cowboy)*, 1989. Ektacolour photograph, 226.1 x 313.1 cm. © Richard Prince. Courtesy Gagosian Gallery.

Plate 10: First World War United States Army poster. Source: Advertising Archive.

Plate 11: The 'Great Britain' campaign. Courtesy of Department for Media, Culture and Sport.

B.I.G. increased when their murders were deemed mysterious. This is part of a human desire to unravel a story (murder-mystery or in reality) and often ends, suggests Hidi and Anderson (1991), only when we have found out 'whodunnit'. Playing on the interest to play detective in both murders and unravelling suicides, impacts on our readings of an artist's material.

Tupac's posthumous output raises interesting questions about the lucrative advertising within the death industry:

> Tupac Shakur's 'Better Dayz', released later this month, is no ordinary album. It is the 16th Tupac release since the gangsta rapper's murder in September 1996. Sixteen albums in six years would be a prodigious feat for an artist who was still breathing, particularly when you bear in mind that many of them are double CD sets. For a dead artist who released only four albums during his lifetime, it smacks of macabre exploitation, not to mention an ever-dipping quality control. Listen carefully to many of the posthumous Tupac releases and you can distinctly hear the bottom of the barrel being scraped.
>
> (Petridis 2002)

> Lucrative licensing agreements and fat royalty checks keep rolling in long after many celebrities have shuffled off this mortal coil. Consider Elvis Presley: Last year the King pulled down an estimated $35 million – $15 million of it from Graceland admissions – making him the richest guy in the graveyard.
>
> (*Forbes* 2001)

What has been an interesting trend to follow with the *Forbes* list is that Elvis has not only retained that spot for seven out of nine years (Kurt Cobain overtook in 2006 and Yves Saint Laurent and Michael Jackson both overtook in 2009), but his income has always increased (from $37m to currently $55m). Dead rock stars have become a valuable commodity. It is also not unusual for musicians to succeed in financial terms better in death than in life – and certainly not uncommon for their music to re-enter the charts. John Lennon, for instance, had more chart number ones after death as a solo artist than in his lifetime, which includes his 'Free as a Bird' demo from 1977, which the remaining Beatles recorded in 1995. Commentary following its release recognised the tradition of bringing the dead back to life through recordings as well as the powerful tool that advertising can play:

> It's a grand tradition that's creepy whenever it occurs. Hank Williams Jnr recorded a track with his dead father and Natalie Cole recently did the same. It's a grotesque idea with only one conceivable motive – money. I think this exercise would bring out all of John's cynicism were he around today.
>
> (Marcus 1995)

and

> Firstly it's a triumph of advertising. It's almost certain to be a number one record. The amount of interest created by the PR people – TV show, albums, etc – is incredible. More importantly it's a treat for Beatles fans who thought they'd heard it all.
>
> (Jensen 1995)

Whether posthumous releases are authorised and therefore advertised in the traditional sense or not (much of Hendrix's post-death release list has been a legal battle) what becomes available to us, is an analytic opportunity around authorship. Post-structurally speaking, if we take Barthes's notion which suggests the author can be separated from their work and more literally then, a musician as author, can be taken away from their music into the hands of their record label's advertising department after death. This relevance becomes more important in nostalgic commemoration of an audience in terms of reading meaning. Author intention imbued into musical artefacts that they knowingly create is read polysemically during their lifetime and beyond. A communicative confusion arises when that encoding is arranged through an advertising campaign with no knowledge of the author's preferred reading.

Death becomes a cultural commodity with exchange value. The Grateful Dead, never once shy for knowing and then breaking the rules of advertising, have inspired a new text on the subject. In *Advertising Lessons from the Grateful Dead: What Every Business Can Learn from the Most Iconic Band in History*, authors Scott and Halligan, suggest that it was the band's ability to give away their work (freeconomics) long before online social networks took it, which allowed them to build up such a strong audience base to which they self-marketed. An advertising department budget is there to leverage returns. To *create* a desire in an audience. So the question that in turn begs is what is it about death that sends a signal to consume a commodity (virtual or otherwise – mp3 or hard copy sales)? We need to continue to unpack what it is that advertisers of the music industry understand on the one hand so intuitively that within weeks of a musician's death recording releases are announced. And yet on the other hand the value of a dead musician's legacy can be so much misunderstood. The latter evident through the video game, Guitar Hero 5 with an avatar based on Kurt Cobain, which Courtney Love threatened to take to court (a year later is then an app for an iPhone) or for sale at Christmas 2010, an 'official' Michael Jackson doll. The answer lies within our cultural and historical specificities of ethics, taste and acceptability. Successful advertising should not be seen as a 'cash-in' but is readily embraced if it is packaged to support a fan to continue their enjoyment or opening new ears to material. That said, the permission of commercial exploitation is one thing when the artist is still alive but after death that may change. For instance, this reminds us that Sony launched its own internal advertising agency, the Arcade Creative Group which *Advertising Age* described as making the relationship between labels and advertising agencies 'cozier' (Moran 2008: 16).

As seen where the legacy in name, rather than music, is incorporated into a commodity, there appears to be a line of taste and decency crossed. Brand Republic (2008), the advertising, media and PR company, commented on Converse's use of dead musicians integrated into the designs of their shoes as 'tasteless' endorsement (Whitehead 2008):

> Instinctively, the soul shrinks when a musician's image is exploited posthumously - think of those loathsome, mocked-up ad images of Ian Curtis and Sid Vicious wearing Converse trainers that appeared in 2008 (both artists, according to the company's advertising boss, 'embodied the values of the brand' – ugh).
>
> (Lewis 2010)

Sullivan (2005) suggests that the afterlife of a musician has been enhanced with digital technologies, which we can see with the viral advertising campaign of Michael Jackson's film *This Is It* (2009). We should consider these elements as part of a huge machine – the release of the video, the relationship and impact on record sales and surrounding hype. It was oiled together with the virality of the dancing inmates video. *This Is It* became the highest grossing documentary and again, after some legal settling with Jackson's estate, earned Sony over $2.1m. Echoing Fiske's comment quoted earlier and the example of the Johnny Cash Project, Jackson fans visually merged into their dead hero by contributing an image of themselves into an online mosaic of Jackson (thisisit-fans.com) over a nine-day period in September 2009 – the finished art work was posted live in the week before the release of the film by Sony.

Music has long been used at funerals to represent the deceased symbolically and across cultures has a particular role in the grieving process as a ritual part of a mourning strategy (Robertson 1968; Pollock 1975). Its purpose wrapped in with a psychological function is as a way to deal with loss: 'music of this type can be thought to function as an object of transitory identification, in that the aesthetic reverie evoked by listening to it implements a fantasy in which the painful reality of loss is denied or disavowed' (Stein 2004: 13).

What we have discovered is that through an analysis of the advertising of dead musicians, what is offered is an examination tool which serves an interrogative purpose to probe social attitudes to death, dying and the manner in which that occurs as well as unearthing ethical issues. Williams's 'magic system' (1961) was concerned with production and offered a critical examination of the construction of advertising strategies. This approach offers insight into the use of the death to enhance the industrial machinery of the music industry. What is much forgotten is the consumption part of the process – what is the psychological need of the living, which is met by those picking up advertising signals to buy that musical experience?

References

Anderson, C. (2006), *The Long Tail: How Endless Choice is Creating Unlimited Demand*, London: Random House.

Anon. (2008), 'In Praise of ... Jeff Buckley', *The Guardian*, 24 December 2008, http://www.guardian.co.uk/commentisfree/2008/dec/24/praise-jeff-buckley. Accessed 5 March 2012.

Barthes, R. (1968), 'The Death of the Author', *Roland Barthes*, London: Papermac.

Baudrillard, J. (1993), *Symbolic Exchange and Death*, London: Sage.

Bolza, F. (2008), 'Music and Technology: Friends Reunited', *The Telegraph*, 11 August 2008.,http://blogs.telegraph.co.uk/technology/shanerichmond/4872757/Music_and_technology_Friends_reunited/. Accessed 5 March 2012.

Cohen, S. (1997), 'More than the Beatles: Popular Music, Tourism and Urban Regeneration', in S. Abram, J. Waldren and D. Macleod (eds) *Tourists and Tourism: Identifying with People and Places*, London: Berg.

Coletti, A. (2004), 'Bare Witness the Making of Nirvana: MTV Unplugged' (DVD: 2007).

Cooper, B. Lee. (2005), 'Tribute Discs, Career Development, and Death: Perfecting the Celebrity Product from Elvis Presley to Stevie Ray Vaughan' in *Popular Music and Society* Vol. 28. No. 2, pp. 229–48.

Cunningham, S., Jones, M. and Jones, S. (2004), 'Organising digital music for use: an examination of personal music collections', ISMIR 2004 – 5th International Conference on Music Information Retrieval.

Doss, E. (2004), *Elvis Culture: Fans, Faith, and Image*, Lawrence: University Press of Kansas.

Duffett, M. (2008), 'Transcending Audience Generalizations: Consumerism Reconsidered in the Case of Elvis Presley Fans', in *Popular Music and Society*. Vol. 24 No. 2, pp. 75–91.

Dunbar, D. (1990), 'Music and Advertising', in *International Journal of Advertising*. Vol. 9, No. 3, pp. 197–203.

Featherstone, M. (1990), *Consumer Culture and Postmodernism*, London: Sage.

Fiske, F. (1992), 'The Cultural Economy of Fandom', in L. Lewis (ed.) *The Adoring Audience: Fan Culture and Popular Media*, New York: Routledge, pp. 37–42.

Foley, M. and Lennon, J. (2000), *Dark Tourism: The Attraction of Death and Disaster*, London: Thompson Learning.

Forbes (2001), 'Earnings from the Crypt', http://www.forbes.com/2001/02/28/crypt.html. Accessed 24 November 2011.

Gibson, C and Connell, J. (2007), 'Music, Tourism and the Transformation of Memphis', *Tourism Geographies*, Issue 2. May 2007, pp. 160–190.

Gorn, G. (1982), 'The Effects of Music in Advertising on Choice Behaviour: A Classical Conditioning Approach', *The Journal of Advertising*, Winter 1982 Vol. 46 Issue 1, pp. 94–101.

Hanusch, F. (2010), *Representing Death in the News: Journalism, Media and Mortality*, Hampshire: Palgrave Macmillan.

Hidi, S. and Anderson, V. (1991), 'Situational Interest and Its Impact on Reading and Expository Writing', in K. Renninger, S. Hidi, A. Krapp, and A. Renninger (eds) *The Role of Interest in Learning and Development*, London: Routledge.

Humphries, P. (1995), 'Dead Pop Stars Mean Big Bucks – are Rock Stars now Worth More Dead than Alive?' *The Guardian*, 18 August 1995.

Hutchence, M. (1993), Interview in Q, cited in Perrone, P. 1997, 'Obituary: Michael Hutchence', *The Independent*, 24 November 1997, http://www.independent.co.uk/news/obituaries/obituary-michael-hutchence-1296068.html. Accessed 24 November 2011.

James, O. (2002), in A. Petridis, 'Albums from the Crypt', *The Guardian*, 1 November 2002, http://www.guardian.co.uk/music/2002/nov/01/artsfeatures.popandrock. Accessed 5 March 2012.

Jenson, J. (1992), 'Fandom as Pathology', in L. Lewis (ed.) *The Adoring Audience: Fan Culture and Popular Media*, New York: Routledge, pp. 9–29.

Jensen, D. (1995), in C. Sullivan, 'Do You Believe in Yesterday', *The Guardian*, 21 November 1995, http://www.guardian.co.uk/thebeatles/story/0,,606548,00.html. Accessed 5 March 2012.

The Johnny Cash Project, http://www.thejohnnycashproject.com/. Accessed 5 March 2012.

Jones, S. and Jensen, J. (2005), *Afterlife as Afterimage: Understanding Posthumous Fame*, New York: Peter Lang.

Kear, A. and Steinberg, D. (1999), *Mourning Diana: Nation, Culture and the Performance of Grief*, London: Routledge.

Keller, K. (1987), 'Memory Factors in Advertising: The Effect of Advertising Retrieval Cues on Brand Evaluations', in *The Journal of Consumer Research* Vol. 14. No. 2, pp. 316–333.

Kubrin, C. (2005), '"I See Death Around the Corner": Nihilism in Rap Music', in *Sociological Perspectives*. Winter 2005, Vol. 48, No. 4, pp. 433–459.

Leaver, D. and Schmidt, R. A. (2009), 'Before they were famous: music-based tourism and a musician's hometown roots', in *Journal of Place Management and Development*. Vol. 2, No. 3, pp. 220–229.

Lewis, L. (2010), 'Are Posthumous Album Releases Ever a Good Idea?' NME.com. 12 March 2010, http://www.nme.com/blog/index.php?blog=121&p=8150&more=1&c=1. Accessed 5 March 2012.

Love, D. (2006), 'Johnny Cash: American VI: Ain't No Grave', in *Uncut*, July 2006, http://www.uncut.co.uk/music/johnny_cash/reviews/14035. Accessed 5 March 2012.

Lowry, T. and Fine, J. (2006), 'Finding Nirvana in a Music Catalogue', *Business Week*, 10 February 2006.

Marcus, G. (1995), in C. Sullivan, 'Do You Believe in Yesterday?' in *The Guardian*, 21 November 1995, http://www.guardian.co.uk/thebeatles/story/0,,606548,00.html. Accessed 5 March 2012.

——— (1999), *Dead Elvis: A Chronicle of a Cultural Obsession*. Cambridge, MA: Harvard University Press.

Michaels, S. (2012), 'Whitney Houston iTunes price hike was a 'mistake', Sony says', *The Guardian*, 15 Feb 2012, http://www.guardian.co.uk/music/2012/feb/15/whitney-houston-itunes-price-hike-sony. Accessed 5 March 2012.

Montano, E. (2001), *Collecting the Past for a Material Present: Record Collecting in Contemporary Practice*, M.A. Dissertation, Institute of Popular Music Studies, Liverpool University.

Moran, C. (2008), 'The Record Label that's also a Creative Agency', *Advertising Age*, 27 October 2008, p. 16.

Music Week (2002), 'Dead Stars Top The Charts', *Music Week*, 21 December 2002.

—— (2011), 'Amy Back in the US Top-10 Albums as Adele Scales New Heights', *Music Week*, 27 July 2011, http://www.musicweek.com/news/read/amy-back-in-us-top-10-albums-as-adele-scales-new-heights/046335 Accessed 20 July 2012.

Petridis, A. (2002), 'Albums from the Crypt', *The Guardian*, 1 November 2002, http://www.guardian.co.uk/music/2002/nov/01/artsfeatures.popandrock. Accessed 5 March 2012.

—— (2004), 'Elliott Smith, From a Basement on a Hill', *The Guardian*, 15 October 2004, http://www.guardian.co.uk/music/2004/oct/15/popandrock.shopping7. Accessed 5 March 2012.

Pollock, G. (1975), 'Mourning and Memorialization through Music'. *The Annual of Psychoanalysis*, 3, pp. 423-36.

Robertson, A. (1968), *Requiem: Music of Mourning and Consolation*. New York: Praeger.

Rodman, G. (1996), *Elvis after Elvis: The Posthumous Career of a Living Legend*. London: Routledge.

Scott, D. M., and Halligan, B. (2010), *Advertising Lessons from the Grateful Dead: What Every Business Can Learn from the Most Iconic Band in History*, Oxon: John Wiley & Sons.

Shuker, R. (2004), 'Beyond the "High Fidelity" Stereotype: Defining the (Contemporary) Record Collector', *Popular Music* Vol. 23, No. 3 (Oct., 2004), pp. 311–330.

Singh, A. (2011), 'Amy Winehouse Unifished Album Set for Release', *The Telegraph*, 24 July 2011, http://www.telegraph.co.uk/culture/music/8658565/Amy-Winehouse-unfinished-album-set-for-release.html. Accessed 5 March 2012.

Slater, L. (2010), 'Elliott Smith's Roman Candle Re-Issue Gets Release Date', *Drownedinsound*, http://drownedinsound.com/news/4139136-elliott-smiths-roman-candle-re-issue-gets-release-date. Accessed 5 March 2012.

Stein, A. (2004), 'Music, Mourning and Consolation', *Journal of the American Psychoanalytic Association*, Vol. 52, No. 3, pp. 783–811.

Stromberg, P. (1990), 'Elvis Alive?: The Ideology of American Consumerism' in *Journal of Popular Culture*, Vol. 2. Issue 3, pp. 11–19.

Sullivan, J. (2005), 'Dead, Ahead', *Macworld* Winter 2005, Vol. 21, Issue 13, p. 86.

Tankel, J. (1990), 'The Practice of Recording Music: Remixing as Recoding', *The Journal of Communication*. Vol. 40. No. 3, pp. 34–46.

This Is It Fans Mosaic – http://www.thisisit-fans.com/. Accessed 5 March 2012.

Time 'Top 10 Celebrity Grave Sites', http://205.188.238.181/time/specials/packages/article/0,28804,1919236_1919237,00.html. Accessed 24 November 2011.

Tom, G. (1990), 'Advertising with music' in: *The Journal of Consumer Advertising* Vol. 7 Issue 2, pp. 49–53.

Topping, A. (2011), 'Amy Winehouse: dozen new songs may be set for release', *The Guardian*, 27 July 2011, http://www.guardian.co.uk/music/2011/jul/27/amy-winehouse-new-album-possible. Accessed 5 March 2012.

Whitehead, J. (2008), 'Converse Follows Sid Vicious Ad with Kurt Cobain Shoe', http://www.brandrepublic.com/News/793786/Converse-follows-Sid-Vicious-ad-Kurt-Cobain-shoe/. Accessed 5 March 2012.

Williams, R. (1961), 'Advertising: The Magic System', in R. Williams (ed.) *Problems in Materialism and Culture: Selected Essays* (1980), London: Verso.

Chapter 7

Art and advertising – circa 1880 to the present

Malcolm Gee ·

Since the late-nineteenth century, advertising and fine art have maintained a symbiotic relationship in Western societies. As the advertising industry expanded and became established it appropriated and adapted visual styles and approaches developed in the sphere of fine art. Conversely, fine art practices themselves have been increasingly influenced by an awareness of the visual characteristics of advertising, and the place that these occupy in modern consciousness. The balance of the relationship has changed, however. At the beginning of the period considered here, advertisers sought to use the established place and prestige of art for their commercial purposes, while numerous artists were excited by the association of advertising with the dynamic of modernity. Today, at a time when the advertising industry has become fully professionalised and the nature of 'fine' art has become constitutionally unstable (although it is institutionally secure), advertising is a realm that artists frequently engage with, but is one which their practice has to be defined against, in a process of constant critical self-renewal. This chapter outlines the history of this relationship: a particular and distinctive case of the overall conjunction of advertising and culture examined in this book.

In the course of the nineteenth century, in the context of widespread urbanisation and facilitated by advances in printing technology, notably in the field of colour lithography, visual impact became increasingly important in advertising. One straightforward way in which fine art could be used in this respect was by simple appropriation. The most famous example of this was the transformation of Millais' image of childhood into an advertisement for Pears Soap – 'Bubbles', in 1888–9 – a move that was immediately emulated by the company's competitor, Lever, with the use of a painting by William Frith. Appropriation of this kind remained a popular strategy in advertising: it mobilised powerful cultural connotations simply and effectively. However it only had limited application since, fundamentally, the advertising image needed to be fit for purpose and therefore, with exceptions, made to order. The most important changes to visual practices in advertising took place from the 1860s onwards in the context of initiatives to improve the quality and the status of the applied arts in general. This led to the poster 'movement' of the 1890s and 1900s, that had a major impact on the appearance of major urban centres, and resulted in advertising being taken seriously as a branch of art practice.

Chéret and poster art

A key role in these developments was played by Jules Chéret, both as designer and entrepreneur. In 1866 he set up a poster studio in Paris with the support of the perfume manufacturer Eugène Rimmel whom he had met while based in London. There was an exploding demand for posters in Paris at this time (boosted in 1881 by the liberalisation of bill-sticking regulations) particularly to advertise consumer products and entertainment venues. Chéret proved himself extremely adept at this business: he understood and exploited the technical possibilities of lithographic printing in colour; he was attentive to the communication imperatives of the medium; and over the years he developed a distinctive style which displayed artistic ambition as well as commercial astuteness. It is possible that he was aware, through Rimmel, who was a member of the Royal Society of Arts, of English initiatives in relation to raising artistic standards in the design field. He was certainly influenced by the Rococo revival of the mid-century and the widespread enthusiasm for Japanese prints in artistic circles in Paris. He realised that aspects of these – the warm colours, crisp drawing, and idyllic mood of eighteenth-century Rococo painting, the distinctive angles, flat-colour planes and spatial compression of the Japanese – were highly suited to the needs of the poster, to be highly visible, easily legible and hedonistically persuasive. The formula that he applied consistently from the mid-1880s onwards, to advertise goods that ranged from entertainment sites to cigarettes and lighting oil, consisted of an elegant, smiling young woman – 'la Chérette' – depicted in bright colours close to the picture plane in an abstract airy space in which the product was also present, succinctly represented and labelled, using a typographical schema that was integrated into the composition (see Plate 5).

These posters were very successful. Chéret also benefited from critical support from writers who argued that his work set an example for advertising as a genuine popular art form. J. K. Huysmans famously urged visitors to the official Salon art show, in 1880, to abandon the boring rows of paintings on display to enjoy the free exhibition that Chéret's posters offered on the streets of the city; Ernest Maindron concluded a historical survey of 'Les Affiches Illustrées' in *La Gazette des Beaux Arts* in 1884 with a presentation of his work where he argued that it merited being 'raised to the level of art' through the quality of its colour, line and composition. For over two decades leading up to the First World War the critic and arts administrator Roger Marx repeatedly cited Chéret as an exemplar of the reformed, democratic art he believed the Third Republic should foster. 'Under the pretext of advertisements, a thousand gay and charming visions have emerged from his capricious inspiration. He has elevated the poster to the level of mural painting – Chéret has made light of the difficult problems of representation that the fever for advertising has presented him with and he has exploited this growing fever to become, over thirty years, the unique decorator of modern Paris', he wrote in 1899 (Marx 1913: 155).

In 1895 the Imprimerie Chaix – which had taken over Chéret's studio but retained him as artistic director – launched a monthly subscription publication *Les Maîtres de l'affiche*.

Each issue consisted of four loose chromolithographic prints that reproduced selected modern posters in a reduced format, one of which every month was by Chéret himself. This initiative was striking testimony to two aspects of the poster phenomenon at the end of the century: its critical recognition as a form of art, and its international scope. These prints were aimed at collectors who were interested in acquiring and conserving, on aesthetic grounds, what were at base ephemeral products, destined to be torn down and replaced after a short period of outdoor display. The selection of work demonstrated the range and quality of contemporary poster design – due in some instances, most notably that of Toulouse-Lautrec, to artists primarily engaged in the fine art field – not only in France but throughout Europe and the United States.

The golden age of the poster

Largely taking their cue from the French example, artists, designers and critics in other countries were very active from the 1890s onwards in promoting the value of quality in commercial art, primarily through the poster. Enthusiasts in England created a periodical with this name in 1898 and which, like *Les Maîtres de l'affiche*, provided material for collectors but also argued the case for higher standards in advertising generally. A journal with the same name and mission – *Das Plakat* – was founded in Berlin in 1912. Advertising was a major theme in initiatives to improve design in Germany in this period, centred on the activities of the *Werkbund* from 1907 onwards. The prominent *Werkbund* member Karl-Ernst Osthaus, a major art collector and the founder of the Folkwang Museum in Hagen, established a museum for Art in Trade and Industry in 1909 in which advertising had a central place, organising touring exhibitions and publishing five monographs on 'advertising artists' between 1911 and 1915.

The supporters of advertising 'art' had a dual goal – to draw the attention of the public to the aesthetic qualities of commercial illustration, and also to convince the business community that investment in quality 'art' advertising was worthwhile. The artists engaged in this work had to develop approaches to style, colour and composition that were both visually satisfying and original, and which highlighted the product concerned effectively. Chéret, as indicated above, resolved this challenge through the use of a style that combined the fantasy and elegance of Rococo art with elements of the urban realism of the Impressionists, communicating the message through the metonymical association of the product with a glamorous young woman, reinforced by visually integrated labelling. Chéret's manner was widely imitated in France and elsewhere, as in the 'Gaiety Girl' devised by Dudley Hardy in England for theatre posters, who was clearly modelled on 'La Chérette'. The styles of Symbolist art and arts and crafts-related design generated a 'modern' version of the formula in the mid-1890s, using organic decorative schema in flat, patterned compositions with one or two, usually female, stylised figures. The young Czech painter Alphonse Mucha, working in Paris, after achieving his breakthrough with a poster for the theatre star Sarah Bernhardt in 1895, produced a series of works, notably for JOB cigarette papers, that were masterpieces of the genre, in which product, label, and personification were held together in a flat, sensual web of undulating lines.

The 'Beggarstaffs' (brothers-in-law William Nicholson and James Pryde), working in England in the 1890s, also used figures to validate products, but they drew on other strands of recent art practice to develop their own style, Toulouse-Lautrec's use of flat colour and Whistler's reductive sobriety of form and line. 'The blank space is my special beauty', the Beggarstaffs' 'Rowntrees Cocoa Man' informed a 'Gaiety Girl', in a humorous 'poster dialogue' which appeared in *The Poster* in 1900 (Campbell 1990: 119–120). In this work the artists emphasised the flat, unreal nature of the advertising space in a restrained, elegant composition, which represented the product discreetly in the company of three male figures evocative of the past – but not explicitly identified. This approach tested the limits of acceptable advertising – the Beggarstaffs were not very successful commercially – but their work was widely admired in professional circles, as abstracting forms of stylisation came to be widely taken up in the field. Leonetto Cappiello applied it successfully in his version of the Chéret formula, where products often acquired an animating spirit, and it was a key feature of the 'object-poster' style championed in Berlin by Lucian Bernhard. This influential method dispensed with the validating, atmospheric, human figure – rich, flat colours were used to hold and present isolated objects – the advertised product became the protagonist of the scene (see Plate 6).

By 1914, the visual presence of advertising had been forcefully asserted, particularly through poster arrays in urban centres, and a history of advertising was beginning to evolve. The advertising image was also becoming increasingly recognised by artists as a key component of the visual component of modern life. Cubist works by Braque and Picasso incorporated fragments of newspaper advertisements and cinema and theatre bills; in 1913 Robert Delaunay, in his painting *The Cardiff Team*, a composite image of a world transformed by modern communications and the machine, linked the aeroplane soaring over Paris with a poster for the aero manufacturer ASTRA. The association of advertising with the 'modern' was reinforced in the post-war years, in the context of its gradual development as a distinctive visual discipline.

Between the wars: consolidation and innovation

In recognition of its importance in the contemporary designed environment, advertising was included as a display category at the 1925 Paris Decorative and Industrial Arts exhibition, in the class 26 – 'Les Arts de la Rue' – and enjoyed considerable success. This initiative was part of the ongoing effort by the French establishment to promote quality in design, which in the field of advertising meant asserting the importance of artistic values to its practice. The catalogue of the exhibition noted that post-Chéret there had been a certain decline in poster design that the section display had helped to rectify – it demonstrated that 'To seduce requires beauty: to fulfil its role advertising must retain an artistic character … Anonymous or not, now the artist has his place in advertising' (Anon. 1926: 48). What this meant in practice was a matter of debate and experiment throughout the period. In a 1922 text on 'Posters and Business', Paul Dermée (co-founder of the periodical *L'Esprit Nouveau*) and Eugène Courmont had argued that poster artists should not 'discover new aesthetic dimensions' – this was the realm of the 'fine artist', although they were strongly supportive of the concept of the art poster in general – Dermée was a great admirer of Jean D'Ylen, who worked in the general style of Cappiello, with a strong focus on the object (Halter 1992: 47). Some critics, possibly including Dermée, thought that the new 'School' of designers that emerged in France in the mid-1920s, whose key figures were Carlu, Cassandre, Colin and Loupot, were too 'avant-garde' in their approach, although they were undoubtedly successful in prestige terms. Cassandre's work throughout the interwar period exemplified a distinctively 'modern' graphic style with its roots in the planar, geometric forms of synthetic cubism. It came to embody a stylish 'Parisian' approach to publicity material that was particularly suited to the promotion of luxury lifestyle goods, including travel. Reductive design, applied to an established iconic product, using precise delineation and smooth flat colour combined with sharp sans serif lettering, generated memorable images that linked their subjects effectively to notions of refinement and advanced taste, for consumers who were attuned to the visual language employed (see Plate 7).

British commentators in this period continued to urge the business community to support aesthetic quality in their advertising, bemoaning the fact that too many of them sought to make economies in this area, or were too prescriptive, and philistine, in their dealings with artists. At the same time they emphasised that artists entering this field needed to accept its limitations and its specific goals. In *Art in Advertising* (1925) Percy Bradshaw praised the distinguished mural painter Frank Brangwyn for his pragmatic and modest approach to advertising illustration that he contrasted with the misplaced belief of some young artists that they were 'above' the taste of the ordinary public (Bradshaw 1925: 1–15). Brangwyn's commercial work included posters for the London North Eastern Railway. Conventional artistic practices could be adapted quite easily to travel advertising, where the pleasures associated with specific destinations could be highlighted. The London Midland Railway, in fact, commissioned a series of posters by Royal Academicians in the 1920s. Besides Brangwyn, the enterprising publicity manager for the London and North Eastern Railway (L.N.E.R.) W. M. Teasdale was responsible for the production of a range of attractive material by other illustrators including Fred Taylor and Tom Purvis that were widely admired for their aesthetic qualities. For Chas Knights, the author of *Lay-out and Commercial Art*, Purvis' work exemplified what a highly trained and skilled professional could achieve, drawing on the modern painting tradition stemming from Impressionism, in response to the need for an advertisement to impose a memorable image with instant effect. He argued that while 'extreme' forms of modernism were inappropriate in the commercial field, the general principle of simplifying abstraction that underlay much modern art was complementary to the aims of advertising. Wilful experimentation was entirely misplaced, but if modern techniques, including photomontage, where photographic images were cut and combined to generate visual impact, were used intelligently in relation to an appropriate concept, they could produce impressive results. He cited Edward McKnight Kauffer as a dedicated, successful 'modernist' in this respect. Some of McKnight Kauffer's most striking work was made for the London Underground which, through the initiative of Frank Pick, was a major commissioner of high quality 'artistic' publicity material throughout the inter-war period. Illustrating it as an example of effective modernist work, Knights described his poster 'Power the nerve centre of London's Underground' as 'Expressionist' (Knights 1932: 49) (see Plate 8). His use of this term indicated an awareness of the German modern art tradition, and it was the case that McKnight Kauffer was influenced by recent German graphic design as well as French. He was, with Purvis, one of a group of international designers invited to contribute to the tenth anniversary issue of the German dual language review *Gebrauchsgraphik-International Advertising Art* in 1933, where he paid a fulsome tribute to its role in disseminating modern ideas in the field, and to the contribution of German designers in making the poster 'a living force in our modern world' (McKnight Kauffer 1933: 15).

As its English title suggests, *Gebrauchsgraphik*'s mission was the promotion of high artistic standards in the advertising field. In his foreword to the anniversary issue its director H. K. Frenzel reiterated his fundamental belief that 'it is only creative imagination which rejoices and inspires mankind, for it is almost always the pictorial element which decides the success or failure of every advertisement' (Frenzel 1933: 1). He was warning, here, against over reliance on prescriptive formulae of 'persuasion' that, he argued, had become too influential over the previous decade. This was symptomatic of the growth of the advertising business generally and the influence, particularly in Germany, of 'scientific' approaches to marketing emerging from the United States. As *Gebrauchsgraphik* demonstrated, the German design community was in fact very successful in producing visually exciting advertising material in this period across a range of platforms. Some designers, including Lucian Bernhard and Ludwig Hohlwein, continued aesthetic approaches developed before the war; others, notably those associated with the Bauhaus, including Lázló Moholy-Nagy and Herbert Bayer, applied radical new ideas of composition and representation to business imagery through the use of reductive geometric forms, a dynamic approach to typography, and the incorporation of photomontage. These were practices that the Russian avant-garde pioneered in the early 1920s, including in the case of Rodchenko and the poet Mayakovsky, in advertising material that they produced for a range of state enterprises including the department store GUM and Gosizdat, the publishing house (Rodchenko 1940). Through the work and presence of El Lissitzky – whose Soviet Pavilion at the 1928 PRESSA exhibition in Cologne was widely admired – German designers were particularly attuned to Soviet achievements in this sphere – *Gebrauchsgraphik*, for example, included a feature on him and on Soviet film posters in its December 1928 issues. El Lissitzky had collaborated with Kurt Schwitters in 1924 on a double issue of the periodical MERZ (8–9), as Schwitters developed his interest in experimental typography. Through his 'Merz' design consultancy and the group he established in 1927, the *ring neue werbegestalter* (the 'circle of new advertising designers'), Schwitters was an important figure in initiatives to apply 'avant-garde' artistic concepts in the field of commercial graphics: this had limited appeal in business circles, naturally, but there were some manufacturers, such as *Pelikan* inks in Hanover, that were receptive to such ideas (Aynsley 2000: 156–162).

As in Europe, the role of artistic quality in advertising and the appropriateness of 'modern' styles of illustration derived from contemporary art were widely debated in advertising circles in the United States between the wars. While art directors in agencies promoted the commercial sense of commissioning work with a modern aesthetic, critics argued that this approach was self-indulgent and insufficiently focused on public taste (Bogart 1995: 137–143; Marchand 1985: 140–148). Lucian Bernhard set up a business in New York in the mid-1920s, seeking with some success to benefit from the dynamism of the American advertising sector. The technical, focused, approach of the Americans impressed him, but this relocation required some adjustments on his part. He found that there was less respect than in Europe for the purely aesthetic aspects of a design. Americans demanded above all 'human interest' in advertisements and were over reliant on enlarged photographs in posters (Aynsley 2000: 83–85). Photomontage did not make a great impact on American design until somewhat later, but American business did appreciate the potential of 'art' photography in the commercial field. Edward Steichen's career from the early 1920s onwards, providing images for J. Walter Thompson campaigns, primarily for advertisements in the burgeoning womens' magazine market, demonstrated the opportunities that existed for talented photographers who were willing to orient their work to the business of selling (Johnston 2000). Photography embodied the 'modern' and above all it allowed fragments of the 'real' to be selected, framed and identified persuasively with a brand. Consequently almost as soon as reproductive technology allowed it – in the late 1920s – the photograph became a key component of advertising, particularly in the fields of fashion and cosmetics.

In an article of 1936, reflecting on art and contemporary visual culture in general, Fernand Léger asked how it was possible for art to compete for the workers' attention, when they were constantly bombarded with 'the enormous photographic compositions of advertising posters ... these enormous modern machines delivering vulgarised art to the power of a thousand' (Léger 1936: 178). With Robert and Sonia Delaunay, Léger had been a key figure in the artistic engagement with the visual signs of modernity in France, including advertising posters: here he recognised that these were also a threat to the existence of art itself. His response was to advocate the reappropriation of the scale and dynamic colour of commercial art for a pure fine art use, moving towards abstraction. A different major strand in art practice of the interwar period, stemming from the Dada and Surrealist movements, destabilised the whole concept of the aesthetic sphere. One form this took, exemplified by Schwitters' MERZ collages and Hannah Höch's photomontage pieces, recycled the 'debris' of contemporary media output, incorporating fragments of posters, newspaper announcements and fashion illustrations into works of art. Another, championed in contrasting ways by René Magritte and Salvador Dalí, applied the principles of collage to painting to make images full of surprise and fantasy, eschewing modernist formal principles. While the former exerted a major influence on art after the Second World War, the latter had a lot to offer to the visual practices of advertising – as was presaged by Dalí's own foray into window display in New York in 1939 and developments in Herbert Bayer's work in 1930s Germany.

Quality in post-war advertising design

McKnight Kauffer, forced by circumstances, moved back to the United States in 1940. His work was well known in art circles in New York – the Museum of Modern Art, which had developed a remit to promote high standards in design, had put on an exhibition of his posters in 1937. However, he found it difficult to penetrate the structured, 'rationalised' world of New York advertising. He did eventually secure a commission to produce posters for American Airlines – the combination of place with the modernity of flight that this work suggested eminently suited his personal style. The approach to advertising imagery that McKnight Kauffer exemplified, which drew on the modern painting tradition, remained a potent strand in advertising output in the post-war period, in various guises. Abram Games, for example, designer of the logo for the Festival of Britain in 1951, produced a series of elegant posters employing the decorative features of geometric abstraction; Bernard Villemot and others in Paris perpetuated the French tradition of authorial, painterly commercial illustration. However, the dominant tendencies in the period 1945–1960, notably in the United States, had a different relationship to the practices of Fine Art, that reflected the maturity and expansion of the advertising industry. A great deal of advertising output continued models that had become established within the design community itself: versions of object-oriented illustration abounded, together with situation 'realism' that drew on (and promoted) stereotypes of gender, family and occupation. In both cases the role of photography became increasingly central, and the advent of television reinforced this pattern. On the other hand, the dissemination of ideas and practices about the specific discipline of graphic design that had been developed in Germany in the interwar period – a process in which central European emigrés played a key role – led to the emergence of design professionals who succeeded in producing powerful innovative work that demonstrated a sophisticated understanding of visual form applied to the distinct needs of commercial communication. Paul Rand was exemplary in this respect. Having studied at the Pratt Institute, Parsons School of Design and the Art Students League, he had wide-ranging knowledge of modernist practice in art and design, and he applied this with intelligence and focus to the needs of advertising, in the fields of magazine layout, posters and trademark design. Rand had a high sense of his calling and in this he, and other major designers of the period, perpetuated the ideas and practices of early-twentieth-century pioneers in advertising 'art'. He was clear that the graphic designer was an artist: the core of his activity was creative invention that drew on a personal response to the visual nature of the world. However, he also completely accepted that the 'popular artist' working in advertising was engaged in the business of selling and should be judged in terms of this. He concluded his essay 'Integrity and Invention' with the stern reminder that 'Graphic design which fulfils aesthetic needs ... is not good design if it is irrelevant. Graphic Design which evokes the symmetria of Vitruvius, the dynamic symmetry of Hambridge, the asymmetry of Mondrian; which is a good gestalt ... is not good design if it does not communicate' (Rand 1985: 237–239).

Rand was versatile in his design work, employing a range of techniques and approaches. What made his output recognizable, and effective, was its concision, the integration of different elements, lightness of touch, often including humour, and the clear focus on communication, combining direct and associative imagery with a verbal message. For Coronet Brandy he devised a series of advertisements in the late 1940s featuring an abstract waiter whose head resembled a brandy glass, holding the Coronet bottle on a range of imaginatively drawn and coloured trays, set against a background of coloured dots evocative of bubbles in soda water. For El Producto cigars he converted the product itself into a personage, through minimal means, which was deployed in a range of lightly drawn settings, with witty captions that underlined the brand. In his work for Jacqueline Cochran cosmetics he combined areas of flat colour with carefully disposed verbal information and striking photomontage details (see Figure 7.1). In the latter half of his career Rand applied his distinctive skills to the growing field of corporate identity, working notably for Westinghouse Corporation and IBM. Through his example, and also his writing and teaching, he was a highly influential figure, standing for the highest professional standards in the production of advertising graphics (while also, through his ousting from the Weintraub agency in 1955, exemplifying the tensions that could still develop between the 'creative' and the 'commercial' sides of the business).

Post-war art and the challenge of advertising

Rand was a continuator of the modernist aesthetic tradition in advertising – indeed he came to embody it – but in a context in which the industry had grown to the point of establishing its independent status as a generator of modern visual culture. Fine art practice in this epoch related to advertising in two distinct ways, one that forcefully distanced itself from the commercial art sphere and one that on the contrary embraced it as a key aspect of contemporary reality. A major trend in painting from the 1940s to the 1960s built on the example of abstraction. Aesthetic, and spiritual, values were asserted free of direct reference to either the natural or the man-made environment. Echoing the radical critique of commercial culture developed by Frankfurt School Marxist theorists, Clement Greenberg argued that art had to combat 'kitsch' – cultural products that reiterated established formats on an industrial scale, appealing to the lowest common denominators of public taste. Advertisements naturally came into this category. The 'high' art that Greenberg championed, and which became very prominent on the Western art scene in the 1950s did, to a degree, answer Léger's call for painting to reclaim the scale and colour of advertising for purely aesthetic ends. This form of painting functioned within

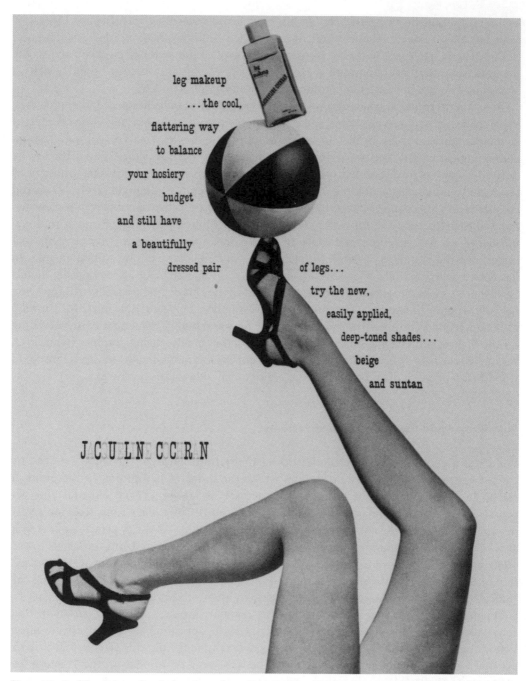

Figure 7.1: Paul Rand, *Jacqueline Cochran leg makeup*, 1944. Paul Rand Papers (MS 1745), Manuscripts and Archives, Yale University Library.

parameters established through the history of modern art over the previous century. It celebrated the originality of the artist and the freedom of art work from all functional constraints, even that of representation. In contrast to this, other currents in avant-garde art, partly influenced by the alternative 'anti-aesthetic' tradition associated with Dada and Surrealism, rejected the abstract route of 'pure', 'modernist' painting, and turned to advertising imagery as source material. They adopted a variety of approaches to its use. The 'affichistes' linked to the French 'New Realism' group – Villeglé, Hains, Dufrêne and Rotella – appropriated multi-layered billboards by 'de-pasting' them, and presented the tattered, fragmented remnants of advertising posters in the gallery environment as 'compositions' that embodied the contemporary urban environment. The artists in Britain and the United States who came to be identified with 'Pop' (a term directly taken from the generic term for commercial art at the time) focused specifically on the imagery associated with advertising. Richard Hamilton made paintings that borrowed from, and imitated, fashion plates and domestic appliance advertisements; James Rosenquist created collage-based work using imagery from the mass media on the scale of billboards; Andy Warhol – who had had a successful early career as a graphic designer – adapted media images, commercial labels and packages and the iconic form of the Coca-Cola bottle, in paintings that blandly challenged the values of originality, uniqueness and technique conventionally associated with 'fine' art. For Arthur C. Danto, Warhol's philosophically significant achievement was that he 'gave objectivity to the common cultural mind' (Danto 1999: 81). His work asserted that all the familiar forms and objects of contemporary American culture could be art: prominent among them, of course, were those associated with advertising.

Postmodern

The centrality of advertising and the images it generates to experience in capitalist societies has been constantly reinforced over the years since Pop Art emerged. One view of the 'postmodern' cultural environment can see advertising effectively as the defining visual art form of our times. Roger Marx's late-nineteenth-century vision of the commercial poster as a key element in a democratic art movement could be said to have been realised, but in a context where aesthetic norms are virtually non-existent and in which this 'art' fulfils needs that its producers work hard not just to meet, but to create, and where they themselves are engaged in constant competitive struggle. It is certainly true that as advertising, through the media forms it uses, has become ever more present in our environment, it has also, through necessity, become increasingly inventive and sophisticated in its use of imagery. Brands use advertising in order to sustain and assert their identity in 'consumer-led' markets, where the consumers are both image-saturated and highly image conscious. Formal elegance, sensuality, wit, surprise and shock are all techniques that have been applied by designers to retain viewers' attention and convey their message. Famous and successful campaigns that have effectively tested the boundaries of 'creative' advertising over the last thirty years include the United Colors of Benetton series by Oliviero Toscani, using extreme 'dislocation' between the image and the product, and the Silk Cut advertisements devised by the Saatchi and Saatchi agency in the context of heightened awareness of the hazards of smoking, from the 1980s onwards. Several of these evoked the styles and methods of contemporary art in their use of objects, shape and colour. In the same way that it has drawn on popular music because of its familiarity and emotional power, as Judith Stevenson demonstrates elsewhere in this volume, modern advertising has also often used art directly for its status and visual impact. Absolut Vodka, which created a market for vodka in the United States in the 1980s from almost nothing, has a long-standing practice of inviting artists to devise campaigns based on its distinctive bottle shape. The 'Absolut Art' series, which was, symptomatically, initiated by Andy Warhol, featured regularly throughout the 1990s inside the back cover of *Artforum* and *Artsmagazine* – the leading art journals of the time in New York (Gibbons 2005: 137–140). Quotation, often employed with humour, is a common device – Michelangelo's David dressed in Levi's denim shorts (1970s) is a good example that draws on the multiple connotations of the original statue, combined with the Surrealist principle of collage, to make a joke and establish brand value (Carrière-Chardon 2000: 100). The highly acclaimed television advertisement for Honda 'Cog' (2005) is a recent example of the industry's ability to incorporate ideas and models from art for its own ends. In this piece the mobile principle of the art film 'Der Laufe der Dinge' (Fischli and Weiss, 1987), in which objects are set in motion to create a narrative of materials 'in action', is appropriated to generate a witty homage to the mechanical perfection encapsulated by the Honda brand.

The 1960s and 1970s marked the end of the hegemonic drive of 'modernist' painting and sculpture as championed by Greenberg, based on a restrictive understanding of what constitutes 'high' art in our time. Fine art in the contemporary era is pluralist, defined not by any essential aesthetic identity but by the institutional, critical and theoretical field in which it functions. Advertising has been used for dual purposes in this context. Numerous artists incorporate and use its features in recognition of its central role in our visual world. As appropriated image and object, its products are also mobilised to articulate the critical interrogation of the concept of art itself, that is an ongoing thread in contemporary practice. At the Dokumenta 7 exhibition in Kassel in 1982 Daniel Buren presented his work in the form of a commercial fête, stringing up abstract, striped pennants with broadcast enumeration of colour terms in different languages as accompaniment. In the same show John Knight turned his name into a logo, made up of collaged tourist brochures (Gintz 1990: 460–466). In each case the artist was simultaneously questioning the formal and conceptual parameters of 'painting' and acknowledging the power and ubiquity of the commercial image. From the 1970s onwards Barbara Kruger has appropriated the visual style of the poster to raise social and political issues within the spaces of art; in a similar vein, in a series of works of the 1970s Victor Burgin used the visual and verbal rhetorical devices of advertising image and copy to expose its ideological basis (Athanassopolous 2009: 141–150). Conversely, Jeff Koons and Takashi Murakami – two of the most successful artists of the early-twenty-first century – have come close to collapsing 'fine' art into the practices of mass-media popular promotion. These examples demonstrate the degree to which the art–advertising relationship has been inverted over the last century. Whereas in the 1890s advertising, via the poster, aspired to the prestige of art, art today is both attracted and threatened by the power of advertising. The advertising industry is integral to the ways in which we experience the world, deploying enormous material and creative resources to communicate its messages. The form and content of these are part of the reality with which many artists seek to engage, even though their power is such that they risk making art itself redundant. The seductive force of the advertising image, and the possibility for art to use it for its own, precarious, ends, is elegantly demonstrated by Richard Prince's *Untitled (cowboy)* series (1980). The 'Marlboro Man' condensed the myth of the frontier, masculine aspiration, and a brand in a formidable demonstration of advertising's ability – using visual means – to encapsulate social values and subvert them to commercial ends. Prince's re-appropriation of the image asserts the power of art to 'show' the world – all the qualities of dream and nostalgia associated with the cowboy are elegiacally displayed, but in a form that also *represents* the presence of advertising at the core of American culture (see Plate 9).

References

Anon. (1926), 'Art Publicitaire. Section Française', in *Encyclopédie des arts décoratifs et industriels modernes au XXème siècle, 2, Architecture: décoration peinte et sculptée,* Paris: Office Central d'Éditions et de Librairie, pp. 47–51.

Athanassopolous, V. (2009), *La Publicité dans l'art contemporain I*, Paris: Harmattan.

Aynsley, J. (2000), *Graphic Design in Germany 1890–1945*, London: Thames and Hudson.

——— (2001), *A Century of Graphic Design: Graphic Design Pioneers of the 20th Century*, London: Mitchell Beazly.

Bogart, M. H. (1995), *Advertising, Advertisers, and the Borders of Art,* Chicago and London: University of Chicago Press.

Bradshaw, P. (1925), *Art in Advertising. A Study of British and American Pictorial Publicity,* London: The Press Art School.

Campbell, C. (1990), *The Beggarstaff Posters: The Work of James Pryde and William Nicholson,* London: Barrie and Jenkins.

Carrière-Chardon, S. (2000), *L'Art dans la Pub.*, Paris: Union centrale des arts décoratifs.

Collins, B. (1981), *Jules Chéret and the Nineteenth-Century French Poster*, London: UMI Press.

Danto A. C. (1999), *Philosophizing Art: Selected Essays,* Berkeley, Los Angeles and London: University of California Press.

Fischli, P. and Weiss, D. (1987) *Der Laufe der Dinge* (The Way Things Go) http://icarusfilms.com/cat97/t-z/the_way_.html Accessed 20 July 2012.

Frenzel, H. K. (1933), '10th Volume', *Gebrauchsgraphik*, 10:1, p. 1.

Gibbons, J. (2005) *Art and Advertising*, London: Tauris.

Gintz, C. (1990), 'Everything is Connected to Everything Else', in *Art & Pub: art et publicité 1890–1990*, Paris: Éditions du Centre Pompidou, pp. 456–477.

Hahn, H. (2007), 'Boulevard Culture and Advertising as Spectacle in Nineteenth-Century Paris', in A. Cowan and J. Steward (eds), *The City and the Senses. Urban Culture since 1500*, Aldershot: Ashgate, pp. 156–175.

Halter, A. (1992), 'Paul Dermée and the Poster in France in the 1920s: Jean d'Ylen as "Maître de l'Affiche Moderne"', *Journal of Design History*, 5:1, pp. 39–51.

Haworth-Booth, M. (2005), *E. McKnight Kauffer: A Designer and his Public*, London: V&A.

Heller, S. (1999), *Paul Rand*, London: Phaidon.

Hiatt, C. (1895), *Picture Posters: A Short History of the Illustrated Placard, with many Reproductions of the Most Artistic Examples in All Countries*, London: George Bell and Sons.

Jobling, P. and Crowley, D. (1996), *Graphic Design: Reproduction and representation since 1800*, Manchester: MUP.

Johnston, P. (2000), *Real Fantasies: Edward Steichen's Advertising Photography*, Berkeley and London: University of California Press.

Jones, S. R. (1924), *Posters and their Designers*, London: The Studio Ltd.

——— (1925), *Art and Publicity: Fine Printing and Design*, London: The Studio Ltd.

Knights, C. C. (1932), *Lay-Out and Commercial Art*, The Library of Advertising, 7, London: Butterworth and Co.

Lamberty, C. (2000), *Reklame in Deutschland 1890–1914. Warhnehmung, Professionalisierung und Kritik der Wirtschaftswerbung*, Berlin: Duncker & Humblot.

Léger, F. (1936), 'Le nouveau réalisme continue', in F. Léger (1975), *Fonctions de la peinture*, Paris: Denoël/Gonthier.

Maindron, E. (1884), 'Les Affiches Illustrées', *Gazette des Beaux Arts*, XXX 2e période, pp. 439–433, 535–547.

Marchand, R. (1985), *Advertising the American Dream: Making Way for Modernity, 1920–1940*, Berkeley/London: University of California Press.

Marx R. (1913), *L'Art Social*, Paris: Charpentier.

McKnight Kauffer, E. (1933), 'Ten Years of "International Advertising Art"', *Gebrauchsgraphik*, 10:1, pp. 13–15.

Rand, P. (1985), *A Designer's Art*, New Haven and London: Yale University Press.

Rodchenko, A. (1940), 'Working with Mayakovsky', D. Elliot (ed.) (1979) *Alexander Rodchenko*, Oxford: Museum of Modern Art, pp. 102–4.

Segal, A. J. (2000), 'Commercial Immanence: The Poster and Urban Territory in Nineteenth-Century France', in C. Wishermann and E. Shore (eds) *Advertising and the European City. Historical Perspectives*, Aldershot: Ashgate, pp. 113–138.

Timmers, M. (ed.) (1998), *The Power of the Poster*, London: V&A Publications.

Various authors (1990), *Art & Pub: Art et publicité 1890–1990*, Paris: Éditions du Centre Pompidou.

Varnedoe, K. and Gopnik, A, (1991), *High & Low: Modern Art and Popular Culture*, New York: Museum of Modern Art.

Chapter 8

On-line digi-ads

David Reid

This chapter outlines the development of digital online technology over the last decade and its impact on advertising form and content within a changing consumer culture context. The twenty-first century has witnessed a technological revolution with the successful implementation and incorporation of digital tools into everyday life. Today, a multitude of digital media platforms are available to individuals, communities, businesses and governments. Whilst some traditional viewing platforms, such as television, maintain a healthy audience, others are losing out in a digitally reinvented world. The all-pervasive impact of digital technology on the advertising of consumer products contributes to changing cultural experiences and in many ways purchasers of goods have gained a consumer power that was denied them in the pre-digital age. Consumption based on traditional brand loyalty is being challenged by price-driven consumerism – an aspect of advertising and marketing enhanced by new digital technology. Change is not just limited to consumer culture. A further consequence of the development of digital online technology has been to impact on culture more generally. This has, since at least the 1990s, been labelled 'virtual culture' (Jones 1998), 'cyber culture' (Levy 2001), 'information culture' (Manovitch 2001) and 'Internet culture' (Castells 1996, Castells 2006). This chapter is interested in the place of online digi-ads within these cultures where longer-term effects and directions resulting from this can only be glimpsed in the present configuration.

Introduction

Whilst advertising has been an element of human experience and culture for many thousands of years, digital advertising is a relatively new phenomenon. But what is meant by the term 'digital technology'? What comprises digital advertising? How does it differ from traditional advertising? A simple definition describes digital as 'information, music, an image, etc. that is recorded or broadcast using computer technology' (Cambridge Dictionaries Online 2011). According to Bassey digital is a form of electronic media that can be distinguished from analogue and 'works by the exchange of digital codes' (2009: 184). However, the birth of digital advertising did not coincide with the development of computer technology. In the early days of computer technology, ENAIC, generally considered to be the first 'computer', was designed for military use by the US Army during the Second World War. Even when computers became commercially available they where functionally limited. Important developments occurred later with Ed Roberts's Altair 8800 computer in 1975, followed shortly afterwards with the creative endeavours of Steve Jobs and Steve Wozniak at Apple in 1976. Such developments enabled individuals and businesses to see new opportunities and uses associated with computer technology.

Connectivity, which is the term used to describe the way computers talk to each other, was initially limited and very local. Towards the end of the twentieth century came arguably one of the biggest technological developments. In 1989, Tim Berners-Lee and his team at the European Organization for Nuclear Research (CERN) developed the World Wide Web. From this point in time, computer interaction grew from local to regional and national to global.

Today, the World Wide Web is immense, allowing a significant proportion of humanity to connect with one another around the globe. Arguably, it is becoming the basis for a new global culture. In 2008, the search engine Google provided an estimate of the sheer volume of data floating in hyperspace: 'recently, even our search engineers stopped in awe about just how big the web is these days – when our systems that process links on the web to find new content hit a milestone: 1 trillion (as in 1,000,000,000,000) unique URLs on the web at once' (Alpert and Hajaj 2008). Research carried out by others in this field such as Maurice de Kunder from Tilburg University in the Netherlands provides findings which give a more conservative estimate. Despite these different estimates for user numbers the Internet remains the system used by most people to communicate with one another across the World Wide Web.

So when did the advertising industry start to use this communication platform? In 1994, the first online advertisement, a simple static banner advertisement for the American Telco brand AT&T was featured on the Hot Wired web site. The advertisement posed a direct question to the computer user: "have you ever clicked your mouse right here?" An arrow pointed to a button that stated: "you will". When users clicked on the button, they were taken to the AT&T site' (Hollis 2005).

Between the mid-1990s and 2000, online advertising and marketing communication went through a boom period. Known as the 'dot.com bubble' it was quickly followed by a dramatic decline, linked to a slow down in the American economy. When the economy started to grow again, online advertising and communication soon regained their momentum. This can be partly attributed to advances in technological development applied to online connectivity – namely broadband. With the introduction of broadband, Web 1.0 officially became Web 2.0.

Advertising change – technology, brands and culture

Culture and cultural experience have been transformed in numerous ways by new technological developments such as the use of digital technology in advertising and elsewhere. The development of digital media in the last few decades has contributed to a huge growth in personal computing and expansion of the World Wide Web, as well as developments in telecommunications that gave rise to the notion of media convergence.

Media convergence involves the integration of the old into the new. What is known as old or traditional media comprises radio, television, cinema, out-of-home billboards, mobile or transit and the newsprint media of magazines, newspapers and directories. Each of these media forms was separate having its own identity and mode of media delivery. Convergence alters the relationship between these existing technologies and forms. Convergence incorporates old media – which was in the main analogue – as digital 'new media'. New or digital media enables forms of advertising and marketing communication to be distributed through different technologies such as the Internet, mobile phone and gaming devices.

The concept of convergence is important to culture attached to new media and the new forms of advertising that it delivers. Convergence is not just about media content. It is also about platforms and the way that content is distributed, all of which help form what Henry Jenkins terms a new media-related 'participatory culture' (2006). A more active physical and mental engagement is often required for participation in new media than was for the old. For instance video game involvement is a different form of behaviour to the more passive mode of television watching. Bricolage and the exchange of content between users are aspects of active involvement in new media culture. Convergence then can also refer to the shared culture of new media users. 'Advertising flow' is a phenomenon traditionally attached to an analysis of radio and television broadcasting, where a succession of advertisements form an 'advertising string' between commercial television programmes and is recognised as a significant, if not defining, feature of the media form. The flow of advertising across new media also forms a continual stream of online digital advertising such as pop ups, e-mail and spam that accompany new media content. (These digi-ads are discussed later in this chapter.) In the 1970s Raymond Williams talked of 'television flow' and 'social flow', describing how television content entered the way of life of a people, similarly today, 'online digital advertising flow' can be seen to enter the culture of new media users (Williams 1974). Digital cultures are increasingly becoming entrenched: 'so deeply embedded in everyday life that they disappear' (Deuze 2006). As Henry Jenkins has suggested, 'content isn't the only thing that flows across multiple media platforms. Our lives, relationships, memories, fantasies, desires also flow across media channels' (Jenkins 2006: 3).

Dramatic technological change underpins economic, social and cultural development. The process of industrialisation in the eighteenth and nineteenth centuries can be seen as a precursor of our current technological revolution. Recent changes in technology have enabled the globalisation of economies and societies. The experience of globalisation, for a rapidly increasing number of people around the world, is real and profound. The communicative power of the Internet, a major component of this technological revolution, was identified in an early media age by the theorist, Marshall McLuhan, who talked of living in a 'global village'. As McLuhan suggested, 'after more than a century of electric technology, we have extended our central nervous system itself in a global embrace, abolishing both space and time' (McLuhan 1994: 3).

The current age of technological transformation coincides with a growth in open economic markets. This in turn has generated an ever-increasing level of sales and exchange of goods and services across international borders – a commercial aspect of globalisation that has given rise to changing cultural practice. Yet, despite globalisation – and its compression of space and time – commerce still maintains its links with culture and tradition often local in nature. Yet as Elliot suggests, 'the meanings of consumer goods are grounded in their social context and the demand for goods derives more from their role in cultural practices rather than from the satisfaction of simple human needs' (Elliot 1997: 287).

The rise of branding is important here, not just to the process of commodifying goods and services and distinguishing one product from another, but in providing these commodities with a global identity. Branding and brand recognition is part of a global consumer culture. As demand has increased, the 'need' for more products has required a sophisticated mechanised manufacture of these goods through large-scale global production. Global production has provided an expanded platform for the manufacturers of branded goods with a concomitant increase in profits. Making use of marketing and communication skills developed by advertising agencies in the late-twentieth century, brands, or more specifically, the businesses and corporations behind the brands, have achieved international recognition and commercial stature within the global marketplace. Familiarity with this system of production and exchange ensures that consumers today are 'brand aware'. As Elliot suggests, 'the exercise of choice through consumption now flows across national boundaries in a global cultural economy through the operation of advertising "mediascapes" which are image-centred strips of reality which offer the consumer a series of elements' (Elliot and Ritson 1995: 740).

Such changes in the economic landscape have made consumers significantly more price aware and their decisions price driven. As competition between brands increases and intensifies, distinctiveness and differentiation between products becomes harder to make and the products harder to sell. Consumer loyalty to a brand is increasingly problematised by advertising and marketing strategies which rather than demonstrate product difference reinforce the similarities products share with those of competitors. In a crowded marketplace of message saturation where an increasing number of advertisements occupy a diminishing space, the clarity of the advertising message becomes critical. In the battle for brand loyalty, communication overload can result in consumer disengagement. Consumers come to distrust information that appears as an advertising overload and they may ultimately lose interest in the brand. Ariely argues that 'as long as any single advertiser is tempted to over-claim ... consumers' trust will be weakened, additional advertisers will be tempted to make exaggerated claims ... ultimately each advertiser will be forced to over-promise and to over-claim' (Clemons, Barnett and Appadurai 2007: 269).

In a highly mediated and advertising-saturated world, advertising 'cut through', that is the ability of advertising and marketing to communicate a message discernibly distinct from other messages becomes increasingly problematic. As Malmelin points out, 'a single advertisement cannot reach the consumer as successfully as it used to ... advertising has expanded, advertisements have become more common' (Malmelin 2003). Business blames poor sales and reduced profits on the nature and quality of advertising and marketing strategies. Continued use of planning, design, production and distribution associated with traditional advertising modes, along with a slow reaction to the changing consumer landscape and technological advances are indeed partly to blame for this. However, Gian Fulgoni of comScore, an international Internet marketing research company, suggests other factors: 'pricing power is rapidly shifting to the consumer. The digital medium has brought transparency to prices and made it easy for anyone with a computer or mobile device to quickly find the lowest price for any product' (Fulgoni 2011).

In an economic recession when there is less to spend on commodities and consumers need to be able to differentiate between similar product lines – the consumer decision model, which emphasises decision making and consumer choice, becomes even more significant. In addition, technology has revolutionised advertising and marketing communication with traditional advertising now competing with new and expanding forms of digital advertising and marketing.

Audience reception is important to marketing and advertising industry research. This is true for audience and potential consumer interpretation of advertisements particularly in a period when new forms of advertising delivery are being introduced. Industry research seeks to create more successful campaigns. From an industry perspective the advertising receiver is primarily identified as a potential consumer of goods and services, and therefore is targeted as such. Similar research is conducted by media studies but this identifies the receiver as primarily part of a media audience and subject to a range of different media texts. Interestingly, film and television research, part of the traditional creative industries, but substantially theorised within academia, is closer to the industry view.

Technological evolution in the last few decades has also been matched by a marked change in the identity and role of the consumer. Previously seen by many as simply the receiver of messages, the consumer is now perceived as an active participant in the design of the advertising message. In the area of computerised and digital technology, 'the consumer increasingly dominates the way the web works ... opinions are being published everyday, which is a massive change in the way that information was previously distributed [in] the top down model of the traditional media world' (Breslauer, Ruoss and Smith 2009). Consumer views are incorporated into ongoing digital advertising design. According to Buzea, 'the power and influence that clients and consumers exercise ... [suggests that] ... in digital, the consumer is in charge, as he/she may hold a direct influence on the brand's image' (2011). This is a further example of cultural change – in this case in a consumer culture progressively identified as being active rather than passive.

These changes have resulted in a two-way conversation between brand and consumer. It would seem, despite everyday observations of frenetic and seemingly spontaneous consumer activity in the globalised shopping mall, the purchase of a commodity is today a more considered and deliberative consumer exercise than previously. More deliberative time is taken before a decision to purchase is made, products and services are reviewed online, details scrutinised, ratings compared; and consultation of social media-based peer reviews provide an opportunity for an information exchange about product function, performance and quality. This is a further instance of change to consumer culture. Working in partnership with the advertising agency Saatchi and Saatchi, Google researchers have explored the consumer purchasing decision process. They have evaluated the changing nature of the brand/consumer relation seeking to clarify how a brand might leverage its position to its favour. The critical moment of purchase is defined as the 'zero moment of truth'. Comparing traditional and new forms of consumption, Lecinski notes that 'today's consumers know so much more before they reach the shelf. They find incredible detail online … They browse, dig, explore, dream and master, and then they're ready to buy with confidence. And what they learn, they share with others' (Lecinski 2011).

It would appear that consumer behaviour, not just in the purchase of a commodity but crucially in the run up to the decision-making process is changed perceptibly by participation in online activity. Furthermore, the experience is extended to post-purchase activity where consumer culture is no longer confined to the street, shopping mall or store but is experienced online and at its centre is shared information, knowledge and judgments about products and processes.

As an expanding and developing area of technology, digital media continues to influence changes in the advertising and marketing communications business. Facing the reality of lower returns from traditional media outlets, advertising agencies have been forced to restructure their businesses by investing in the development of digital departments or the buying up of digital companies and incorporating them into existing businesses.

This section has outlined the rise of new media forms with digital advertising as an important part of the mix. This has helped enable, and added to, the sense of a globalised market culture. The intensity of branding in an advertising-saturated world has consequences and more price-aware consumers; part of a new online consumer culture are displaying changed consumer behaviour. In the next section, the forms that online and some offline digital advertising take are organised into a typology.

Online digi-forms

Like other areas of advertising, the digital arena can be broken down into a series of different forms. These take their place as part of digital content and also come to help shape consumer and wider cultural formations. These can be roughly grouped into the following categories: display, rich media, e-mail, viral, classified, search, moving image, social network, virtual environments, mobile, and out-of-home. This section will provide an outline, description and evaluation of advertising forms using online digital technology.

Display

The simplest form of web-based advertising is known as the 'banner'. Essentially a print style advertisement, this form of display is a miniature version of an outdoor banner or similar in form to a billboard advertisement. In the UK, the Internet Advertising Bureau (IAB) provides guidelines which have standardised the structure and design of banner style advertisements. The simplest banner style advertisement, known as the 'rectangle', is required to be a specific dimension, 180 × 150 pixels (picture elements). Additionally, there are other aptly titled forms and shapes: leader board (728 × 90), skyscraper (160 × 200), half page (300 × 600), button (120 × 60) and the micro (88 × 31).

Digital technology enables the user to interact with online information in a way which allows for advertising to extend the real-time connection with viewers and potential consumers. The banner's interactive function is simple. Information is activated by clicking on a display advert with a mouse pointer or touch-screen action. This opens up another URL (uniform resource locator) which is likely to be an advertising message from the brand. The process known as 'click through' has in itself become a measurement of online advertising success. Further advances in digital technology have enabled the development of more sophisticated and creative interactive forms such as the billboard, filmstrip, portrait, pushdown, sidekick and slider; however, these require additional software such as java script, adobe flash or media streaming to function.

Rich media

Interactive types of web advertising are also referred to as Rich Media. The IAB defines these as web page format advertisements that a user can interact with 'as opposed to solely animation and excluding click-through functionality ... used either singularly or in combination with various technologies, including but not limited to sound, video, or Flash, and with programming languages such as Java, JavaScript, and DHTML' (Internet Advertising Bureau 2011).

Just as with display-type web advertising, rich media has been standardised into a number of formats including 'in page video', a video advertisement that appears in a fixed size and placement on a web page, 'expandable/retractable units', a banner-style advertisement that enlarges or reduces in physical size, 'pop-up or pop-under units', an advertisement that appears in a new web-browser window above or below an existing web page, 'floating units', an advertisement which floats above or across the content on screen and 'between-the-page units', an advertisement that displays in between current and destination pages.

Like all forms of advertising, digital is constantly evolving. An annual review of web-based advertising is carried out by top agency creative directors, media executives, publishers and advertising operations specialists in association with the IAB to maintain advertising's creative and business credibility within the creative industries sector.

E-mail

E-mail advertising or EDM (Electronic Direct Mail) has become a complex area of marketing. It is a communication form that causes anxiety for brands and their respective advertising communications partners as well as being loathed by consumers for whom it is known as electronic junk mail or 'spam'. As Rushkoff points out, 'Email gives direct marketers almost all the advantages of junk mail without the high costs of postage and paper. Spam is crafted to elicit a maximum response, then blasted out to literally millions of people at once' (Rushkoff 1999, 278–9).

Whilst advertisers and their clients see the commercial benefits of e-mail advertising – state and government institutions are concerned about its detrimental effects. In August 2011, Symantec estimated that 75.5% of e-mail traffic on the Internet consisted of spam (Wood 2011), and as the Internet continues to grow the call to regulate becomes imperative. In 2003, under the auspices of the Australian Government, the Australian Communications and Media Authority (ACMA) implemented the Spam Act to regulate and control the use of EDM for commercial purposes. The act identifies three important requisites for commercial e-mail advertising communication: consent, the e-mail message must be sent with the consumer's permission; identification, the originator of the message must be clearly identifiable; and subscription, the consumer must be given the opportunity to opt out or unsubscribe. If the EDM communication does not meet these requisites it is defined as spam.

With e-mail being utilised by '65.1% of the global online community' (The Nielson Company 2009) there is a clear and simple case for a prospective advertiser to develop an e-mail advertising communication strategy as either stand alone or as part of an integrated campaign. The reach can be significant and the cost low.

Viral

A type of EDM communication, viral, is also known as electronic word-of-mouth. Reliant upon audience engagement and motivation, information is sent predominantly via e-mail through individual networks. Some of the most successful viral campaigns have included Hotmail, which was launched in July 1996. By the time it was sold to Microsoft in 1997 Hotmail had '8.5 million subscribers' (Pelline 1997). Its exponential growth can be partly attributed to its viral marketing message placed at the bottom of all e-mails. Somewhat like a branded signature, the recipient of the message is encouraged to sign up for a free Hotmail account. Another example, created by the advertising agency, Ogilvy & Mathers in 2006, Dove Evolution was originally developed as an afterthought from funds left over in that year's marketing budget. Within weeks of its launch 'Evolution', a seventy-five-second online video viral received '1.7 million views on video sharing site YouTube', at the time a significant response which ensured creative and critical success. Nike's success using viral marketing can be seen in its Touch of Gold 'Crossbar' video viewed on YouTube in 2006. The viral featured the world-famous footballer Ronaldinho hitting the crossbar four times, without the ball touching the floor. The product on display was a Nike football boot. It became an immensely popular viral, eventually garnering 'more than 23 million views globally' (Maymann 2008).

Classified

Online classified advertising portals are pretty much a carbon copy of their print-based cousins. They are considered a low cost form of advertising and are generally simple in design and content. This form is popular with automotive, property and recruitment industries and services. One of the key benefits online classifieds have over print is that they are searchable. At the time of Britain's last economic recession in 2008, 'a fall off in newspaper classified advertising expenditure was reversed in online classified with growth of 5–6%' (James and Whiteside 2008).

Search

As an advertising tool, search, clearly has advantages over other digital advertising forms and Google, the online search engine, is by far the biggest player in this field. Search-based advertising started in 1995 when Infoseek, one of the earlier search engines for the web (which is no longer active), began to target banner advertising in their system to the keywords users entered. The 'click through' or 'cost-per-click' (CPC) model was introduced in a deal Proctor and Gamble struck with Yahoo in 1996.

Search is a very simple process whereby the consumer chooses an online search engine, such as Google, to find a product or service. When the result is returned, the search engine places paid for advertising on the web page along with the results of the search. What search offers over most other forms of digital advertising is reach and its unique ability to connect with the consumer using contextual, behavioural and geo-targeting methods. Although Google currently dominates the search arena, others such as Yahoo, Baidu, Bing, Ask and AOL are competing for market share. As the dominant and most innovative player in the field, Google is the search engine of choice for companies advertising and marketing the world's leading brands.

Google operates a system known as Search Engine Marketing (SEM) by selling the use of Ad Words, a 'cost-per-click' online advertising tool, to prospective advertisers. If a potential consumer searches Google using one of the keywords the advertiser has listed, an advertisement, which may take the form of a variety of formats including text, image and video, appears in the side column of the search page. Google only receives payment if the user continues the click-through process to the advertisers' designated URL.

Search can also contextualise information to target users with advertisements for products and services based on their consumer preferences. Adware programs are employed to analyse a user's Internet surfing habits to determine the type of goods and services they are likely to purchase. As a result of this analysis, 'contextual ads' are made to pop up periodically. 'Behavioural' targeting is where advertising is delivered to consumers based on their past search behaviour. Since user behaviour reveals their interests, these types of consumers are considered highly motivated. In addition 'geo-targeting' describes a situation where the content of a search is returned to the consumer based on the specific physical location. This may include the actual street address, the ISP details or the actual IP address.

With traditional forms of advertising communication the message delivery process works best; it is understood more clearly and is more likely to have an impact when an Integrated Marketing Communication (IMC) strategy is considered. In considering search as an online tool, it's also critical to view it as part of the marketing mix, the advertisers' media marketing plan, or in 'digital speak' as part of an integrated digital campaign. This inclusive route may include, for example, search engine advertising, advertising on websites (such as e-mail sites, news sites, video-sharing sites), paid online directories (Yellow Pages), online classified (real estate, automotive, recruitment), in-video advertising (catch-up television) as well as social network advertising.

Whilst Google is a dominant player, their own research points to a current dis-connect between media consumption and purchasing. Whilst the consumer spends a significant time on the Internet compared to other forms of media, this does not currently translate into the purchasing of goods and services online.

Video

Another area of significant growth is video. The development of key infrastructure such as fibre-optic connectivity has significantly aided the roll out of high-speed Internet connection (broadband). High-speed Internet is particular important for online products that require high bandwidth and faster connections to run smoothly. Gaming and video are two such products. Major search engines and a number of video-sharing platforms like Google (via YouTube), Yahoo and AOL offer these advertising services.

Social Network Services

Advertising within Social Network Services (SNS) has risen sharply in parallel with the rise in the use of SNS globally. Facebook, the leading player in the SNS market with '750 million users globally' (Facebook 2011), offers a significant number of unique advertising services to brands. Just as with Google its strength lies in its 'reach' and its ability to connect to the consumer using contextual, behavioural and geo-targeting methods. SNS are rapidly becoming a significant aspect of not only youth cultures but of contemporary culture more generally and the process of social networking is seemingly all pervasive.

What then fuels our need to socially network? We can consider here the concept of 'neo-tribes' which relates to lifestyle and habitation and the changing nature of social groups. Bauman and May note that 'neo-tribes are, in essence, life-styles and these relate to styles of consumption' (2001: 156). Elliott goes further: 'the development of individual self-identity is inseparable from the parallel development of collective social identity' and 'self-identity must be validated through social interaction' (1998: 100). Ultimately therefore it would seem that we have a need to interact, to engage and communicate 'socially'; SNS are both serving and fuelling that need in the global age of Internet technology. The reach of SNS is a significant cultural factor. Research data from Pew Internet suggests that over 50% of all adults use SNS – evidence of the rapid growth in social networking worldwide. Social networking and new media are becoming central to the formation of new aspects of culture.

As their reach is so wide and collection of data so immediate, SNS offer the prospective advertiser an opportunity to target the consumer in a very precise way. Specialist online services for photo sharing, such as Flickr and video-sharing sites such as YouTube are being superseded by the larger SNS which offer similar services but all in a 'one stop shop'.

Social media is generally used as a personal and private space and as such advertisers have had had difficulty in utilising it to market brands. The projection of advertising and marketing communication into that space can have a negative effect; Breslauer et al. suggest that 'social media involvement for brands is more around the idea of building direct relationships with consumers, creating communities and distributing content through these platforms – a big shift that many companies have been slow to embrace, and in some cases are fearful of doing, lest interactions with consumers go wrong' (Breslauer, Ruoss & Smith 2009).

In a recent development, and in line with the current trend to utilise lifestyle options for further expansion of consumer activity, Facebook announced a major strategic move away from its original creative position as a social network to that of a newly envisioned role – that of 'Online Life Manager'. 'Facebook, in short, aims not to be a website you spend a lot of time on, but something that defines your online – and increasingly offline – life' (Sengupta and Sisario 2011). This has much to do with its ongoing battle with Google and aggressive monetisation strategy whilst also playing into the hand of the prospective advertiser who is happy to pay for more knowledge of existing and potential consumers.

Gaming and virtual environments

As digital environments can be offline as well as online, advertising and marketing companies have developed unique approaches to reaching consumers in such places. Gaming, an entertainment medium which has seen rapid growth in the last few decades offers additional digital opportunities for companies to advertise and market their products. There are many different types of games namely 'alternate reality', 'applications', 'social games', 'virtual worlds' and 'casual games' all of which can be experienced using a multitude of platforms such as a gaming console, personal computer and handheld device.

Advertising communication takes different forms in gaming. Brands are able to be incorporated into the structure and narrative of the game itself - making use of specific sites and elements of games such as a stadium hoarding in a rugby football game, or on a vehicle in a motor racing game. According to Willifer, 'In-game advertising has very sophisticated metrics in terms of measuring eyeballs – the number of people who have been exposed to the brand and for how long. It also has very sophisticated ways of serving the advertising, via dynamic advertising schedules' (Willifer 2010). A brand-created game might be free or retailed.

Other games such as Second Life, an online virtual world where the user creates an avatar to engage in the different experiences and activities the virtual world has to offer provides opportunities for advertisers to reach huge audiences. According to Philip Rosedale, creator of Second Life, the current 'population' of the platform is approximately '1 million active users' (Singularity University 2011). In the manufactured online world, advertising and marketing can mirror and copy its real-world cousin making use of sites and locations such as billboards for the display of the brand. In addition, brand interaction can occur through avatar 'agents', who like salespeople in a real shop, offer detailed information on a product or service.

Mobile

The development of broadband infrastructure, a major technological advance, enabled the Internet to deliver high-speed communication. In mobile phone technology, a similar advance has occurred with the development of high-speed wireless networks, 3G and 4G, at the same time as the launch of the smart-phone. Reaching the consumer wherever they are is the key advantage mobile communication has over all other digital platforms. Advertising and marketing communication delivered to mobile can include instant messaging (IM), Bluetooth promotions, barcode scanner promotions, mobile apps, as well as mobile web-based digital marketing.

Out-of-home

Across the UK digital screens are slowly replacing older style billboards. Currently these new digital screens offer the flexibility of the average plasma screen found in the home. Importantly this digital technology allows advertisers to measure audience metrics, noting their presence, notice and dwell time, as the digital marketing industry terms it, twenty-four hours a day, seven days a week.

However if we look to the future of outdoor advertising and its use of digital technology, we can see a new environment emerging. As Steinbichler anticipates, 'A totally new form of advertising, dubbed "gladvertising", will be one of the first innovations to arrive. Gladverts are envisaged as digital-out-of-home ads that react to consumers' moods by using emotion recognition software (ERS) and cameras to detect whether consumers are happy, tailoring ads to their mood' (Steinbichler 2011).

Conclusion

This chapter has explored the genesis of computer technology and digital advertising recognising that this has taken place within a developing advertising culture. The relationship between the consumer, the economy and the commodities on offer has changed dramatically with both globalisation and technology playing significant parts. The impact of the Internet and World Wide Web has allowed advertisers to reach the consumer more quickly and more precisely. A new form of consumer culture has developed in which product information and shared consumer knowledge are central. Digital culture is becoming an important element of new cultural formulations and online digi-ads are a significant aspect of this content. This chapter has outlined the various forms that online and in some cases offline digital advertising are taking. This is important not only to consumer culture but is likely to have deep seated and perhaps as yet unknown ramifications for culture in general. Digital advertising and marketing communication might appear to advertisers and consumers alike as the 'bee's knees' of advertising technology. However the consumer spends a significant part of his or her life offline. As Les Binet of advertising agency Doyle Dane Bernbach (DDB) suggested at a recent London 'advertising effectiveness' conference 'over 83% of media consumption … over 90% of communication … and over 90% of retail sales are offline' (Binet 2011).

References

Alpert, J. and Hajaj, N. (2008), 'We Knew the Web was Big … ', http://googleblog.blogspot.com/2008/07/we-knew-web-was-big.html. Accessed 1 October 2011.

Australian Communications and Media Authority (2011), 'Spam', http://www.acma.gov.au/WEB/STANDARD/pc=PC_310294. Accessed 25 November 2011.

Bassey, J. (2009), 'Advertising and New Media', in H. Powell, J. Hardy, S. Hawkin and I. MacRury (eds) *The Advertising Handbook*, London: Routledge.

Bauman, Z. and May, T. (2001), *Thinking Sociologically*, 2nd edn, Oxford: Wiley-Blackwell.

Binet, L. (2011), 'Beyond the Click', WARC, http://www.warc.com/. Accessed 1 October 2011.

Breslauer, B., Ruoss, S. and Smith, T. (2009), 'Social Media Trends around the World! – The Global Web Index', ESOMAR, http://www.warc.com/. Accessed 1 October 2011.

Buzea, C. (2011), *Rise of 2.0: Digital Agencies Set New Marketing Trend*, http://business-review.ro/links/rise-of-2-0-digital-agencies-set-new-marketing-trend/10853/. Accessed 1 October 2011.

Cambridge Dictionaries Online (2011), http://dictionary.cambridge.org/dictionary/british/digital?q=digital. Accessed 1 October 2011.

Castells, M, (1996), *The Information Age: Economy, Society and Culture Volume I, The Rise of the Network Society*, Oxford: Blackwell.

—— (2005), *The Network Society: A Cross-Cultural Perspective*, Northampton: Edward Elgar Publishing.

Clemons, E., Barnett, S. and Appadurai, A. (2007), 'The Future of Advertising and the Value of Social Network Websites: Some Preliminary Examinations', in ICEC '07, *Proceedings of the ninth international conference on electronic commerce*, 19–22 August 2007, University of Minnesota, Minneapolis. New York: ACM, pp. 267–276.

De Kunder, M. (2011), 'The Size of the World Wide Web', http://www.worldwidewebsize.com/. Accessed 1 October 2011. http://www.different-uk.com/ 'Different Advertising'. Accessed 1 October 2011.

Deuze, M. (2006), *Participation, Remediation. Bricolage: Considering Principle Components of a Digital Culture*, http://scholarworks.iu.edu/dspace. Accessed 19 March 2012.

Elliot, R. (1997), 'Existential Consumption and Irrational Desire', *European Journal of Marketing* (online), http://www.emeraldinsight.com/. Accessed 1 October 2011. Vol. 31, No.3/4, pp. 285–296.

———— (1998), 'A Model of Emotion-Driven Choice', *Journal of Marketing Management* (online), http://www.ebscohost.com/academic/business-source-complete. Accessed 1 October 2011. Vol. 14, pp. 95–108.

Elliot, R. and Ritson, M. (1995), 'Practicing Existential Consumption: The Lived Meaning of Sexuality in Advertising', http://www.ebscohost.com/academic/business-source-complete. Accessed 1 October 2011. Volume 22, pp. 740–745.

Facebook (2011), *Statistics*, https://www.facebook.com/press/info.php?statistics. Accessed 1 October 2011.

Fulgoni, G. (2011), *Pricing Power is Moving to the Consumer – Is it Time for a Renaissance in Advertising?* http://www.comscore.com/Press_Events/Presentations_Whitepapers/2011/Is_it_Time_for_a_Renaissance_in_Advertising_Webinar. Accessed 24 November 2011.

Hollis, N. (2005), Ten Years of Learning How Online Advertising Builds Brands, in *Journal of Advertising Research*, Vol. 45, No. 2, pp. 255–268.

Internet Advertising Bureau (IAB) (2011), http://www.iab.net/iab_products_and_industry_services/1421/1443/1452. Accessed 1 October 2011.

James, L. and Whiteside, S. (2008), *The WARC Advertising Outlook for Autumn 2008*. WARC, http://www.warc.com/. Accessed 1 October 2011.

Jenkins, H. (2006) *Convergence Culture: Where Old and New Media Collide*, New York: New York University Press.

Jones, S. (1998), *Cybersociety 2.0: Revisiting Computer-Mediated Community and Technology*, London: Sage.

Lecinski, J. (2011), *Winning the Zero Moment of Truth*, http://www.zeromomentoftruth.com/. Accessed 10 November 2011.

Levy, P. (2001), *Cyberculture*, Minneapolis: University of Minnesota Press.

Malmelin, N. (2003), *Mainonnan lukutaito: Mainonnan viestinnällistä luonnetta ymmärtämässä*, Helsinki: Gaudeamus, cited in Puustinen, L. (2006), *The Age of Consumer-Audience: Conceptualising Reception in Media Studies, Marketing, and Media Organisations*, Working Paper 5, University of Helsinki (online), http://www.valt.helsinki.fi/comm/fi/english/. Accessed 1 October 2011.

Manovitch, L. (2001), *The Language of New Media*, Cambridge: MIT Press.

Marshall, P. (2011), 'Newly Mediated Media: Understanding the Changing Internet Landscape of Media Industries', in M. Consalvo and C. Ess (eds), *The Handbook of Internet Studies*, Chichester: Wiley-Blackwell, pp. 406–423.

Maymann, J. (2008), *For Virals, Pack a Shotgun or a Stiletto?* WARC. http://www.warc.com/. Accessed 1 October 2011.

McLuhan, M. (1994), *Understanding Media: The Extensions of Man* 2nd edn, Cambridge, MA: MIT Press.

Pelline, J. (1997), *Hotmail, Microsoft Talk Deals*, http://news.cnet.com/2100-1023-206039.html. Accessed 1 October 2011.

Rushkoff, D. (1999), *Coercion*, New York: Riverhead Books.

Sengupta, S. and Sisario, B. (2011), *Facebook as Tastemaker*, http://www.nytimes. com/2011/09/23/technology/facebook-makes-a-push-to-be-a-media-hub. html?_r=2. Accessed 1 October 2011.

Singularity University (2011), *Philip Rosedale, Creator of Second Life*, http://www.youtube.com/watch?v=C04wwLjJ0os. Accessed 1 October 2011.

Steinbichler, D. (2011), 'Digital Out-of-Home: The real Minority Report', *Admap*, http://www.warc.com/. Accessed 1 October 2011.

The Nielson Company (2009), *Global Faces and Networked Places: A Nielsen report on Social Networking's New Global Footprint*, http://www.nielsen.com/us/en/insights/reports-downloads/2009/Social-Networking-New-Global-Footprint.html Accessed 1 October 2011.

Williams, R. (1974), *Television, Technology and Cultural Form*, London: Fontana.

Willifer, M. (2010), 'Gaming's Role in the Marketing Mix', *Admap*, http://www.warc.com/. Accessed 1 October 2011.

Wood, P. (2011), *Symantec Intelligence Report: August 2011*, http://www.symantec.com/business/theme.jsp?themeid=state_of_spam. Accessed 1 October 2011.

Chapter 9

Selling politics - the political economy of political advertising

Andrew Mullen

Introduction

The selling of politics as a product – rather than politics as a process of active citizen engagement with the public sphere (Habermas 1989) – is a long-standing objective of the corporate elite and their political allies in capitalist, liberal-democratic regimes. Like art, fashion and music, politics increasingly reflects and reinforces a particular fusion of advertising and culture which is individualised and instrumentalist in nature. Advertising and its techniques – market research, neuroscience, psychology, public opinion polling, symbol manipulation, etc. – are not only used by the private sector to promote and sell goods and services to the masses, they are also used by politicians, political parties and governments to promote their products to the public. Politicians seek to convey their personal attributes, personalities and trustworthiness so as to convince the electorate of their suitability for public office; political parties strive to publicise their ideologies, programmes and visions; while governments aim to communicate their messages, policies and services (i.e. e-government). This chapter looks at how advertising has been used to sell politics to the masses. Much of the existing literature on political advertising limits itself to the nature of the communication (i.e. the message), the means by which it was transmitted (i.e. the medium) and/or the impact it had on the target audience (i.e. the effect). This chapter, by contrast, makes the case for an alternative, holistic, critical political economy approach to studying political advertising within the 'propaganda-managed democracies' (Chomsky 1995: vi) that have developed in Britain, the United States and other capitalist, liberal-democratic societies over the past one hundred years. The chapter is divided into four main sections. The first section defines political communication and identifies its main forms: political education, political persuasion and political propaganda. The second section summarises the existing literature on political advertising. Going beyond the work to date, much of which tends to focus upon political advertising during election campaigns, the third section discusses the different types of political advertising that have developed – from the micro-level of selling individual politicians to the macro-level of selling nations. The fourth section makes the case for a critical political economy approach to understanding and explaining political advertising.

Political communication as education, persuasion and propaganda

Political communication is a sub-field of media and communication studies and political science. Sanders (2009: 9) argued that 'as practice, political communication has existed as long as there have been human beings engaged in one of two activities: persuasive communication directed towards political goals and informational communication about politics'. Swanson and Nimmo (1990: 8) observed that by 1990 political communication had developed 'as a more or less distinct domain of scholarly work' – encompassing election communication, political attitudes, political behaviour and information, political communication and news, and political rhetoric (Johnston 1990). Consequently, 'the scope of practice and research in political communication is now vast' (Sanders 2009: 1) – exemplified by Blumler and McQuail (1968), Seymour-Ure (1968, 1974, 2003), Blumler and Katz (1974), Kaid (1981, 2004), Franklin (1994), Blumler and Gourevitch (1995), McNair (1995), Scammell (1995), Negrine (1996, 2008), Norris (2000), Hallin and Mancini (2004), Lilleker and Lees-Marshment (2005) and Negrine and Stanyer (2006). Political communication encompasses political education, political persuasion and political propaganda, however, and this begs an important question: what is the difference between these? To answer this question, it is useful to draw upon the liberal-pluralist versus elitist versus critical-Marxist debate about the nature of political and media systems in capitalist, liberal-democratic regimes.

Political education is central to the liberal-pluralist conception of democracy because an informed electorate, with access to accurate and unbiased information and news, is widely accepted as an essential precondition for the effective functioning of a democratic society (Mill 1975). The desire to defend the putatively liberal-pluralist media system from corporate concentration and globalisation (Herman and McChesney 1997) precipitated demands for increased media regulation in Britain from the Campaign for Press and Broadcasting Freedom, established in 1979, and the Coordinating Committee for Media Reform created in 2011. The desire to defend the putatively liberal-pluralist political system in Britain from the corrosive effects of popular disenchantment from politics (Power Inquiry 2006) led to the introduction of citizenship education in schools (Hargreaves 1994; Wilkinson and Mulgan 1995; Roberts and Sachdev 1996; Crewe 1997; Qualifications and Curriculum Authority 1998; Electoral Commission/Hansard Society 2004; Ofsted 2006, 2010), calls for the reinvigoration of political education (Crick and Porter 1978; Davies 1999; special issue of *Oxford Review of Education* Vol. 25, No. 1 1999) and the launch of the Campaign for Political Education, The 'Hand's Up Who's Bored' campaign and the HM Government e-petition on compulsory political education in 2011.

Political persuasion, in the form of political advertising, is an essential component of the elitist conception of democracy (i.e. representative rather than direct) as rival elites compete for an electoral mandate to govern (Schumpeter 1942). The definition of political advertising has changed over time in response to significant economic, political, social and technological developments. Political advertising was defined in the *Handbook of Political Communication* in 1981 as 'the communication process by which a source (usually a political candidate or party) purchases the opportunity to expose receivers through mass channels to political messages with the intended effect of influencing their political attitudes, beliefs and/or behaviours' (Kaid 1981: 250). The fact that not all countries permitted political advertising and the point that some political advertising opportunities were provided for free prompted Kaid and Holtz-Bacha (1995: 2) to widen the definition to include 'all moving image programming that is designed to promote the interests of a given party or candidate' and to incorporate 'any programming format under the control of the party or candidate and for which time is given or purchased on a broadcast (or narrowcast) outlet'. This formulation, however, neglected the print media and advocacy advertising – which aims to influence the public policy agenda rather than the electorate (Sethi 1977) – and predated the emergence of the Internet. Consequently, the concept was further refined: 'the defining characteristics of modern political advertising are (1) control of the message and (2) use of mass communication channels for message distribution' (Kaid 1999: 243). This definition possessed several notable features. Firstly, it stipulated that the message had to be controlled by the source, thus distinguishing it from news content. Secondly, it had to employ mass media channels such as broadcasts, cable, direct mail, the Internet, newspapers, pamphlets, posters, etc., whether these were free or purchased, thus differentiating it from interpersonal communication. Thirdly, it allowed for advocacy advertising but excluded other forms of political communication, such as speeches, which were subjected to interpretation and/or filtering by the media (Kaid 2004).

Political propaganda plays a key role in the critical-Marxist conception of democracy as the capitalist class seeks to defend its hegemony over the masses through its control of the economy, the media and the state (Miliband 1969). Propaganda, euphemistically described as spin or public relations (PR) by many academics, businesspeople, journalists and politicians, is a controversial and elusive concept (Miller and Dinan 2008). The term 'propaganda' was first used by Pope Gregory XV who established the Office for the Propagation of the Faith in 1622 to supervise the missionary efforts of the Catholic Church in the face of an expanding Protestantism. Propaganda is perceived in different ways, leading to a wide variety of definitions. Indeed, Marlin (2002) identified three categories. Lasswell (1927), Doob (1948), Russell (1967), Carey (1995) and the *Encyclopaedia Britannica* (2005) advanced negative definitions of propaganda, McKenzie (1938) and Taylor (1999) offered neutral definitions, while Bracken (1944), the British Minister of Information during the Second World War, defended a positive definition. Nevertheless, Marlin (2002: 22) argued that 'one feature, common to all, should be present in any definition of propaganda: it is an organized and deliberate attempt to influence many people, directly or indirectly'.

Following the First World War and the concerted propaganda campaigns in Britain and the US to demonise the Germans (Ponsonby 1928; Axelrod 2009), propaganda acquired the negative connotation that we commonly associate it with today. Indeed, as one of the founders of the modern PR industry, Edward Bernays explained, 'propaganda got to be a bad word ... So what I did was to try to find some other words [and I came up with] public relations' (quoted in Curtis 2002).

Regarding the more recent label, Miller and Dinan (2008: 2) argued that spin was a 'ubiquitous term for public relations' and that, although it was 'initially applied to the news management techniques of political parties and the image-polishing of politicians, particularly during election campaigns', it 'has recently come to be used in relation to corporate and government activity. Spin is generally thought of as deceptive or manipulative communications'. Miller and Dinan (2008: 2) further argued that the power of the corporate elite and their political allies to 'manage the public agenda' was not 'limited to questions of communications alone' however. These social forces 'invented public relations and used its skills and techniques to impose business interests on public policy and limit the responsiveness of the political system to the opinions and preferences of the masses' (1). Propaganda thus implied 'the unity of communication and action; it is communication for a purpose' (5) and this purpose was the 'engineering of consent':

> To win the consent of the public might be desirable for the rulers of the world but it is not always necessary. The key is to ensure political and public compliance. It is not that the decision-makers or public actively agree and support the policy ideas promulgated by business lobbies and the corporations. What is critical is that they do not actively ... oppose them. This is what makes the melding of action and ideology so powerful. In other words, the aim and effect of much corporate propaganda is the manufacture of compliance.
>
> (5–6)

Having defined education, persuasion and propaganda, it is now possible to distinguish between them. Carey (1995: 20) juxtaposed education and propaganda:

> Propaganda refers to communications where the form and content is selected with the single-minded purpose of bringing some target audience to adopt attitudes and beliefs chosen in advance by the sponsors of the communications. Propaganda, so defined, is to be contrasted with education. Here, at least ideally, the purpose is to encourage critical enquiry and to open minds to arguments for and against any particular conclusion, rather than close them to the possibility of any conclusion but one.

Jowett (1987: 101) contrasted persuasion and propaganda: 'definitions varied in the specificities regarding issues of control and intent, but it was generally agreed that propaganda was distinguished from mere persuasion by the elements of deliberateness and manipulation'.

As a form of political communication, political advertising usually aims to persuade and/or propagandise rather than educate. More specifically, political advertising may attempt to persuade the audience of the merits, or otherwise, of one candidate, ideology, party or project over another. Political advertising may adopt a propagandistic approach and deliberately mislead the audience about a particular candidate, ideology, party or project through lies, omissions and half-truths. Political advertising rarely strives to educate the audience, however, and the sponsors of political advertising are not required to communicate or explain the range of choices and options that exist; indeed given that the sponsors have particular economic and/or political objectives, they have a vested interest in not doing so. The goals and outputs of the sponsors of political advertising therefore have a considerable impact upon the nature and trajectory of politics.

Existing literature on political advertising and its limitations

The existing literature on political advertising can be categorised into two main groups. One set of studies concentrated upon the message and the medium, particularly the role of televised political advertising during election campaigns (Mullen 1963, 1968; Bowers 1972; Humke et al. 1975; Jones and Kaid 1976, 2004; Patterson and McClure 1976; Kaid and Davidson 1986; Kern 1989; Johnson-Cartee and Copeland 1991, 1997; Philo 1993; Kavanagh 1995; Scammell 1995; Kaid 1999; Norris et al. 1999; Johnston and Kaid 2002; Kaid 2002; Baker 2008). The second set focused upon the effects of these campaigns on audiences (Becker and Doolittle 1975; Jacobson 1975; Basil et al. 1991; Johnston and White 1993; Lau and Sigelman 2000; Hollihan 2001; Bystrom and Kaid 2002; Goldstein and Ridout 2004; Sanders and Norris 2005). Sethi (1977) studied the achievements of advocacy advertising by corporations in the US, while Kaid and Holtz-Bacha (1995) and Plasser (2002) conducted international comparisons of political advertising in terms of content and effects.

While the existing literature has generated a great deal of insight into political advertising, it suffers from three main limitations. Firstly, the existing literature has primarily focused upon political advertising during election campaigns and has neglected to consider the other domains where political advertising is deployed. Secondly, the point of departure for much of the existing literature, in terms of the origins of political advertising, is the 1950s when British and US political parties and US presidential candidates used the new mass medium of television to great effect. It is implicit within this work that political advertising was developed within civil society (i.e. political parties) and the private sector (i.e. advertising agencies), drawing upon the knowledge about, and the techniques associated with, commercial advertising as designed and tested during the nineteenth century when mass consumption societies emerged. It is also implicit within this work that the knowledge and techniques of commercial advertising – having been finessed in the form of the 'depth approach' which aimed to 'channel our unthinking habits, our purchasing decisions and our thought processes by the use of insights gleaned from psychology and the social sciences' (Packard 1957: 31), and, more recently, from neuroscience (Alexander et al. 2011; Gannon and Lawson 2011) – were then applied to politics; advertisers 'did not turn their attention to politics in a serious way until the 1950s' (Packard 1957: 171). These claims are mistaken, however, because the foundations of political advertising were established much earlier, during the 1910s, and the state played a major role in the development of political advertising. Thirdly, following the generalised retreat from grand theories– particularly Marxism and other critical perspectives – within the social sciences from the 1970s, the existing literature has failed to adequately situate political advertising within the wider economic, political and social context of modern capitalism. In short, the existing literature has failed to explore the economic and political objectives (i.e. the political economy) of the sponsors of political advertising. These limitations result in analyses which are all too often ahistorical and apolitical. What follows is an attempt to address these deficiencies.

A typology of political advertising

The consensus within the existing literature that political advertising is concerned with the promotion of political parties and presidential candidates during elections is far too narrow, as this section will demonstrate. Likewise, the contention that political advertising emerged in the 1950s, having been developed within civil society and the private sector, misses some important history, which this section will present.

Selling war

Political advertising has been used to sell war to the public. Deployed on a mass scale and in a systematic manner, political advertising was pioneered during the First World War as part of the much broader propaganda campaigns devised by Britain, Germany and the US (Ponsonby 1928; Axelrod 2009). The British campaign had four main objectives: to promote conscription to the British Army, to deter anti-conscription and anti-war sentiment, to solicit the support of neutral countries (particularly the US) and to demonise the Germans. Once it had joined the war, the US campaign also promoted conscription (see Plate 10) and attempted to demonise the Germans.

The pro-war campaigns developed by Britain and the US possessed four notable features. Firstly, the state played a central role in developing and coordinating these campaigns. In Britain, the War Propaganda Bureau – established in 1914 by the Liberal Prime Minister Herbert Asquith – was supervised by the Foreign Office (Sanders 1975). The Department of Information, created in 1916, launched political advertising and propaganda operations against enemy populations overseas, while the War Aims Committee, founded in 1917, coordinated domestic and overseas campaigns and combated pacifism at home. In the US, the Committee on Public Information (CPI), formed in 1917, strove to sell the war to Americans and it counted army and navy secretaries and secretaries of state amongst its members.

Secondly, the state formed strategic partnerships with private sector organisations to pursue these campaigns. The Central Committee for National Patriotic Associations, which was set up in 1914 with Asquith as president, organised lectures, patriot clubs and rallies in Britain and across the British Empire (Buitenhuis 1987). In 1918, the Conservative-Liberal Coalition Government appointed some of the owners of the press to manage the propaganda offensive against enemy and neutral countries (Taylor 1999). In the US, the CPI worked with film studios and other private sector organisations (Wells 2002), while Bernays was an advisor to the CPI (Ewen 1996).

Thirdly, these campaigns utilised a broad range of techniques which encompassed interpersonal communication and political advertising and propaganda via the mass media. The work of the CPI, for example, was recounted in the book produced by its chair, George Creel, in 1920:

> There was no part of the Great War machinery that we did not touch, no medium of appeal that we did not employ. The printed word, the spoken word, the motion picture, the telegraph, the cable, the wireless, the poster, the signboard – all these were used in our campaign to make our own people and other peoples understand the causes that compelled America to take arms. All that was fine and ardent in the civilian population came at our call until more than one hundred and fifty thousand men and women were devoting highly specialized abilities to the work of the Committee, as faithful and devoted in their service as though they wore the khaki.
>
> (1920: 5)

Fourthly, these campaigns were judged effective in terms of generating a pro-war consensus. The German campaign, by contrast, was widely considered to be amateurish. Indeed, Adolf Hitler, in *Mein Kampf*, praised the British and US campaigns and conceded that they had contributed to Germany's defeat. What the Germans learnt from these offensives helped them to devise much more effective propaganda during the Second World War. The private sector also noted how effective these campaigns had been and they used the associated knowledge and techniques to sell both goods and services (i.e. commercial advertising) and the capitalist system as a whole (i.e. corporate propaganda). At the end of the war, for example, Bernays set up a private advertising agency and applied the methods that he had pioneered with the CPI. In other words, Bernays and others honed their knowledge and skills in the public sector and later transferred them to the private sector.

Selling ideas

Political advertising has been used to sell ideas, such as capitalism, to the public. Carey observed that the twentieth century was 'characterized by three developments of great political importance: the growth of democracy, the growth of corporate power and the growth of corporate propaganda as a means of protecting corporate power against democracy' (1995: 18). The extension of the franchise and the expansion of trade unionism

> presented corporations with potential threats to their power from the people at large (i.e. from public opinion) and from organized labour. ... corporations have met this threat by learning to use propaganda, both inside and outside the corporation, as an effective weapon for managing governments and public opinion.
>
> (18)

Put simply, democracy is dangerous for corporations because the masses may vote to radically reform, if not abolish, capitalism. Corporate propaganda was thus developed as alternative means of population control to prevent such change without recourse to state violence; in effect it allowed the corporate elite and their political allies to 'take the risk out of democracy' (Lohrey 1995: 2). Indeed, the success of the First World War campaigns prompted Bernays (1928: 37) to confidently declare the following:

> The conscious and intelligent manipulation of the organized habits and opinions of the masses is an important element in democratic society. Those who manipulate this unseen mechanism of society constitute an invisible government which is the true ruling power of our country.

Moreover,

> [l]eaders, with the aid of technicians in the field who have specialized in utilizing the channels of communication, have been able to accomplish purposefully and scientifically what we have termed 'the engineering of consent'. This phrase quite simply means the use of an engineering approach – that is, action based on thorough knowledge of the situation and on the application of scientific principles and tried practices to the task of getting people to support ideas and programs.
>
> (Bernays 1947: 114)

Corporations, on an individual basis, use advertising as a means of maximising market share and sales – and therefore profits. Corporations have two broader objectives however: to protect the corporate sector as a whole from state regulation and higher taxes and to safeguard the capitalist system from rival ideologies such as anarchism, communism and socialism. To achieve these objectives, corporations act collectively and employ a variety of methods, including corporate propaganda and political advertising, to safeguard their interests. Corporations have, over the course of the past one hundred years, developed sophisticated and well-resourced campaigns to protect corporate power from democracy. The existence and history of these campaigns, however, has been denied and/or marginalised within the disciplines of media and communication studies, politics, sociology and the sub-disciplines of political advertising and political communication.

Following Hughes (1994), Carey (1995), Fones-Wolf (1994), Beder (2006a, 2006b) and Miller and Dinan (2008), it is possible to identify three waves of corporate propaganda during the twentieth century. The first wave, in the 1910s and 1920s, attempted to quell the growing radicalisation of the labour movement in Britain and the US. The second wave, from the 1930s to the 1950s, aimed to neutralise the threat posed by the economic nationalism of the New Deal in the US and the nationalisation programme in Britain, while the third wave, from the 1970s, effectively prepared the way for the neo-liberal counter-revolution. Adopting the successful strategy developed during the First World War, these pro-business and anti-labour campaigns utilised a broad range of techniques which encompassed interpersonal communication and political advertising and propaganda via the mass media. Unlike the pro-war campaigns, however, these offensives were organised by private sector organisations – albeit with the active support of the state.

In terms of the third wave in the US, the American Advertising Council (AAC) launched its pro-business campaign, which aimed to 'create greater understanding of the American economic system' (AAC 1976: 1), in 1976. It was described by Rippa (1984: 306) as 'the most elaborate and costly PR project in American history'. The AAC ran dozens of 'public service' campaigns every year on different aspects of corporate activity, became the largest advertiser in the US (thanks to donations from individual corporations and free space and time from media and publishing companies), extended the provision of 'economic education' campaigns and was financially supported by the US Department of Commerce. The five-year, multi-million dollar campaign involved:

> media advertisements, dedicated newsletters, films, teaching materials and training kits, booklets, point of sale displays, and messages on envelopes and flyers included with bank statements, utility bills and insurance premium notices. The media contributed $40 million of free space and time to the campaign in the first two years.
>
> (AAC 1976: 6)

The AAC distributed millions of copies of publicity materials to communities, schools and workplaces – some 13 million by 1979 – and these were advertised free by 400 television stations, 1000 radio stations, 3000 daily and weekly newspapers, 400 business and consumer magazines, in thousands of banks, libraries and shops and in 110,000 transport venues (Beder 2006b: 68). In addition, individual corporations deployed their own political advertising and propaganda campaigns to complement that of the AAC. Consequently, it was reported to a Congressional inquiry in 1978 that US corporations were 'spending $1,000 million per year on propaganda' (cited in Carey 1995: 89).

Like the pro-war campaigns during the First World War and the pro-business and anti-labour campaigns during the first and second waves, the AAC campaign was judged a success. A poll commissioned by the AAC in 1980 found that 'the proportion of Americans who think there is too much government regulation' rose 'from 42 per cent to 60 per cent' (cited in Carey 1995: 89), while an organisation that monitored public opinion for business observed that 'between Jimmy Carter's election in 1976 and Ronald Reagan's victory in 1980, the outlook of the American people underwent one of those decisive shifts that historians generally label as watershed events' (89). Carey concluded that 'as in 1919–21 and 1945–50, a corporate-sponsored assault on public opinion brought about a dramatic nationwide swing to conservatism' (1995: 89).

Selling political parties and presidential candidates

Political advertising has been used to sell political parties and presidential candidates to the public. In Britain, the Labour Party created the Press and Publicity Department in 1917 and, from the 1920s, debated whether election campaigns should be 'image'- or 'issue'-driven (Wring 2004). The 'persuasionists' (i.e. those who believed in the power of symbols) scored an early victory against the 'educationalists' (i.e. those who believed in rational argument) when the Labour Party formally adopted a logo in 1924 (Wring 1996). The logo was changed in 1986 when the red flag was replaced with a red rose as Labour 'modernisers' attempted to re-position the party in the public mind. Similarly, the Conservative Party logo was changed in 2006 when the torch was replaced by a tree as part of an attempt to 'detoxify' the Conservative 'brand' after three general election defeats. The importance of political symbols was established.

The Conservative Party employed Holford-Bottomley Advertising Services and S. H. Benson and Press Secretaries Ltd. to help them design and distribute millions of leaflets and posters during the 1929 General Election. The Labour Party, by contrast, abandoned plans to use an advertising agency for the 1935 General Election and it was not until the local elections of 1937 that it sought the assistance of external professionals. Following the Conservatives' defeat in 1945, the party appointed a new advertising agency, Colman Prentis Varley, that produced the slogan, 'Life's better with the Conservatives, don't let Labour ruin it', which helped the Conservatives win the 1959 General Election. The utility of slogans and soundbites was established.

The Conservatives created the Public Opinion Research Department in 1948 and it was tasked with conducting private polling to inform the party's electoral strategy. Following an extensive study of 5000 voters in 1949, the Public Opinion Research Department produced a report, titled 'The Floating Vote', which identified the age, gender, newspaper readership, occupation and recreation activities of floating voters (Street 1992). During the 1980s, Experian – a transnational corporation (TNC) headquartered in Ireland – developed its ACORN and Mosaic geo-demography systems. Drawing upon private and state sources of data (e.g. census information, credit histories, shopping habits, etc.), Experian categorised every household in Britain. Originally produced at the postcode level (i.e. covering twenty properties), the 2009 version of Mosaic provided a detailed classification at the household level by dividing the population into 15 distinct socio-economic groups and, within these, sixty-seven different types of persons. The ACORN and Mosaic systems were sold to private and public sector organisations that wanted to improve their marketing efforts. These systems, in turn, underpinned the 'Voter Vault' system developed by the British Conservatives and US Republicans, the 'DataMart' system devised by the US Democrats and the 'Contact Creator' system used by the British Labour Party. The benefits of polling and targeting swing voters in marginal constituencies were established.

In the US, the Republican candidate, General Dwight Eisenhower, won the 1952 Presidential Election using the new mass medium of television to reach a much wider audience than the traditional methods of public meetings, rallies, bus tours, etc. A subsequent study of the election found

> some interesting differences in the place occupied by professional publicists in the councils of the opposing parties. The strategy, treatment of issues, use of media, budgeting, and pacing of the Eisenhower campaign showed the pervasive influence of professional propagandists. The Democrats used fewer professionals, were less apt to draw upon commercial and industrial public relations experience in their thinking, and their publicity people apparently had less of a voice in the policy decisions of the campaign.
>
> (cited in Packard 1957: 172)

The Democrats 'learned their lesson' and made 'greater use of advertising and public relations in 1956' (Packard 1957: 172). Britain's political parties also competed to harness the new mass medium of television. Tasked with modernising Labour's communication strategy, more specifically its use of televised political election broadcasts during the 1959 General Election, Tony Benn declared that 'one television broadcast more than equals a lifetime of mass rallies and street-corner oratory; old methods of campaigning are ... obsolete' (cited in Adams 1992: 142).

More recently, the Internet has been used by British and US political parties and US presidential candidates for fundraising, networking and political advertising activities. The pioneering use of this medium by the US Democrat contender Howard Dean in 2004 was later emulated and successfully expanded upon by Barack Obama in 2008. Moreover, Republican contenders for the nomination for the 2012 US presidential election, such as Michelle Bachmann, used the new advertising tools developed by Facebook to produce more customised campaigns (Knapp 2011). The value of exploiting new technologies, such as television and the Internet, was established.

Packard recalled that a New York-based advertising agency conducted

> a test study during the 1952 campaign with the 'I don't know' voters, used ... projective techniques to spot affinities for brand images to identify voters' underlying emotional tone. After the election it called up the people who had been probed (all of them professedly undecided) and found that it had been 97 per cent right in predicting how each one would vote. The spokesperson for the agency said that the undecided voter is not the thoughtful 'independent' ... often pictured.
>
> (1957: 173)

Subsequent studies confirmed the power of irrationality in voters' thinking and behaviour (Zajonc 1984; Bornstein 1989; Damasio 1994; Westen 2007; Crompton 2010). The critical role of emotion was established.

In the US, an important shift in political parties' electoral strategy was acknowledged by sections of the media in the early 1950s:

[T]he politicians are beginning to apply all the smart advertising techniques used by mass production America to merchandise autos, bath salts and lawn-mowers [and that] … under chairperson Leonard Hall and Robert Humphreys, publicity director, the Republican Congressional Committee has made-to-order productions for the candidate who wants to use television, movies built around cartoons and charts, dramatized radio spot announcements … newsletters, street interview techniques, etc.

(Cited in Packard 1957: 172)

Corporations were also cognisant of the transformation; the Chamber of Commerce observed in 1956 that

[b]oth parties will merchandise their candidates and issues by the same methods that business has developed to sell goods. These include scientific selection of appeals; planned repetition … No flag-waving faithful will parade the streets. Instead, corps of volunteers will ring doorbells and telephones … Radio spot announcements will repeat phrases with a planned intensity. Billboards will push slogans of proven power … Candidates need, in addition to rich voice and good diction, to be able to look 'sincerely' at the TV camera.

(Cited in Packard 1957: 172)

The need for professional electioneering was established.

Sociologists such as David Riesman pointed to a positive correlation between the advent of television and the growing importance of personality in US politics. As part of the trend towards other-directedness (i.e. being guided by values derived from external influences), it seemed that 'Americans, in their growing absorption with consumption, have even become consumers of politics' (Packard 1957: 174). Indeed, Reisman contended in 1950 that

just as glamour in packaging and advertising of products substitutes for price competition, so glamour in politics, whether as charisma – packaging – of the leader or as the hopped-up treatment of events by mass media, substitutes for the type of self-interest that governed the inner-directed.

(cited in Packard 1957: 174)

The significance of candidate and party image was established.

The 1970s witnessed the emergence of a new approach to selling political parties and presidential candidates. Political marketing 'is not just about campaigning, communication or public relations. Parties are acting like businesses, using market intelligence to inform the design of the political product they offer, becoming market- (or voter-) orientated rather than focused on selling' (Lees-Marshment 2009: 28). Put simply, policy content – more specifically the appeal, or otherwise, of certain policies to particular sections of the population as gleaned from focus groups and private polling – and policy presentation were viewed as being of equal importance in electoral terms. In Britain, the Conservative Party employed the services of Saatchi and Saachi advertising agency for its 1979 General Election campaign (see Figure 9.1), and for subsequent election campaigns and these were informed by this new approach.

Figure 9.1: 'Labour isn't working' Conservative Party General Election poster, 1979. Courtesy of Bodleian Library University of Oxford.

Under Bill Clinton, in the US, the 'New Democrats' successfully utilised this approach in 1992. Likewise in Britain, the creation of Labour's Shadow Communications Agency in 1986 and the 1987 Policy Review effectively prepared the way for the construction of the 'New Labour' project which, under Tony Blair, was voted into office in 1997. The efficacy of the marketing approach was established.

Expenditure on political advertising during election campaigns in Britain and the US has increased exponentially over time. The spending on US presidential elections totalled $67 million in 1976, $92 million in 1980, $103 million in 1984, $210 million in 1988, $192 million in 1992, $240 million in 1996, $343 million in 2000, $718 million in 2004 and $1.3 billion in 2008. Following the unsuccessful attempt in the Supreme Court to limit campaign donations by corporations and other organisations in 2010, the Center for Responsive Politics estimated that the 2012 election may cost more than $6 billion. In Britain, political parties spent £25 million during the 2001 General Election campaign, £43 million in 2005 and £31 million in 2010. The advantages gained by access to substantial campaign financing were established.

Selling policies

Political advertising has been used to sell particular policies to the public. In 1946, the Labour Government replaced the wartime Ministry of Information with the peacetime Central Office of Information (COI). Opposed by the Conservatives and sections of the media, the COI was tasked with informing individuals about government policies which impacted upon their lives. Early COI campaigns promoted the government's nationalisation of the coal, electricity and gas industries (Crofts 1989; Scammell 1995).

Following the Conservatives' adoption of the political marketing approach in the 1970s, the party in government increasingly utilised the COI to publicise its policies. As one Cabinet Minister observed in 1988, 'government programmes are like cornflakes; if they are not marketed, they will not sell' (cited in Franklin 1994: 73). COI expenditure on political advertising expanded significantly during the 1980s as the Conservative Government promoted its privatisation programme (see Figure 9.2). Indeed, by financial year 1989–1990, the government had become Britain's biggest advertiser, spending £98 million, and the trend continued under New Labour with spending peaking at £192 million in the financial year 2000–2001.

Selling nations

Political advertising has been used by governments to sell their nations to the rest of the world. Following the end of the Cold War, the US increasingly emphasised the efficacy of 'soft power', understood as the manipulation of culture, ideology and public opinion

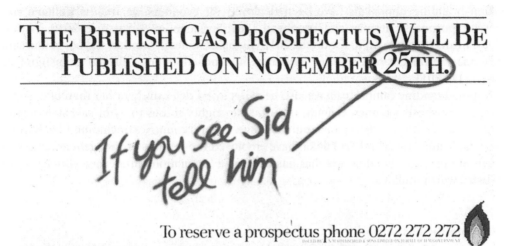

THE BRITISH GAS PROSPECTUS WILL BE PUBLISHED ON NOVEMBER 25TH.

If you see Sid tell him

To reserve a prospectus phone 0272 272 272

Figure 9.2: 'Tell Sid' British Gas privatisation poster. Source: History of Advertising Trust.

(Nye 1990, Nye 2004), in terms of pursuing foreign policy objectives. 'Soft power' methods, together with the more traditional deployment of 'hard power' (i.e. military action), were fused in the strategy of 'full spectrum dominance' (Department of Defense 2000; Miller 2004) which aims to maintain the US as the global hegemonic power. Public diplomacy (i.e. political advertising and propaganda) was integrated into US national security planning and operations (Department of Defense 2004, 2006).

Britain emulated the US trend by further expanding the COI and by establishing the Government Communication Network in 2005 on the basis that the government needed 'an overarching public diplomacy strategy' that would shape 'the core messages that we wish to put across to our target audiences' (Leonard 2002: 2). The official embrace of public diplomacy in the 2003 and 2006 Foreign Office White Papers (Foreign Office 2003, 2006) was inspired by the work of the Foreign Policy Centre think tank, the 1998 'Rebranding Britain' Panel, the Foreign Office 'Panel 2000' taskforce, and the 2002 (Wilton) and 2005 (Carter) reviews of the propaganda work undertaken by the Foreign Office, British Council and British Broadcasting Corporation World Service (Foreign Office 2002, 2005, 2008; Miller 2004).

Many other countries followed suit and embraced nation-branding and public diplomacy. Following the 9/11 attacks in 2001, US public opinion polls indicated a significant fall in support for Pakistan and Saudi Arabia – two key US allies. The problem, in part, was that Pakistan and Saudi Arabia were implicated in the global export of radical Islamist ideology (Curtis 2010). Pakistan and Saudi Arabia responded to the changes in US public opinion by placing advertisements in the US media in an attempt to demonstrate their allegiance to the US and their reliability as partners in the 'war on terror'.

Nation-branding campaigns have been deployed for economic as well as military and strategic purposes (Herman and Brodhead 1985; Sussman 2005, Sussman 2010; Wilson 2005). In an attempt to capitalise on the 2012 Olympic Games in London and boost tourism, the Conservative-Liberal Coalition Government launched its 'Great Britain' campaign (see Plate 11) in 2011.

Nation-branding campaigns have also been deployed defensively rather than offensively by regimes whose activities, ranging from human rights abuses to wholesale state terror, have adversely affected their global public image. Several countries, including Kazakhstan, Rwanda, Saudi Arabia and Sri Lanka, have employed the services of PR agencies, many of which are based in London, in what has become a 'reputation laundering' (Booth 2010) industry worth millions.

Selling politicians and political candidates

Political advertising has been used to sell individual politicians and political candidates. In an attempt to 'detoxify' the Conservative 'brand' and appeal to women voters, David Cameron, as party leader in opposition, launched 'Webcameron' in 2006. Using webcam technology and social networking sites, the Conservatives aimed to bypass the traditional media and reach voters via their personal computers. Live streams of Cameron doing the washing up – thus projecting Cameron as an everyday family man – while talking politics were broadcast from the Camerons' kitchen. In a further attempt to 'detoxify' the Conservative 'brand' and appeal to environmentally conscious voters, Cameron invited a media entourage to accompany him as he sledged with huskies in the Arctic in 2006 while promising that a future Conservative government would tackle global warming and address other environmental problems. A similar strategy was adopted by Sarah Palin, the former Governor of Alaska and the US Republican vice-presidential candidate in 2008. Projecting herself as a 'soccer mom' – a married, middle-class, suburban woman with children – Palin established PalinTV to communicate with US voters, 'in her own words – unfiltered', and starred in an eight-week television programme in 2010, 'Sarah Palin's Alaska', in which she presented herself as a hardworking and wholesome mother and politician who liked to 'get back to nature'.

The case for a critical political economy approach

The dominant view within the existing literature that political advertising in capitalist, liberal-democratic societies contributes to, and functions within, political and media systems which are essentially liberal and pluralistic is flawed, as this section will show. Likewise, the assumption that there is a diversity of political communication (i.e. political education as well as persuasion and propaganda) in contemporary societies such as these is questionable, as this section will evidence. As Herman and Chomsky (1988: xi) warned,

> [i]f the powerful are able to fix the premises of discourse, to decide what the general populace is allowed to see, hear and think about, and to manage public opinion by regular propaganda campaigns, the standard [liberal-pluralist] view of how the [political and media systems work] is at serious odds with reality.

This contention begs two important and interrelated questions: (1) Which model – liberal-pluralist, elitist or critical-Marxist – best explains the operation of political and media systems in capitalist, liberal-democratic societies such as Britain and the US? (2) In terms of political communication within such systems, is there a healthy marketplace of ideas and a vibrant public sphere?

The campaign for democracy and trade unionism in Britain was launched in the seventeenth century. The US population followed suit in the eighteenth century. By the early-twentieth century, after hundreds of years of struggle, universal suffrage had been introduced and mass-membership trade unions were commonplace. During this period, the aristocracy, the corporate elite and their political allies devised a myriad of techniques to manage the political system (Ginsberg 1986). State violence was commonplace.

In the twenty-first century, as a result of their financing of political parties (Ferguson 1995; Challen 1998), lobbying and advocacy advertising efforts (Sethi 1977; Balanyá et al. 2000; Monbiot 2001; Corporate Europe Observatory 2005; McRae 2005; Weissman and Donahue 2009; Alter-EU 2010), manipulation of the 'revolving door' between business and politics (Project on Government Oversight 2004; Dinan and Miller 2009) and privileged access to the policy-making process (Alter-EU 2008), corporations exert considerable influence over political systems at the national, regional (e.g. European Union) and global levels. Corporations have, in effect, colonised and purchased the political system. The liberal-pluralist thesis that power is dispersed; that governments pursue the 'common good'; that the state is neutral; and that there is a level playing field in terms of influencing the policy process is therefore fundamentally flawed.

Ruling-class management of the political system necessitated control over the media system and the wider public sphere. To protect aristocratic, capitalist and state power from democracy and ideologies such as anarchism, communism and socialism and the trade unions, the ruling class launched a war for the 'hearts and minds' of the population. While progressive social forces aimed to educate the masses about the iniquities of the economic system and persuade them of the virtues of alternative social systems, the ruling class deployed a range of population-control techniques and eventually settled upon propaganda. The last 400 years has thus witnessed an ongoing conflict over the dominant form of political communication in society and this conflict intensified with the democratisation of the political system a century ago.

During the seventeenth century, progressive social forces in Britain such as the Diggers and the Levellers aimed to educate the largely illiterate and formally uneducated masses about the unfairness of feudalism and private property, and to persuade the masses of the benefits of common ownership and democracy, through public meetings and word-of-mouth. Their efforts were terminated by state violence (Hill 1972).

During the eighteenth and nineteenth centuries, following the widespread adoption of the printing press and the rise of literacy and formal schooling, progressive social forces such as the Chartists and the Suffragettes strove to educate the people about democracy and equality, and to persuade the people to organise for radical change, through pamphlets, public meetings and the radical press. Their efforts were countered using legal means (e.g. blasphemy laws and sedition), economic measures (e.g. the bond system, stamp duty and taxes) and state repression (e.g. the confiscation of printing presses). By the mid-nineteenth century, however, state efforts to control the media were abandoned in favour of market forces. The media became increasingly dependent upon commercial advertising and, given the demographics of their readership (i.e. the lack of disposable income) and their political orientation (i.e. anti-capitalism), much of the radical press was boycotted by advertisers; out-competed and out-priced, it was forced to moderate its political stance and/or close (Curran and Seaton 1994). The range of opinion expressed in the mass media was narrowed significantly.

In the twentieth century, with the advent of near universal literacy and formal schooling and the emergence of the mass media, progressive social forces such as the trade union movement attempted to educate the public about the realities of the economic system and to persuade the public of the need to reform if not abolish capitalism, through pamphlets, public meetings and the working-class press. As with the earlier radical press, however, advertisers discriminated against the working-class press and it too was forced to moderate its political stance and/or close (Curran and Seaton 1994). The range of opinion expressed in the mass media was further narrowed.

By the mid-twentieth century, factors such as the private and/or corporate ownership of the media, journalists' dependence on corporations and the state for information and news (i.e. sourcing) and their use of corporate-funded think tank 'experts', the media's reliance on advertising for revenue, the threat of 'flak' from right-wing media monitoring organisations, and the routine promotion of capitalism and denigration of rival ideologies, resulted in a media system which effectively performed a propaganda function. Put simply, dissenting views were routinely filtered out in the service of private and state power. Furthermore, the US model was exported elsewhere as US media corporations such as News Corporation, Disney and Viacom, plus the European Bertelsmann, became global media empires (Herman and Chomsky 1988; Franklin 1994; Herman and McChesney 1997; McChesney 1999; McChesney et al. 1998; Bagdikian 2004).

The shift from labour-intensive, mass organisation-based democracies to capital-intensive, communication-based ones from the 1970s provided the corporate elite and their political allies with additional management tools. These include the use of focus groups and private polling to identify the key issues of swing voters in marginal constituencies, direct mail-shots, broadcast media (i.e. television), PR, social media and social networking sites, telephone canvassing and other means. The use of these, together with political advertising, has boosted 'the political fortunes of those social forces – usually found on the political right – whose sympathizers are better able to furnish the large sums of money now needed to compete in elections' (Ginsberg 1986: 150).

In the twenty-first century, 'integrated corporate communications' (Jansen 2011) as provided by TNCs such as Aegis, Havas, Interpublic, Omnicom and WPP have become a reality. These global entities, with both corporate and political clients, aim to colonise media and political systems across the world (Jansen 2011). More specifically, this alliance between the corporate media, corporate-funded political parties and the corporate communication industry aims to further blur the distinction between political advertising (i.e. persuasion) and PR (i.e. propaganda) so that, according to one PR practitioner, 'it may by indistinguishable at some point where one ends and another begins' (cited in *The Economist* 2010).

The results of this new trend are evident, as these two examples illustrate. An important element within contemporary election campaign strategy is to incorporate the key messages of the political parties into the media coverage of the election itself (Franklin 1994). Meanwhile, PR is playing an increasingly important role in shaping how the media function (Davis 2002; Sussman 2011). In Britain, Davies (2008) commissioned research which surveyed more than 2000 news items from four daily broadsheets – *The Times, The Telegraph, The Guardian* and *The Independent* – plus *The Daily Mail*. The researchers found that only 12 per cent of these stories were wholly composed of material researched by reporters, while 80 per cent were wholly, mainly or partially constructed from second-hand material provided by news agencies and by the PR industry. Furthermore, the researchers also found that in only 12 per cent of cases had the facts been thoroughly checked.

Given these realities, it is difficult to reconcile the liberal-pluralist view that the media functions as an independent 'fourth estate' with the actual corporate colonisation of the media. Furthermore, the evidence suggests that, over time, the media have become less diverse and, under the influence of PR, more propagandistic. Consequently, there is even less space in the public sphere for political communication that is educational. The great hope that the Internet would democratise and open up the media system and the political system also seems misplaced, as the Internet is being colonised by corporations (Morozov 2011; Pariser 2011; Wu 2011).

Conclusion

Political advertising was developed over a century ago by the state – two important facts which much of the existing literature seems ignorant of – and these early campaigns proved effective in shaping the political attitudes, beliefs and behaviours of the audience. Over the course of the twentieth century, political advertising expanded in three main ways. Firstly, following its pioneering use in selling war, political advertising was later applied to selling ideas such as capitalism, selling political parties and presidential candidates, selling nations, and selling individual politicians and political candidates. Secondly, the amount spent on political advertising increased significantly over time. It therefore played an increasingly important role in the operation of the political system. Thirdly, political advertising was increasingly integrated into PR and other corporate communication strategies and thus became an important weapon in the extensive arsenal deployed by the ruling class in their struggle to maintain a system of 'propaganda-managed democracies' (Chomsky 1995: vi).

Employing a critical political economy approach illuminates the economic and/or political objectives of the sponsors of political advertising, which the existing literature largely neglects, and thus helps to situate political advertising within the wider economic, political and social context of modern capitalism. Put simply, political advertising has become a tool for population control and a mechanism through which corporations colonise the media system, the political system and the wider public sphere. Over the course of the twentieth century, political education and persuasion have been eclipsed by ever more effective propaganda. The space within the public sphere for informed and lively debate is constantly under attack. The problem is compounded by an education system which fails to properly inform citizens about advertising, the media, politics and sociology, etc. Given that these subjects do not fully figure in the national curriculum alongside English, maths and science, the vast majority of people – with the exception of those who study these subjects at college or university – are largely confused, uninterested and/or ignorant about how the political and media systems function and how the social world is organised. Politics as a consumptive, individualised and private activity, rather than a collective and deliberative activity in the public sphere, has produced a 'society of the spectacle' (Debord 1977) and such a situation prompted Sussman (2011: 7) to lament that 'we are living in a propaganda society'.

References

Adams, J. (1992), *Tony Benn*, London: Macmillan.
Alexander, J., Crompton, T. and Shrubsole, G. (2011), *Think of Me as Evil? Opening the Ethical Debates in Advertising*, London: Public Interest Research Centre/WWF-UK.
Alter-EU (2008), *Secrecy and Corporate Dominance: A Study on the Composition and Transparency of European Commission Expert Groups*, Brussels: Alter-EU.
―――― (2010), *Bursting the Brussels Bubble: The Battle to Expose Corporate Lobbying at the Heart of the EU*, Brussels: Alter-EU.
American Advertising Council (1976), 'Program to Last Three to Five Years', *Economic Communicator*, May, p. 1.
Artz, L., Macek, S. and Cloud, D. (2006), *Marxism and Communication Studies: The Point is to Change It*, New York: Peter Lang.

Axelrod, A. (2009), *Selling the Great War: The Making of American Propaganda*, Basingstoke: Palgrave Macmillan.

Bagdikian, B. (2004), *The New Media Monopoly*, Boston: Beacon Press.

Baker, F. (2008), *Political Campaigns and Political Advertising*, New York: Greenwood Press.

Balanyá, B., Doherty, A., Hoedeman, O., Ma'anit, A. and Wesselius, E. (2000), *Europe Inc. Regional and global Restructuring and the Rise of Corporate Power*, London: Pluto.

Basil, M., Schooler, C. and Reeves, B. (1991), 'Positive and Negative Political Advertising: Effectiveness of Ads and Perceptions of Candidates' in F. Biocca (ed.) *Television and Political Advertising Vol. 1*, Hillsdale, NJ: Lawrence Erlbaum.

Becker, L. and Doolittle, J. (1975), 'How Repetition Affects Evaluation of and Information Seeking about Candidates', *Journalism Quarterly* Vol. 52, pp. 611–617.

Beder, S. (2006a), *Suiting Themselves: How Corporations Drive the Global Agenda*, London: Earthscan.

––––––– (2006b), *Free Market Missionaries: The Corporate Manipulation of Community Values*, London: Earthscan.

Benn, T. (1994), *Years of Hope: Diaries, Papers and Letters, 1940–1962*, London: Arrow Books.

Bernays, E. (1928), *Propaganda*, New York: H. Liveright.

––––––– (1947), 'The Engineering of Consent', *Annals of the American Academy of Political and Social Science*, Vol. 250, pp. 113–120.

Berry, D. and Theobald, J. (eds) (2006), *Radical Mass Media Criticism: A Cultural Genealogy*, London: Black Rose Books.

Blumler, J. and McQuail, D. (1968), *Television in Politics: Its Uses and Influences*, London: Faber.

Blumler, J. and Katz, E. (1974), *The Uses of Mass Communications*, Beverly Hills, CA: Sage Publications.

Blumler, J. and Gurevitch, M. (1995), *The Crisis of Political Communication*, London: Routledge.

Booth, R. (2010), 'PR Firms Make London World Capital of Reputation Laundering', *The Guardian*, 3 August 2010.

Bornstein, R. (1989), 'Exposure and Affect: Overview and Meta-analysis of Research, 1968–1987', *Psychology Bulletin* Vol. 106, No. 2, pp. 265–289.

Bowers, T. (1972), 'Issue and Personality Information in Newspaper Political Advertising', *Journalism Quarterly* Vol. 49, pp. 446–452.

Bracken, B. (1944), Speech to Parliament, *Parliamentary Debates (Hansard) House of Commons Official Report*, Fifth Series, Vol. 401, Col. 926, London: Hansard.

Buitenhuis, P. (1987), *The Great War of Words: British, American and Canadian Propaganda and Fiction, 1914–1933*, Vancouver: University of British Columbia Press.

Bystrom, D. and Kaid, L. (2002), 'Are Women Candidates Transforming Campaign Communication? A Comparison of Advertising Videostyles in the 1990s', in C. Rosenthal (ed.) *Women Transforming Congress*, Norman, OK: University of Oklahoma Press.

Carey, A. (1995), *Taking the Risk Out of Democracy: Propaganda in the US and Australia*, Sydney: University of New South Wales Press.

Challen, C. (1998), *The Price of Power: The Secret Funding of the Tory Party*, London: Vision.

Chomsky, N. (1995), 'Foreword' in A. Carey *Taking the Risk Out of Democracy: Propaganda in the US and Australia*, Sydney: University of New South Wales Press.

Corporate Europe Observatory (2005), *Lobby Planet Guide: Brussels – The EU Quarter*, 3rd edn, Brussels: Corporate Europe Observatory.

Creel, G. (1920), *How We Advertised America*, New York: Harper and Brothers.

Crewe, I. (1997), *Citizenship and Civic Education*, London: Citizenship Foundation.

Crick, B. and Porter, A. (1978), *Political Education and Political Literacy: The Report and Papers, and the Evidence Submitted to, the Working Party of the Hansard Society Programme for Political Education*, London: Longman.

Crofts, W. (1989), *Coercion or Persuasion? Propaganda in Britain after 1945*, London: Routledge.

Crompton, T. (2010), *Common Cause: The Case for Working with Our Cultural Values*, London: WWF-UK.

Curran, J. (2011), *Media and Democracy*, London: Routledge.

Curran, J. and Seaton, J. (1994), *Power without Responsibility: The Press and Broadcasting in Britain* (Fourth Edition), London: Routledge.

Curtis, A. (2002), 'Interview with Edward Bernays' in 'Happiness Machines', *The Century of the Self*, Part 1, BBC 2, 29 April.

Curtis, M. (2010), *Secret Affairs: Britain's Collusion with Radical Islam*, London: Serpent's Tail.

Damasio, A. (1994), *Descartes' Error*, New York: G. Putman's Sons.

Davies, I. (1999), 'What Has Happened in the Teaching of Politics in Schools in England in the Last Three Decades and Why?' *Oxford Review of Education* Vol. 25, No. 1, pp. 125–140.

Davies, N. (2008), *Flat Earth News*, London: Chatto and Windus.

Davies, A. (2002), *Public Relations Democracy: Public Relations, Politics and the Mass Media in Britain*, Manchester: Manchester University Press.

Debord, G. (1977), *The Society of the Spectacle*, Detroit, MI : Black and Red.

Dinan, W. and Miller, D. (2009), *Revolving Doors, Accountability and Transparency: Emerging Regulatory Concerns and Policy Solutions in the Financial Crisis*, Paris: Organization for Economic Cooperation and Development.

Doob, L. (1948), *Public Opinion and Propaganda*, New York: Shoe String Press.

Electoral Commission/Hansard Society (2004), *An Audit of Political Engagement*, London: Electoral Commission/Hansard Society.

Encyclopaedia Britannica (2005), 'Propaganda', *Encyclopaedia Britannica*, 15th edn, London: Encyclopaedia Britannica Inc.

Ewen, S. (1996), *PR! A Social History of Spin*, New York: Basic Books.

Ferguson, T. (1995), *Golden Rule*, Chicago: University of Chicago Press.

Fones-Wolf, E. (1994), *Selling Free Enterprise: The Business Assault on Labor and Liberalism, 1945–60*, Chicago: University of Illinois Press.

Foreign Office (2002), *Changing Perceptions: Review of Public Diplomacy*, 22 March, London: Foreign Office.

——— (2003), *UK International Priorities: A Strategy for the FCO*, Cm.6052, London: Foreign Office.

—— (2005), *Public Diplomacy Review*, London: Foreign Office.

—— (2006), *Active Diplomacy for a Changing World: The UK's International Priorities*, Cm.6762, London: Foreign Office.

—— (2008), *Engagement: Public Diplomacy in a Globalized World*, London: Foreign Office.

Franklin, B. (1994), *Packaging Politics: Political Communications in Britain's Media Democracy*, Second Edition, London: Arnold.

Gannon, Z. and Lawson, N. (2011), *The Advertising Effect*, London: Compass.

Ginsberg, B. (1986), *The Captive Public: How Mass Opinion Promotes State Power*, New York: Basic Books.

Goldstein, K. and Ridout, T. (2004), 'Measuring the Effects of Televised Political Advertising in the United States', *Annual Review of Political Science* Vol. 7, pp. 205–226.

Gurevitch, M., Bennett, T., Curran, J. and Woollacott, J. (eds) (1982), *Culture, Society and the Media*, London: Routledge.

Habermas, J. (1989), *The Structural Transformation of the Public Sphere: An Inquiry in a Category of Bourgeois Society*, Cambridge, MA: MIT Press.

Hallin, D. and Mancini, P. (2004), *Comparing Media Systems: Three Models of Media and Politics*, Cambridge: Cambridge University Press.

Hargreaves, D. (1994), *The Mosaic of Learning*, London: Demos.

Herman, E. and Brodhead, F. (1985), *Demonstration Elections: United States-Staged Elections in the Dominican Republic, Vietnam and El Salvador*, Boston, MA: South End Press.

Herman, E. and Chomsky, N. (1988), *Manufacturing Consent: The Political Economy of the Mass Media*, New York: Pantheon.

Herman, E. and McChesney, R. (1997), *The Global Media: The New Missionaries of Corporate Capitalism*, London: Cassell.

Hill, C. (1972), *The World Turned Upside Down: Radical Ideas during the English Revolution*, Harmondsworth, Middlesex: Penguin.

Hollihan, T. (2001), *Uncivil Wars: Political Campaigns in a Media Age*, New York: Bedford/St Martin's.

Hughes, M. (1994), *Spies at Work*, Bradford: 1 in 12 Publications.

Humke, R., Schmitt, R. and Grupp, S. (1975), 'Candidates, Issues and Party in Newspaper Political Advertisements', *Journalism Quarterly* Vol. 52, pp. 499–504.

Jacobson, G. (1975), 'The Impact of Broadcast Campaigning on Electoral Outcomes', *Journal of Politics* Vol. 37, No. 3, pp. 769–793.

Jansen, S. (2011), 'International Public Relations: Neo-Liberal Fixer and Diplomat without Portfolio', in G. Sussman (ed.) *The Propaganda Society: Promotional Culture and Politics in Global Context*, New York: Peter Lang.

Johnson-Cartee, K. and Copeland, G. (1991), *Negative Political Advertising: Coming of Age*, Hillsdale, NJ: Lawrence Erlbaum.

—— (1997), *Manipulation of the American Voter*, Westport, CT: Praeger.

Johnston, A. (1990), 'Trends in Political Communication: A Selective Review of Research in the 1980s' in D. Swanson and D. Nimmo (eds) *New Directions in Political Communication: A Resource Book*, Newbury Park, CA: Sage.

Johnston, A. and Kaid, L. (2002), 'Image Ads and Issue Ads in Presidential Advertising: Using Videostyle to Explore Stylistic Differences in Televised Politics Ads from 1952–2000', *Journal of Communication* Vol. 52, pp. 281–300.

Johnston, A. and White, A. (1993), 'Communication Styles and Female Candidates: A Study of the Political Advertising during the 1986 Senate Elections', *Journalism Quarterly* Vol. 71, pp. 321–329.

Jones, C. and Kaid, L. (1976), 'Constitutional Law: Political Campaign Regulation and the Constitution', *Oklahoma Law Review*, Vol. 29, pp. 684–711.

Jowett, G. (1987), 'Propaganda and Communication: The Re-Emergence of a Research Tradition', *Journal of Communication* Vol. 37, No. 1, pp. 97–114.

Kaid, L. (1981), 'Political Advertising', in D. Nimmo and K. Sanders (eds) *Handbook of Political Communication*, Beverley Hills, CA: Sage.

—— (1999), 'Political Advertising: A Summary of Research Findings', in B. Newman (ed.) *The Handbook of Political Marketing*, Thousand Oaks, CA: Sage.

—— (2002), 'Political Advertising and Information Seeking: Comparing Exposure via Traditional and Internet Channels', *Journal of Advertising* Vol. 31, No. 1, pp. 27–35.

—— (2004), *Handbook of Political Communication Research*, Mahwah, NJ: Lawrence Erlbaum Associates.

Kaid, L. and Davidson, D. (1986), 'Elements of Videostyle: A Preliminary Examination of Candidate Presentation through Televised Advertising', in L. Kaid, D. Nimmo and K. Sanders (eds) *New Perspectives on Political Advertising*, Carbondale, IL: Southern Illinois University Press.

Kaid, L. and Holtz-Bacha, C. (eds) (1995), *Political Advertising in Western Democracies*, Thousand Oaks, CA: Sage.

Kaid, L. and Jones, C. (2004), 'The New US Campaign Regulations and Political Advertising', *Journal of Political Marketing* Vol. 3, No. 4, pp. 105–110.

Kavanagh, D. (1995), *Election Campaigning: The New Marketing of Politics*, Oxford: Blackwell.

Kern, M. (1989), *Thirty-Second Politics: Political Advertising in the Eighties*, New York: Greenwood Books.

Knapp, E. (2011), 'Here's how Politicians are Using Facebook's New Targeted Advertising Tools', 26 September, http://wallstcheatsheet.com/stocks/heres-how-politicians-are-using-facebooks-new-targeted-advertising-tools.html/. Accessed 20 October 2011.

Lasswell, H. (1927), *Propaganda Technique in the World War*, London: Kegan Paul.

—— (1938), 'Foreword' in G. Bruntz *Allied Propaganda and the Collapse of the German Empire in 1918*, Stanford, CA: Stanford University Press.

Lau, R. and Sigelman, L. (2000), 'Effectiveness of Negative Political Campaigning' in J. Thurber, C. Nelson and D. Dulio (eds) *Crowded Airwaves: Campaign Advertising in Elections*, Washington DC: Brookings Institute.

Lees-Marshment, J. (2009), *Political Marketing: Principles and Applications*, Abingdon, Oxfordshire: Routledge.

Leonard, M. (2002), *Public Diplomacy*, London: Foreign Policy Centre.

Lilleker, D. and Lees-Marshment, J. (eds) (2005), *Political Marketing: A Comparative Perspective*, Manchester: Manchester University Press.

Lohrey, A. (1995), 'Introduction' in A. Carey *Taking the Risk Out of Democracy: Propaganda in the US and Australia*, Sydney: University of New South Wales Press.

Marlin, R. (2002), *Propaganda and the Ethics of Persuasion*, Ormskirk: Broadview Press.

Marsh, D. and Stoker, G. (eds) (2010), *Theory and Methods in Political Science*, 3rd edn, Basingstoke: Palgrave Macmillan.

McChesney, R. (1999), *Rich Media, Poor Democracy: Communication Politics in Dubious Times*, Chicago: University of Illinois Press.

McChesney, R., Meiksins Wood, E. and Bellamy Foster, J. (eds) (1998), *Capitalism and the Information Age: The Political Economy of the Global Communication Revolution*, New York: Monthly Review Press.

McKenzie, V. (1938), *Through Turbulent Years*, London: Geoffrey Bless.

McNair, B. (1995), *An Introduction to Political Communication*, London: Routledge.

McRae, S. (2005), *Hidden Voices: The CBI, Corporate Lobbying and Sustainability*, London: Friends of the Earth.

Miliband, R. (1969), *The State in Capitalism Society*, London: Weidenfeld and Nicholson.

Mill, J. S. (1975), *Three Essays: 'On Liberty', 'Representative Government' and 'The Subjugation of Women'*, Oxford: Oxford University Press.

Miller, D. (2004a), 'Information Dominance: The Philosophy of Total Propaganda Control', http://www.coldtype.net. Accessed 20 October 2010.

Miller, D and Dinan, W. (2008), *A Century of Spin: How Public Relations Became the Cutting Edge of Corporate Power*, London: Pluto.

Monbiot, G. (2001), *Captive State: The Corporate Takeover of Britain*, London: Pan Books.

Morozov, E. (2011), *The Net Delusion: How Not to Liberate the World*, London: Allen Lane.

Mullen, J. (1963), 'Newspaper Advertising in the Kennedy-Nixon Campaign', *Journalism Quarterly* Vol. 40, pp. 3–11.

—— (1968), 'Newspaper Advertising in the Johnson-Goldwater Campaign', *Journalism Quarterly* Vol. 45, pp. 219–225.

Negrine, R. (1996), *The Communication of Politics*, London: Sage.

—— (2008), *The Transformation of Political Communication: Continuities and Change in Media and Politics*, Basingstoke: Palgrave Macmillan.

Negrine, R. and Stanyer, J. (2006), *The Political Communication Reader*, London: Routledge.

Norris, P. (2000), *A Virtuous Circle: Political Communications in Post-industrial Societies*, Cambridge: Cambridge University Press.

Norris, P., Curtice, J., Sanders, D., Scammell, M. and Semetko, H. (1999), *On Message: Communicating the Campaign*, London: Sage.

Nye, J. (1990), *Bound to Lead: The Changing Nature of American Power*, New York: Basic Books.

—— (2004), *Soft Power: The Means to Success in World Politics*, New York: Public Affairs.

Ofsted (2006), *Towards Consensus? Citizenship in Secondary Schools*, London: Ofsted.

—— (2010), *Citizenship Established? Citizenship in Schools, 2006–2009*, London: Ofsted.

Packard, V. (1957), *The Hidden Persuaders*, New York: McKay.

Pariser, E. (2011), *The Filter Bubble: What the Internet is Hiding from You*, London: Viking.

Patterson, T. and McClure, R. (1976), *The Unseeing eye: Myth of Television Power in Politics*, New York: Putnam.

Philo, G. (1993), 'Political Advertising, Popular Belief and the 1992 General Election', *Media, Culture and Society* Vol. 15, No. 3, pp. 407–418.

Plasser, F. (2002), *Global Political Campaigning: A Worldwide Analysis of Campaign Professionals and their Practices*, Westport, CT: Praeger.

Ponsonby, A. (1928), *Falsehood in Wartime: Propaganda Lies of the First World War*, London: George Allen and Unwin.

Power Inquiry (2006), *Power to the People*, York: York Publishing.

Project on Government Oversight (2004), *The Politics of Contracting*, http://www.pogo.org/pogo-files/reports/government-corruption/the-politics-of-contracting/gc-rd-20040629.html. Accessed 6 October 2011.

Qualifications and Curriculum Authority (1998), *Educating for Citizenship and the Teaching of Democracy in Schools*, London: Qualifications and Curriculum Authority.

Rippa, A. (1984), *Education in a Free Society: An American History*, New York: Longman.

Roberts, H. and Sachdev, D. (1996), *Young People's Social Attitudes: Having their say – the Views of 12–19 Year Olds*, London: Barnados.

Russell, B. (1967), *Education and the Social Order*, London: Allen and Unwin.

Sanders, D. and Norris, P. (2005), 'The Impact of Political Advertising on the 2001 General Election', *Political Research Quarterly* Vol. 58, No. 4, pp. 525–536.

Sanders, K. (2009), *Communicating Politics in the Twenty-First Century*, Basingstoke: Palgrave Macmillan.

Sanders, M. (1975), 'Wellington House and British Propaganda during the First World War', *Historical Journal* Vol. 18, pp. 119–146.

Scammell, M. (1995), *Designer Politics*, Basingstoke: Macmillan.

Schumpeter, J. (1942), *Capitalism, Socialism and Democracy*, London: Allen and Unwin.

Sethi, S. (1977), *Advocacy Advertising and Large Corporations*, Lexington, MA: Lexington Books.

Seymour-Ure, C. (1968), *The Press, Politics and the Public*, London: Methuen.

—— (1974), *The Political Impact of Mass Media*, London: Constable.

—— (2003), *Prime Ministers and the Media: Issues of Power and Control*, Oxford: Wiley-Blackwell.

Street, S. (1992), 'The Conservative party Archives', *Twentieth Century British History* Vol. 3, No. 1, pp. 103–111.

Sussman, G. (2005), *Global Electioneering: Campaign Consulting, Communications and Corporate Financing*, Oxford: Rowman and Littlefield.

—— (2010), *Branding Democracy: US Regime-change in Post-Soviet Eastern Europe*, New York: Peter Lang.

—— (2011), *The Propaganda Society: Promotional Culture and Politics in Global Context*, New York: Peter Lang.

Swanson, D. and Nimmo, D. (eds) (1990), *New Directions in Political Communication: A Resource Book*, Newbury Park, CA: Sage.

Taylor, P. (1999), *British Propaganda in the Twentieth Century: Selling Democracy*, Edinburgh: Edinburgh University Press.

The Economist (2010), 'Public Relations in the Recession', *The Economist*, 14 January 2010.

United States Department of Defense (2000), *Joint Vision 2020*, Washington DC: Department of Defense.

—— (2004), *Report of the Defense Science Board Task Force on Strategic Communication*, Washington DC: US Government Printing Office.

—— (2006), *Quadrennial Defense Review*, Washington DC: US Government Printing Office.

Wayne, M. (2003), *Marxism and Media Studies: Key Concepts and Contemporary Trends*, London: Pluto Press.

Weissman, R. and Donahue, J. (2009), *Sold Out: How Wall Street and Washington Betrayed America*, Washington DC: Essential Information/Consumer Education Foundation.

Wells, R. (2002), 'Mobilizing Public Support for War: An Analysis of American Propaganda during World War 1', paper presented at the annual meeting of the International Studies Association, Los Angeles, 24–27 March.

Westen, D. (2007), *The Political Brain*, New York: Public Affairs.

Wilkinson, H. and Mulgan, G. (1995), *Freedom's Children: Work, Relationships and Politics for 18–34 Year Olds in Britain Today*, London: Demos.

Wilson, A. (2005), *Virtual Politics: Faking Democracy in the Post-Soviet World*, London: Yale University Press.

Wring, D. (1996), 'Political Marketing and Political Development in Britain: A "Secret" History', *European Journal of Marketing*, Vol. 30, No. 10, pp. 1–17.

—— (2004), *The Politics of Marketing the Labour Party*, Basingstoke: Palgrave Macmillan.

Wu, T. (2011), *The Master Switch: The Rise and Fall of Information Empires*, New York: Alfred Knopf.

Zajonc, R. (1984), 'On the Primacy of Affect', *American Psychologist*, Vol. 39, pp. 151–175.

Chapter 10

Media and advertising – the interests of citizens and consumers

Monika Metykova

This chapter concentrates on advertising as a source of finance for commercial media and indeed other branches of the cultural/creative industries[1] and its impact on the production, distribution and access to symbolic goods. While previous chapters have concentrated on how culture has been shaped in relation to advertising and advertisements, the current one shifts attention to the role of advertising within the broader context of media industries and the roles these play in democratic societies. Some of the issues particularly those associated with a discussion of power are also highlighted in Andrew Mullen's exploration in the previous chapter. This chapter discusses the detrimental impact that marketisation has on public communication and its contribution to the erosion of citizens' (as opposed to consumers') interests. Arguably, marketisation and ever present promotion also impact on culture and cultural production. The distinction between citizens' interests linked to public communication and those of consumers and particularly the impact of advertising on these represent a complex field, as 'the identities of citizen and consumer are continuously in tension since the possessive individualism promoted by consumerism is deeply corrosive of the sense of shared fate and equal entitlement required by a culture of citizenship' (Murdock 2004: 34). This chapter argues that there is a need for communicative spaces operating outside the market, which are not funded by advertising income. Furthermore, the funding and regulatory models that are currently in place need to be (radically) rethought if such spaces are to be sustainable.

Explorations of citizens' and consumers' interests in communication are rife in academia. Stuart Hall, for example, argues that there is 'such a thing as "the public interest" – *a social interest* – at stake in broadcasting' (1993: 24, original emphasis), he goes on to identify some of the roles of broadcasting in modern societies (source of knowledge, creator of a discursive space, a key pass between 'the governed' and 'the governors') to argue that 'access to broadcasting has thus become a condition, a *sine qua non*, of modern citizenship' (25, original emphasis). There is an abundance of studies showing that the media play a key role in enabling democratic participation, in keeping a check on those in power and in creating a public sphere, but also in promoting social cohesion. For instance, Charles Husband argues that mass media are 'a core element in civil society and a fundamental prerequisite for the promotion of civic trust in complex multi-ethnic societies' (1998: 136). These discussions have also involved policy-makers, for example in the UK The Communications Act 2003 makes it Ofcom's (the UK communications regulator) duty '(a) to further the interests of citizens in relation to communications matters; and (b) to further the interests of consumers in relevant markets, where appropriate by promoting competition.'[2]

At the same time advertising is 'a cultural formation in its own right' (Murdock 2004: 31). There are several critical threads that run through the literature on advertising as a cultural formation, with some writers suggesting that advertising is a euphemism for social control in that it creates a 'false consciousness'. Advertising has been criticised as a cultural activity through which advertisers 'manipulate the symbols that serve as the social fabric of human association' (Schultze 1981: 376). Judith Williamson's key *Decoding Advertisements: Ideology and Meaning in Advertising* explored advertising as a symbolic currency serving not only the economic but also the ideological interests of advertisers.

Markets, media and public interest

Before focusing on advertising as a funding mechanism for commercial media, it is useful to outline the main arguments that concentrate on more general issues linked to the financing of media, some of these relate to the particular nature of media and telecommunications industries.

In modern societies we find examples of sources that are regulated in the public interest, these include basic infrastructure as well as basic telecommunication services. Telecommunication services are part of businesses that are considered to be 'affected with a public interest' (Melody in McQuail 1992: 21) due to the essential nature of the service, its tendency to monopoly and the requirement of universal accessibility. McQuail notes that difficulties with applying the term public interest to an area like communication have their source in misunderstandings according to which features of mass communication are essential and whether interferences with free market mechanisms are justified in order to secure these. It is probably not surprising that apart from difficulties with pinpointing public interest in mass communication there are also various notions about how best to ensure that it actually serves the public.

This debate has been dominated by two opposing views. On the one hand, we find advocates of privately run commercial media systems who argue that this is the way of guaranteeing independence from political and economic interference and that the market will serve the interests of all consumers – it will 'provide them with what they want'. However, as John Keane argues in *The Media and Democracy*, unrestricted competition does not necessarily ensure freedom of entry into the market place, in many cases – and media and creative industries have been noted for this – the costs of entering into a market are high and hence out of the reach of some players. Moreover, free market competition restrains the choices of some and if we accept that mass communication is a public good, it is in economic terms non-excludable and non-exhaustible – in other words those who do not want to pay for such goods cannot be excluded from receiving them, for example, national defence systems protect all – and in addition they have to be constantly available. Berger suggests 'public goods must be produced by institutions other than a market economy and distributed by a mechanism different from markets' (quoted in Raboy 1996: 7).

Also, advertising, which plays a central role in market competition, reduces the supply of minority interest programmes and tends to shut off non-commercial opinions and non-market forms of life. Or to put it simply, if the audience is not sizeable enough to be sold to an advertiser, it is unlikely to have media contents produced for it. For example, ethnic minority media have been acknowledged for their role in maintaining the identities, cultures as well as contributing to the democratic participation of ethnic minority populations (see e.g. Cottle 2000; Lind 2003; Geissler and Potker 2008). Yet in their case, advertising as a funding mechanism is very limited because the audience for such output is too small (e.g. Browne 2005). Non-market goods do not have observable monetary value yet they are extremely valuable – they include activities such as recreation in open-access wilderness areas, as well as access to resources such as clean water or the ozone layer.

Another shortcoming of the advertising funding model has been identified in relation to its potentially detrimental impact on journalism. The increasing exposure of media to profit-generating objectives will result in normative journalism being replaced by market journalism. 'Advertisers do not pay for high-level quality journalism, but for the requested "quality" of the sector of society to be reached. Market journalism, however, provides for a different construction of reality in the media and for a substantially different media reality. Its first and foremost objective is not to inform but to satisfy the targeted sector of society' (Meier and Trappel 1998: 57, original emphasis). The commercialisation of news production has been studied widely. Hardt (1996) has proclaimed the end of journalism in the public interest while others, including Erjavec (2004), map the rise of promotional news, exploring the intersections between advertising and public relations discourses and news.

Some of those who criticise the role of commercial (advertising) funding in media industries propose the view that public service media can best serve the interests of consumers as well as citizens. James Curran, for example, advocates an alternative approach to the question of public service broadcasting[3] that takes into account the fact that people are not only consumers but also citizens within a democratic system with a right to be adequately informed about matters relating to public interest. A right, he argues, that is best guaranteed by public service broadcasting because 'it gives due attention to public affairs, and is less dominated by drama and entertainment than market-based broadcasting generally is' (1998: 190).

In terms of the arguments proposed here it is crucial that public service broadcasting is characterised by the principle of direct funding and universality of payment (Raboy 1996; see also Blumler 1993). James Curran (1998) draws upon the work of neo-Keynesians to critique the free market in broadcasting according to which public service media serve 'public good' without incurring additional costs, that all advertising-funded markets are imperfect as they are biased against quality (favour high ratings as opposed to highly rated programmes) and favour majority programmes which renders them insensitive to intensities of demand.

Apart from serving the public good, broadcasting also represents a merit good which Doyle characterises as 'one where the Government takes the view that more of it should be produced than people would choose to consume, if left to their own devices. Several different motives may be implied when something is treated as a merit good' (2002: 66). She goes on to argue that broadcasting can confer positive externalities,[4] 'there are some forms of content that are collectively desirable and that everyone benefits from (e.g. documentaries, educational and cultural programmes) but which viewers, on an individual basis, might not tune into or be prepared to pay for' (66). It is then a question whether advertising-funded media are geared towards the production of such socially desirable outputs. Doyle, among others, has no doubts that this cannot be the case as 'advertising … creates an incentive for the broadcaster to maximize not overall viewer welfare but the supply of whatever mix of programming yields the audience volumes, while patterns of intensity of viewer demand for different sorts of output may be ignored' (67).

Peter Dahlgren (2001: 11) has argued that the link between public service media and the democratic character of society has a cultural dimension, namely that of civic culture, which is manifested on a daily basis in a 'civic loyalty to the democratic vision'. While commercial media play a role in eroding civic culture, public service media, in turn, play a key role in both demonstrating a commitment to the democratic project at the level of people's everyday life and also in creating a sense of community that challenges an outdated understanding of the nation. Graham Murdock (1992) argues in a similar vein when he explores the relationship between public service broadcasting and social and cultural rights that underline citizenship. He concludes that British commercial television will always have to be supplemented by 'public finance for programmes of a public service kind supported by people in their capacity as citizens and voters but unlikely to be commercially self-supporting in the view of broadcasting entrepreneurs' (Peacock Committee report as quoted in Murdock 1992: 37).

Reliance on advertising as a source of funding for media undermines public interest in communication and promotes consumer – rather than civic – culture. Competition for advertising revenue means that audience volumes determine media contents while their social desirability and the intensity of consumers' demand for such outputs are ignored.

Regulating media, regulating advertising

Before discussing trends in media and advertising regulation, it is important to discuss some general characteristics of media markets. Doyle (2002: 12) reminds us that media generate two commodities, content (sold to audiences) and audiences (sold to advertisers) thus they represent a so-called dual-product market. We should also remember that media industries are characterised by economies of scale (the so-called fixed costs of making a television programme are high but the cost of distributing it to an extra consumer is nil or very low) and scope (a single news gathering organisation that supplies contents to its print, broadcast as well as online media makes significant savings).

Advocates of commercial financing of media stress that undistorted competition best serves the interests of consumers. However, 'perfect competition exists when there are many sellers of a good or a service that is homogeneous (i.e. exactly the same or not differentiated) and no firm(s) dominate(s) the market. In such a situation economic forces operate freely. ... It is very rare to find an example of perfect competition in the real world.

(Doyle 2002: 8)

Rather, what we face is imperfect competition where 'cost advantages associated with size will dictate that an industry should be an oligopoly unless some form of market intervention or Government regulation prevents the firms from growing to their most efficient size' (8). Without such intervention existing firms in a given industry may create barriers to entry to (potential) competitors and this can easily lead to the industry being dominated by a handful of large firms.

Government intervention (regulation) is set up in order to promote and maintain competition (for example, by preventing the concentration in a given market). Media ownership concentration is one demonstration of market failure[5] – 'a failure by the market system to allocate resources efficiently' (Doyle 2002: 64) while another is a 'failure of the market to advance socially desirable goals other than efficiency, such as preserving democracy and social cohesion' (64). This links back to the failure of advertising-funded media to produce socially desirable products (or positive externalities) and also to contribute to civic - rather than consumer – culture. While in the first case regulatory interventions are justified on the basis of economic interest[6] (securing undistorted market competition) public service justifies government regulation in order to secure the provision of merit goods (Feintuck 1999). Moreover, some believe that government intervention (regulation) is justified in this respect also because 'individual choices by individual viewers are highly likely to produce too little public interest programming in light of the fact that the benefits of viewing such programming are not fully "internalized" by individual viewers' (Sunstein quoted in Cooper 2003: 43).

In the field of media we thus find regulatory interventions that support public as well as economic interests. In terms of a general trend in regulating media and creative industries we can identify 'a fundamental reorientation of regulatory regimes in which established conceptions of the "public good" were effectively dismantled and redefined as primarily about open markets, unimpeded competition and consumer protection' (Murdock 2004: 30). McQuail (1992: 143) identifies 'a more general "liberalizing" and deregulation political-economic trend in Europe'. Liberalisation was combined with deregulation which implies a minimalist regulatory approach on the part of the state as well as increased stress on self-regulation. This trend has been widely explored (see e.g. Murdock 1990 and McChesney 2004) and claims have been made to a major shift in the policy rationale; moreover, the change has been characterised as a move away from regulation in the public interest to regulation in corporate interest, a shift from citizen-oriented to consumer-oriented regulation.

Self-regulatory authorities are usually set up by the industry itself, however, their establishment can be supervised by a government body. A report on self-regulation prepared by the Programme in Comparative Media Law and Policy at Oxford University (April 2004) deals in detail with aspects of self-regulation in print media, broadcasting, film industry, electronic game industry and the Internet. The authors of the report identified the following reasons for setting up self-regulatory codes: to provide an alternative to direct statutory regulation; to prevent direct statutory regulation by the state; to build public trust/ consumer confidence; to avoid legal or user-perceived liability; to protect children and other consumers; to exert moral pressure on those who would otherwise behave 'unprofessionally'; to reinforce the competitive advantage of a group of industry players; to mark professional status and to raise the public image of the given industry (17–18).

Bearing in mind the earlier discussions about the impact of advertising funding on media contents, it is important to outline ways in which advertising is regulated in the case of public service media as well as commercial media. I have already suggested that advertising underpins the operations of commercial media while, in contrast, its role in the funding of public service broadcasting of European countries is severely limited. We find European public service broadcasters who are not allowed to broadcast any advertising but may gain income from other commercial activities (such as hiring studios) while in other cases strictly set amounts of advertising are permitted on public service channels. It is in the jurisdiction of individual European Union member states to decide if and what commercial income public service broadcasters can make, however, the broadcasters must comply with European Union competition law.

The amount of broadcast advertising in European Union member states is regulated by the EU's Audiovisual Media Services Directive. It sets minimum rules for advertising (including teleshopping, product placement, sponsorship, etc.) on television (linear service) and video-on-demand (non-linear services). In the UK the amount of broadcast advertising and its distribution is regulated by Ofcom. For example, the amounts of advertising in television news programmes and children's television programmes have been limited since 1 December 2009 in line with minimum rules applying across the European Union by virtue of the Audiovisual Media Services Directive. News programmes may only include one advertising or teleshopping break for each scheduled period of at least thirty minutes; breaks are not permitted in schools programmes while other programmes for children with a scheduled duration of thirty minutes or less may not include an advertising or teleshopping break.

In contrast, other aspects of advertising (namely, content of broadcast and non-broadcast advertising) tend to be self-regulated in European countries. Various bodies, including the Health and Consumer Protection Directorate General of the European Commission, use the same justification for this type of regulation – 'the European Union at present sets a high priority on the identification of the most effective, least costly public policy interventions. Better regulation must provide the least costly, most effective, most proportionate and sufficiently legitimate response to public policy interventions at EU level' (Health and Consumer Protection DG 2006: 10).

The role of self-regulatory bodies is rather limited in terms of achieving major public policy goals, 'the EASA [European Advertising Standards Alliance] participants made it clear that advertising self-regulation does not and cannot carry the burden of expectations that other stakeholders may have of the advertising business as a whole'. The document goes on to stress that self-regulatory organisations (SROs) 'by effectively enforcing good codes, may contribute to the solution of complex societal problems such as ill health caused by alcohol abuse or obesity. But the SROs could not solve such issues alone, nor should SROs be judged solely on their role in such issues' (Health and Consumer Protection DG). Similarly, the report by the Programme in Comparative Media Law and Policy at Oxford University points out that 'if criteria such as those recently outlined in the UK by Ofcom are to justify a shift to self-regulation there must also be some reflection on the nature of the public policy objectives concerned, and whether they are likely to be coterminous with the aims of the industry itself' (April 2004: 86). In some countries self-regulators co-regulate advertising with statutory regulators and there are also legal mechanisms in place to ensure compliance with the codes through so-called legal backstops.

In the UK advertising is in the main regulated by two bodies: Ofcom (Office for Communications, a statutory regulator) – regulates the amount and distribution of broadcast advertising – and ASA (the Advertising Standards Authority, a self-regulatory organisation) – responsible for regulating the content of advertisements.[7] In June 2011 Ofcom launched a review into the UK's TV advertising trading market. The main objective is to identify whether 'a feature or a combination of features of the market or markets for the sale and purchase of TV advertising prevents, restricts or distorts competition, in particular, in connection with: possible poor transparency of pricing signals; bundling of airtime may limit switching; and possible barriers to evolution of the way in which TV advertising is traded' (Ofcom 2011: 81). The consultation document makes no reference to the inefficiencies of advertising funding in ensuring public good (including cultural elements); its arguments concentrate purely on free market and undistorted competition.

The Advertising Standards Agency is funded by a levy on advertising spend and its advertising codes are written, revised and enforced by the Committee of Advertising Practice (CAP) and the Broadcast Committee of Advertising Practice (BCAP). The two organisations represent advertisers, agencies, media space owners, direct marketers and broadcasters. The ASA Council is the body that adjudicates on complaints about advertisements, two-thirds of the Council's members are independent of the advertising industry. ASA can judge that advertisements are in breach of the codes, have them withdrawn and prevent them from appearing again. In cases when ASA cannot achieve compliance with adjudication it can refer these to its legal backstops: the Office of Fair Trading and Ofcom.

There are a number of questions that arise in relation to the accountability, transparency and efficiency of self-regulatory bodies. The question always is to what extent the interests of the industry overlap with the interests – and these interests include a cultural element – of consumers, respectively citizens, and to whom the self-regulatory bodies are made accountable. The already mentioned report by the Health and Consumer Protection Directorate of the European Commission (2006: 37) acknowledges that the 'perceived lack of openness, independence and transparency are seen as critical points for the public acceptability of the self-regulation on advertising. ... The effective contribution of the stakeholders (consumers, parent associations, academics etc.) to the elaboration of codes deserves reinforced attention by EASA [European Advertising Standards Alliance]'. This point also applies to the way advertising codes are developed by the Advertising Standards Authority. The work of ASA and Ofcom has been criticised particularly in the case of advertising codes on alcohol and food, for example, by the British Medical Association.[8] The public relations and lobbying strategies employed by food and alcohol industries and their impacts on elite decision makers (particularly in relation to regulation for health reasons) have also been examined (see e.g. Miller and Harkins 2010).

A UK self-regulatory organisation that has been under the spotlight recently is the Press Complaints Commission (PCC). The failures of the self-regulatory approach exercised by the PCC unfolded in the summer of 2011 when it came under fire in the aftermath of the disclosure of the apparently widespread use of unlawful methods of gathering and intercepting information (the so-called phone hacking scandal) and the subsequent closure of Britain's best-selling tabloid newspaper *News of the World* and the resignation of senior media industry figures as well as the Metropolitan Police Commissioner and Assistant Commissioner. The way in which the 'phone hacking scandal' has evolved suggests that there may be space for a rethinking of issues that this chapter has outlined – the key amongst them being regulation that supports public good and addresses market failure.

It appears that the 'phone hacking scandal' has renewed discussions about a number of issues linked to the role of media in democratic societies, including independence of the press from commercial and political pressures and possibly the role of media in facilitating civic culture. In the aftermath of the scandal, the conflation of citizen and consumer identities came to the foreground. The first indication in this respect was the withdrawal of subscriptions to the *News of the World* as well as *The Times*,[9] once again demonstrating that 'people's decisions in the sphere of consumption may be invested with a sense of effective agency that has increasingly disappeared from their working lives and periodic opportunities to vote in elections'[10] (Murdock 2004: 35). Consumers were mobilised not only to boycott *News of the World* and *The Times* but also to encourage advertisers (using Twitter) to withdraw from the papers.[11] It is without doubt that advertisers react to the civic/democratic aspirations of the consumers they target, yet, it also appears that such mobilisation may lose its momentum relatively quickly – and civic culture (as understood by Dahlgren) requires a more sustainable daily feeding ground.

Conclusions

This chapter has argued that communication is an area affected by public interest. Although it is difficult to identify which of its features are essential in this respect, it has been demonstrated that a market-based approach favouring advertising as a source of finance poses a threat to citizens' interests. Also, it has been argued that while commercial media (with advertising as a main source of income) are closely linked to consumer culture, public service broadcasters have an obligation and commitment to civic culture. Hence when we think about advertising and media, we need to make a distinction between the interests of consumers and of citizens, this distinction – as the chapter has argued – is often a complex one.

The chapter has discussed various aspects of advertising as a faulty mechanism for funding media. It has argued that advertising-funded media fail to promote socially desirable goals and concentrate on audience volume rather than on the intensity of demand for media outputs.

It has highlighted the crucial importance of regulation in securing public interest in communication. The general trend of re-regulation and de-regulation has characterised approaches to advertising and media industries. This has resulted in a shift away from citizen-oriented regulation to competition regulation and this development has been coupled with increasing reliance on self-regulation as an alternative to direct statutory regulation. Apart from acting as regulators, governments have also become major advertisers; the impact of this development is discussed in detail in Chapter 9 of this volume.

Various governmental, pan-European and non-statutory bodies play a role in the regulation of advertising. At the pan-European level the recent Audiovisual Media Services Directive sets rules for advertising on television as well as video-on-demand. In general, we can detect a move towards self-regulation of advertising contents in European countries. In enforcing their decisions self-regulatory bodies may be backed up by statutory regulators.

Overall, the chapter has argued that we should not underestimate the connections between the roles that media play in democratic societies, the ways in which they obtain funding for their activities and the regulatory frameworks that governments put in place. The interplay between these factors is decisive in shaping what type of culture we live in, an issue that various chapters in this volume explore in relation to a variety of cases.

References

Bagdikian, B. (1997), *The Media Monopoly*, 5th edn, Boston: Beacon Press.

Bakan, J. (2004), *The Corporation: The Pathological Pursuit of Profit and Power*, London: Constable & Robinson.

Baker, C. E. (2002), *Media, Markets and Democracy*, Cambridge: Cambridge University Press.

Blumler, J. G. (1993), 'Meshing Money with Mission: Purity versus Pragmatism in Public Broadcasting', *European Journal of Communication*, 8:4, pp. 403–424.

British Medical Association (September 2009), *Under the Influence: The Damaging Effect of Alcohol Marketing on Young People*, http://www.bma.org.uk/images/undertheinfluence_ tcm41-190062.pdf. Accessed 27 July 2011.

Browne, D. E. (2005), *Ethnic Minorities, Electronic Media and the Public Sphere: A Comparative Approach*, Cresskill, NJ: Hampton Press.

Compaine, B. (1982), *Who Owns the Media? Concentration of Ownership in the Mass Communications Industry*, 2nd edn, White Plains, NY: Knowledge Industry Publications.

Cooper, M. (2003), *Media Ownership and Democracy in the Digital Information Age*, Stanford: Centre for Internet and Society, Stanford Law School.

Cottle, S. (ed.) (2000), *Ethnic Minorities and the Media*, London: Open University Press.

Curran, J. (1998), 'Crisis of Public Communication: A Reappraisal', in T. Liebes and J. Curran (eds), *Media, Ritual and Identity*, London: Routledge.

—— (2002), *Media and Power*, London: Routledge.

—— (May 2002), *Global Media Concentration: Shifting the Argument*, www.opendemocracy. net/media-globalmediaownership/article_37.jsp. Accessed 28 July 2011.

—— (July 2011), *OurKingdom Forum: The Fall of Murdoch – What Next?*, http://www. opendemocracy.net/ourkingdom/james-curran-nick-couldry-ryan-gallagher-suzanne-moore-julian-sayarer/ourkingdom-forum-fa. Accessed 28 July 2011.

Dahlgren, P. (2001), 'Public Service Media, Old and New: Vitalizing a Civic Culture', *Canadian Journal of Communication*, 24:4, pp 495–514.

Doyle, G. (2002), *Media ownership: The economics and politics of convergence and concentration*, London: Sage.

Erjavec, K. (2004), 'Beyond Advertising and Journalism: Hybrid Promotional News Discourse', *Discourse and Society*, 15: 5, pp. 553–578.

Feintuck, M. (1999), *Media Regulation: Public interest and the Law*, Edinburgh: Edinburgh University Press.

Garnham, N. (2005), 'From cultural to creative industries: An analysis of the implications of the "creative industries" approach to arts and media policy making in the United Kingdom', *International Journal of Cultural Policy*, 11, pp. 1–14.

Geissler, R. and Potker, H. (2008), *Media, Migration, Integration: The European and North American Perspective*, Rutgers: Transaction Publisher.

Hall, S. (1993), 'Which Public, whose Service?', in W. Stevenson (ed.) *All our Futures: The Changing Role and Purpose of the BBC*, London: The British Film Institute.

Hallin, D. (1986), *The 'uncensored war': The Media and Vietnam*, Oxford: Oxford University Press.

—— (1994), *We Keep America on Top of the World: Television Journalism and the Public Sphere*, London: Routledge.

Hardt, H. (1996), 'The End of Journalism: Media and Newsworkers in the United States', *Javnost/ The Public*, 3:3, pp. 21–42.

Health and Consumer Protection Directorate General (July 2006), *Self-Regulation in the EU Advertising Sector: A Report of Some Discussion among Interested Parties*, http://www.asa. co.nz/pdfs/Madelin%20Report.pdf. Accessed 21 July 2011.

Husband, C. (1998), 'Differentiated Citizenship and the Multi-Ethnic Public Sphere', *The Journal of International Communication*, 5:1&2, pp. 134–148.

Keane, J. (1991), *Media and Democracy*, Cambridge: Polity Press.

Lind, R. A. (ed.) (2003), *Race/Gender/Media: Considering Diversity Across Audiences, Content and Producers*, Boston, MA: Allyne & Bacon.

McChesney, R. and Herman, E. (1997), *The Global Media: The New Missionaries of Corporate Capitalism*, London, Washington, DC: Cassell.

McChesney, R. W. (2003), 'Theses on Media Deregulation', *Media, Culture and Society*, 25:1, pp. 125–133.

McChesney, R. (2004), *The Problem of the Media: US Communications Politics in the 21st Century*, New York: Monthly Review Press.

McQuail, D. (1992), *Media Performance: Mass Communication and the Public Interest*, London: Sage.

Meier, W. and Trappel, J. (1998), 'Media Concentration and the Public Interest', in D. McQuail and K. Siune (eds), *Media Policy: Convergence, Concentration and Commerce*, London: Sage.

Miller, D. and Harkins, C. (2010), 'Corporate Strategy, Corporate Capture: Food and Alcohol Industry Lobbying and Public Health', *Critical Social Policy*, 30:4, pp. 564–589.

Murdock, G. (1990), 'Redrawing the Map of the Communications Industries: Concentration and Ownership in the Era of Privatisation', in M. Ferguson (ed.), *Public Communications: The New Imperatives*, London: Sage.

Murdock, G. (1992), 'Citizens, Consumers, and Public Culture', in M. Skovmand and K. C. Schrøder (eds), *Media Cultures: Reappraising Transnational Media*, London: Routledge.

——— (2004), 'Past the Posts: Rethinking Change, Retrieving Critique', *European Journal of Communication*, 19:19, pp. 19–38.

Murdock, G. (2004a), 'Building the Digital Commons: Public Broadcasting in the Age of the Internet', The 2004 Spry Memorial Lecture, http://www.com.umontreal.ca/spry/spry-gm-lec.htm. Accessed 21 July 2011.

Ofcom (June 2011), *Competition Issues in the UK TV Advertising Trading Mechanism: Consultation on the Potential Reference to the Competition commission*, http://stakeholders.ofcom.org.uk/binaries/consultations/tv-advertising-investigation/summary/TV_advertising_MIR.pdf. Accessed 21 July 2011.

Press Complaints Commission (November 2009), *PCC Report on Phone Message Tapping Allegations*, www.pcc.org.uk/assets/111/Phone_Hacking_report_2009.pdf. Accessed 27 July 2011.

Programme in Comparative Media Law and Policy (April 2004), *Self-Regulation of Digital Media Converging on the Internet: Industry Codes of Conduct in Sectoral Analysis*, http://pcmlp.socleg.ox.ac.uk/sites/pcmlp.socleg.ox.ac.uk/files/IAPCODEfinal.pdf. Accessed 21 July 2011.

Raboy, M. (ed.) (1996), *Public Broadcasting for the 21st Century*, Luton: University of Luton Press.

Schultze, Q. J. (1981), 'Review Essay: Advertising, Culture, and Economic Interest', *Communication Research*, 8, pp. 371–384.

Williamson, J. (1978), *Decoding Advertisements: Ideology and Meaning in Advertising*, London & Boston: Marion Boyars.

Notes

1 For a discussion on the shift in terminology from cultural to creative industries, see Garnham (2005).

2 Part 1, 3(1) http://www.legislation.gov.uk/ukpga/2003/21/pdfs/ukpga_20030021_en.pdf. Accessed 20 July 2011.

3   The already mentioned UK regulator Ofcom provides the following brief description of public service broadcasting: '[it] refers to TV programmes that are broadcast for the public benefit rather than for purely commercial purposes. These programmes include local news coverage, arts programmes and religious broadcasts.' See http://ask.ofcom.org.uk/help/ television/what_is_psb. Accessed 15 October 2011. In the UK, for example, the BBC has a public service remit as well as ITV, Channel 4 and Channel 5.

4   In the words of the economist Milton Friedman, 'an externality is the effect of a transaction … on a third party who has not consented to or played any role in the carrying out of that transaction' (Bakan 2004: 61). In the case of media, for example, high quality news reporting will benefit society at large although due to its high costs it is unlikely to generate large profits.

5   See, for example, the discussion related to media concentration at www.opendemocracy.net as well as McChesney and Herman (1997), Compaine (1982), Curran (2002), Hallin (1986, 1994), Doyle (2002) and Bagdikian (1997).

6   McChesney argues that 'all media systems are the result of explicit government policies, subsidies, grants of rights and regulations. … Indeed, to have anything close to competitive markets in the media requires extensive government regulation in the form of ownership limits and myriad other policies' (2003: 126).

7   Originally ASA regulated only non-broadcast advertising; it was on 1 November 2004 that the Office for Communications in an attempt to deregulate broadcast advertising contracted out its regulation to ASA.

8   The BMA has repeatedly called for a ban on alcohol advertising and on food advertising for children; see e.g. BMA's response to the 2007 Ofcom/ASA research *Young People and Alcohol Advertising* or its 2009 report *Under the Influence*.

9   In an interview to the newspaper *The Guardian*, James Harding, editor of *The Times*, acknowledges that following the allegation of hacking into Milly Dowler's phone the paper lost readers, according to industry data on some days this amounted to as many as 20,000. See www.guardian.co.uk/media/2011/jul/27/times-editor-ni-phone-hacking.

10 Murdock goes on to argue that such actions although small in themselves 'as they accumulate, they prepare the ground for a definition of citizenship that moves beyond national borders and insists on the universality of equal entitlement. This cosmopolitan counter-conception … offers the only comprehensive schema to set against the empire of capital's meta ideology of transnational consumerism'.

11 On 7 July 2011 *The Guardian* published the list of 50 top advertisers in *News of the World* (between January and May 2011), how much they spend, their Twitter account and whether they withdrew from the paper. See www.guardian.co.uk/news/datablog/2011/jul/06/ news-of-the-world-top-50-advertisers-spend. For more on the twitter campaign see www. guardian.co.uk/commentisfree/2011/jul/06/news-of-the-world-twitter-campaign.

Contributor details

Hilary Fawcett is a fashion historian. She worked as a senior lecturer at the University of Northumbria in Newcastle upon Tyne for many years. Her specialisms are post-war British fashion and issues of gender and femininity in relation to fashion cultures. She also has an interest in regional histories and identities.

Professor John Fenwick works in the Faculty of Business and Law of Northumbria University. He teaches in the areas of public management, local government and organisational studies, and has long-established research interests in public participation and methods of policy research. His recent research has included political management in local government and the growth of the third sector, and theoretical developments in public management and public policy. He has published *Managing Local Government* and a large number of papers in journals such as *Local Government Studies*, *Public Money and Management* and *Public Policy and Administration*. He co-edited a collection of essays titled *Public Management in the Postmodern Era* in 2010.

Dr Malcolm Gee is principal lecturer in Art History at Northumbria University. He has written extensively on the history of the modern art market, Surrealism and the urban cultures of Paris and Berlin in the early-twentieth century.

Paula Hearsum is a senior lecturer in Media Studies at the University of Brighton specialising in Popular Music, Journalism and professional placements teaching both on the BA (Hons) Media Studies and MA in Creative Media. Her background is in music journalism and her research covers the relationship between theory and practice in this area, particularly around the coverage of the death of popular musicians.

Dr Monika Metykova works as a lecturer in media and journalism at the University of Sussex in Brighton. She has held research and teaching positions at the University of Sunderland, Goldsmiths and Northumbria University. Her research involves media regulation, media and democracy, migration and cosmopolitanism, European media spaces and policy. She has produced academic texts and reports for non-governmental organisations on these subjects. She is currently working on a monograph titled *Transforming Media Cultures: Cosmopolitan Communications in Europe.*

Dr Andrew Mullen is a senior lecturer in politics in the Department of Social Sciences at Northumbria University. He is the co-convenor of the International Propaganda Model Project and the Austerity Discourses Project. Andrew is the author of *The British Left's 'Great Debate' on Europe,* co-author of *The 1975 Referendum on Europe Vol.2* and the author of several journal articles on the Herman-Chomsky Propaganda Model. His forthcoming titles include *Anti and Pro European Propaganda in Britain* (Continuum) and *The Political Economy of the European Social Model* (Routledge).

Dr Tony Purvis was, until July 2011, programme director for media and cultural studies at Newcastle University and is currently living and working with a lay religious community. His research interests and publications focus on television studies and media theory. In addition, he is researching the work and life of American Cistercian monk, Thomas Merton.

David Reid is originally from New Zealand, and is a lecturer in advertising at Charles Sturt University in NSW, Australia. After working in the creative industries in New Zealand and England for over a decade he joined the award-winning British advertising agency DiFFERENT. He has taught at Northumbria University in England and at Curtin University in Malaysia. His areas of research focus primarily around the impact of technology on advertising and marketing communication.

Judith Stevenson has taught Art History and Contextual Studies since 2003. She is currently studying for a PhD in Art History with the Open University.

Dr Chris Wharton is a senior lecturer in the Department of Media in the Faculty of Arts, Design and Social Sciences at Northumbria University. His writing encompasses media, politics and culture, including *the room project* of 2008 and more recent work on the themes of cities, branding and culture. His forthcoming book *Critical Advertising* is to be published by Routledge in 2013.

Index